STUDY GUIDE

ESSENTIALS OF MANAGERIAL FINANCE

Eighth Edition

STUDY GUIDE

ESSENTIALS OF MANAGERIAL FINANCE

Eighth Edition

J. Fred Weston
University of California
at Los Angeles

Eugene F. Brigham
University of Florida

THE DRYDEN PRESS

Chicago New York Philadelphia
San Francisco Montreal Toronto
London Sydney Tokyo Mexico City
Rio de Janeiro Madrid

ISBN 0-03-009963-3
Printed in the United States of America
789-066-98765432

Address orders:
111 Fifth Avenue
New York, NY 10003

Address editorial correspondence:
One Salt Creek Lane
Hinsdale, IL 60521

The Dryden Press
Holt, Rinehart and Winston
Saunders College Publishing

PREFACE

This *Study Guide* is designed primarily to help you develop a working knowledge of the concepts and principles of financial management. Additionally, it will familiarize you with the types of true/false and multiple choice test questions that are being used with increasing frequency in introductory finance courses.

The *Study Guide* follows the outline of *Essentials of Managerial Finance*. You should read carefully the next section, *How To Use This Study Guide*, to familiarize yourself with its specific contents and to gain some insights into how it can be used most effectively.

We would like to thank Dana Aberwald, Stephen Ambrose, Susan Ball, Lou Gapenski, Kimberly McCollough and Carol Stanton for their considerable assistance in the preparation of this Edition, and Bob LeClair for his helpful ideas in prior editions which we carried over to this one.

We have tried to make the *Study Guide* as clear and error-free as possible. However, some mistakes may have crept in, and there are almost certainly some sections that could be clarified. Any suggestions for improving the *Study Guide* would be greatly appreciated and should be addressed to Professor Brigham. Since instructors almost never read study guides, we address this call for help to students!

J. Fred Weston
Graduate School of Management
University of California
at Los Angeles
Los Angeles, CA 90024

Eugene F. Brigham
College of Business Administration
University of Florida
Gainesville, FL 32611

HOW TO USE THIS STUDY GUIDE

Different people will tend to use the *Study Guide* in somewhat different ways. This is natural, because both introductory finance courses and individual students' needs vary widely. However, the tips contained in this section should help all students use the *Study Guide* more effectively, regardless of these differences.

Each chapter contains (1) an overview, (2) an outline, (3) some definitional questions, (4) some conceptual questions, and (5) answers to the questions. In addition, all but the first chapter (Chapter 1) contain a set of problems with solutions. You should begin your study by reading the overview; it will give you an idea of what is contained in the chapter and how this material fits into the overall scheme of things in managerial finance.

Next, read over the outline to get a better fix on the specific topics covered in the chapter. It is important to realize that the outline does not list every facet of every topic covered in the textbook--the *Study Guide* is intended to highlight and summarize the textbook, not to supplant it. Also, note that appendix material is clearly marked as such within the outline. Thus, if your instructor does not assign a particular appendix, you may not want to study that portion of the outline.

The definitional questions are intended to test your knowledge of, and also to reinforce your ability to work with, the terms and concepts introduced in the chapter. If you do not understand the definitions thoroughly, review the outline prior to going on to the conceptual questions and problems.

The conceptual questions focus on the same kinds of ideas that the textbook end-of-chapter questions address, but in the *Study Guide* the questions are set out in a true/false or multiple choice format. Thus, for many students these questions can be used to practice for the types of tests that are being used with increasing frequency. However, regardless of the types of tests you must take, working through the conceptual questions will help drive home the key concepts of financial management.

The numeric problems are also written in a multiple choice format. Generally, the problems are arranged in order of increasing difficulty. Also, note that some of the *Study Guide* problems are convoluted in the sense that information normally available to financial managers is withheld, and information normally unknown is given. Such problems are designed to test your knowledge of a subject, and you must work "backwards" to solve them. Furthermore, such problems are included in the *Study Guide* in part because they provide a good test of how well you understand the material, and in part because you may well be seeing similar problems on your exams.

Finally, each *Study Guide* chapter provides the answers and solutions to the questions and problems. The rationale behind a question's correct answer is explained where necessary, but the problem solutions are always complete. Note that the problems in the early chapters generally provide both "table-based" and "financial calculator" solutions. In later chapters, only calculator solutions are shown. You should not be concerned if your answer differs from ours by a small amount which is caused by rounding errors.

Of course, each student must decide how to incorporate the *Study Guide* in his or her overall study program. Many students begin an assignment by reading the *Study Guide* overview and outline to get the "big picture," then read the chapter in the textbook. Naturally, the *Study Guide* overview and outline is also used extensively to review for exams. Most students work the textbook questions and problems, using the latter as a self-test and review tool. However, if you are stumped by a text problem, try the *Study Guide* problems first, because their detailed solutions can get you over stumbling blocks.

CONTENTS OF THE STUDY GUIDE

CHAPTER 1
AN OVERVIEW OF MANAGERIAL FINANCE

OVERVIEW

The evolution of managerial finance from 1900 to the present time has seen the financial manager playing an increasingly important role in the business organization. Decisions made by managers within the organization should be consistent with the goals of the firm. The primary goal of most publicly owned firms is stock price maximization. Actions that result in stock price maximization not only are good for the firm, but benefit society as well. Yet managers, because they usually do not own 100 percent of the firm's stock, are not always motivated to act in the best interest of the shareholders. However, there are reasons, such as proxy fights, hostile takeovers, and performance-linked compensation, which tend to force managers to respect the shareholders' interests. Further, the threat of paying abnormally high interest rates or of being barred from debt markets forces management (acting on shareholders' behalf) to also respect the firm's creditors, and labor unions and competitive forces ensure that employees' and customers' interests are observed. Ultimately, the combination of management's efforts and external uncontrollable factors such as inflation, tax law changes, and the general stock market interact to determine the stock price of the firm.

OUTLINE

I. **Managerial finance has undergone significant changes over the years:**

   A. During the early 1900s, the emphasis was on legalistic matters such as mergers, consolidations, the formation of new firms, and the various types of securities issued by corporations. At that time, capital markets were relatively primitive, and the critical problem firms faced was obtaining capital for expansion.

   B. The depression of the 1930s shifted the focus of finance to bankruptcy, reorganization, corporate liquidity, and governmental regulation of securities markets. The emphasis changed from expansion to survival.

   C. During the 1940s and early 1950s, finance continued to be viewed descriptively from an outsider's point of view rather than from the standpoint of the firm's internal management.

   D. In the late 1950s, new methods of financial analysis began to develop:
      1. Emphasis shifted from liabilities and capital to asset analysis.
      2. Mathematical models were applied to the analysis of inventories, cash, receivables, and fixed assets.

   E. Finance in the 1960s and 1970s focused (1) on the optimum mix of securities and the cost of capital, and (2) on the theory of asset selection, or *portfolio management,* and its implications for corporate finance. It was recognized that the results of a firm's investment decisions depend on its stockholders' reactions to those decisions, and that recognition led to a merging of investments and corporate finance.

F. Thus far in the 1980s, three issues have received the most emphasis:
1. Inflation and its effects on interest rates.
2. Deregulation of financial institutions, and the trend away from specialized institutions toward broadly diversified financial service corporations.
3. The dramatic increase in the use of computers for the analysis of financial decisions.

II. There has been a dramatic increase in the importance of managerial finance.

A. Modern business decisions require coordination among marketing, engineering, production, and financial managers.

B. The financial manager is generally responsible for the control process and for corporate planning.

III. The three major forms of business organization are the sole proprietorship, the partnership, and the corporation.

A. About 80 percent of businesses operate as sole proprietorships, 10 percent as partnerships, and 10 percent as corporations.

B. However, 80 percent of business (when measured by dollar value of sales) is conducted by corporations, 13 percent by sole proprietorships, and about 7 percent by partnerships.

C. A sole proprietorship is a business owned by one individual.
1. *Advantages:* (1) A sole proprietorship is easily and inexpensively formed since no formal charter is required; (2) it is subject to few government regulations; and (3) it pays no corporate income taxes (however, all earnings of the business are taxed as personal income to the owners).
2. *Disadvantages:* (1) A sole proprietorship is limited in its ability to raise large sums of capital, (2) it has unlimited personal liability for business debts, and (3) it has a life limited to the life of the individual who created it.

D. A partnership exists when two or more persons associate to conduct a business.
1. *Advantage:* Partnerships are easy and economical to form.
2. *Disadvantages:* 1) Each partner is exposed to unlimited personal liability for business debts, 2) the business' life is limited to the life of the owners, 3) there is difficulty in transferring ownership, and 4) it has difficulty raising large amounts of capital because of the disadvantages previously mentioned.
3. Taxation of a partnership is similar to that of a proprietorship. This can be an advantage or disadvantage, depending on the situation.

E. A corporation is a legal entity (or "person") created by a state, and it is separate from its owners and managers.
1. *Advantages:* (1) A corporation has an unlimited life, (2) one can easily transfer ownership through the transfer of stock, (3) it permits limited liability, and (4) it can more easily attract capital. The value of any business other than a very small one will probably be maximized if the business is organized as a corporation, because of these advantages.

2. *Disadvantages:* Setting up a corporation is more involved than forming a proprietorship or partnership. A charter must be filed with the state where the firm is headquartered and bylaws which govern the management of the company must be prepared. Also, corporations are taxed differently from proprietorships and partnerships, and under certain conditions, this may be a disadvantage (however, it may also be an advantage, depending on the circumstances).

IV. **The goals of managerial finance are based on the goals of the firm.**

    A. Management's primary goal is to maximize the wealth of the firm's stockholders.

    B. This goal translates into maximizing the price of the firm's common stock. This is not the same as maximizing net income or earnings per share.

    C. Other objectives--personal satisfaction, employee welfare, and the good of the community--also have an influence, but for publicly-owned companies they are less important than stock price maximization.

    D. Tying management's compensation to company performance tends to reinforce stock price maximization as a goal.

    E. Tender offers and proxy fights have also stimulated management to maximize share price.

V. **Should firms emphasize social responsibility as well as wealth maximization?**

    A. Socially responsible acts that raise costs will be difficult if not impossible in industries subject to intense competition.

    B. Even firms with above-average profits will be constrained in exercising social responsibility by capital market forces, because investors will normally prefer the firm that concentrates on profits over one excessively devoted to social action.

    C. Socially responsible actions that increase costs may have to be put on a mandatory rather than a voluntary basis to insure that the burden will fall uniformly across all businesses.

    D. Industry and government must cooperate in establishing rules for fair hiring, product safety, environmental protection, and other programs that affect all businesses.

VI. **The same actions that maximize stock price also benefit society.**

    A. Stock price maximization requires efficient, low-cost operations that produce the desired quality and quantity of output.

    B. Stock price maximization also requires the development of products that consumers want and need, which leads not only to new products but also new technology and new jobs.

    C. Stock price maximization necessitates efficient and courteous service, adequate stocks of merchandise, and well-located business establishments.

VII. An agency relationship exists when one or more persons (the principals) hire another person (the agent) to act on their behalf, delegating decision-making authority to that agent. In the financial management framework, this relationship exists (1) between stockholders and managers and (2) between creditors and stockholders.

A. A potential agency problem exists whenever a manager owns less than 100 percent of the firm's common stock.
  1. Since the firm's earnings do not go solely to the manager, he or she may not concentrate exclusively on maximizing shareholder wealth. Also, because costs are borne by all stockholders, the manager may tend to obtain too many perquisites.
  2. Another potential conflict between management and stockholders is the leveraged buyout, due to the fact that management might attempt to *minimize* the stock price just prior to the buyout.

B. To insure that managers act in the best interest of the shareholders, the shareholders must incur agency costs, which include the following:
  1. Expenditures to monitor managerial actions.
  2. Expenditures to structure the organization to minimize undesirable managerial behavior.
  3. Opportunity costs associated with lost profits due to an organizational structure which does not allow managers to act on a timely basis.

C. Complete monitoring of managerial activity would solve the agency problem, but it would be costly and inefficient. Managerial compensation solely in the form of shares of the firm's stock would also solve the problem, but it would also be ineffective because it would be difficult to hire managers on this basis. The optimal solution includes some monitoring as well as compensation that includes both fixed salary and performance incentives.

D. There are several mechanisms which tend to force managers to act in the shareholders' best interest, thus minimizing the agency problem.
  1. Because stock ownership is so heavily concentrated in the funds of large institutions, the firing of management by unhappy stockholders has become a reality. Unhappy shareholders can remove inefficient managers through a *proxy fight* in which proxy votes are obtained by a majority of shareholders who vote to elect new management. Also, unhappy stockholders can agree to merge the firm with a better-run corporation.
  2. Any managerial decision that results in the undervaluation of a firm's stock price makes the firm more likely to be the target of a hostile takeover. In a hostile takeover, management is either fired or else loses a great deal of autonomy.
  3. Tying managers' compensation to the company's performance motivates managers to operate in a manner consistent with stock price maximization. The main tool being used now, which is based on factors over which managers have control, is performance shares. These shares are given to executives on the basis of performance as measured by such criteria as growth in earnings per share and return on assets.

E. An agency problem also exists between a firm's creditors (usually bondholders) and its stockholders (or managers acting on behalf of stockholders). Conflict arises if (1) stockholders (management) take on projects that have greater risk than was anticipated by creditors or (2) the firm increases its level of debt higher than was anticipated. Both of these actions decrease the value of the debt outstanding. It is in the firm's best interest to deal fairly with its creditors in order to assure future access to debt markets at reasonable interest costs.

VIII. **The financial manager has an important role in maximizing stock price.**

A. The financial manager can affect the firm's stock price by influencing the following factors:
   1. Future earnings per share
   2. Timing of the earnings stream
   3. Riskiness of projected earnings
   4. The manner of financing the firm
   5. Dividend policy

B. Every significant corporate decision should be analyzed in terms of its effects on these factors and, through them, on the price of the firm's stock. Other factors influence stock price but are not controllable by managers. Included are:
   1. External constraints such as antitrust laws and environmental regulations
   2. The general level of economic activity
   3. Taxes
   4. The conditions of the stock market

IX. **The organization of the eighth edition of Essentials of Managerial Finance reflects the primary goal of stock price maximization.**

A. Finance cannot be studied in a vacuum. Thus, Chapters 1 through 3 introduce the economic environment, which has a profound influence on financial decisions and about which the financial manager must have a good working knowledge.

B. It is necessary for the financial manager to estimate stockholders' reactions to alternative actions or events. Chapters 4 through 6 provide the valuation models which are used to help evaluate financial decisions in terms of effects on the price of the firm's stock.

C. Chapters 7 through 9 deal with financial statements, financial analysis, and financial planning. Since both short-run and long-run plans are analyzed in terms of future financial statements, it is important to understand how statements are developed and then used by both managers and investors.

D. Financial managers are involved in current, on-going operations. Chapters 10 through 14 first consider the question of how current operations should be financed and then examine the role of the financial manager in insuring that cash, inventories, and other current assets are used most effectively.

E. Chapters 15 and 16 consider the vital subject of fixed asset acquisitions, or capital budgeting. Since major capital expenditures take years to plan and execute, and since decisions in this area are generally not reversible and affect operations for many years, their impact on the firm is profound.

F. Chapters 17 through 19 focus on (1) how the use of different types of long-term capital affects the value of the firm, (2) the cost of each type of capital, and (3) the impact of dividend policy decisions on the firm's capital budget and capital structure.

G. Finally, Chapters 20 through 23 discuss in detail the principal sources and forms of long-term capital.

DEFINITIONAL QUESTIONS

1. In the early 1900s, the finance function concentrated on _____ matters such as mergers, consolidations, and the various types of securities issued by corporations.

2. The _____ of the 1930s caused an emphasis on bankruptcy, liquidity, and _____ regulation of securities markets.

3. During the _____, asset management techniques, especially mathematical _____, began to be developed and applied to financial decision making.

4. Financial managers had been mostly concerned with _____ and capital in earlier times, but in the late 1950s, attention shifted to _____ analysis.

5. A renewed interest in the liabilities-capital side of the balance sheet during the 1960s focused on (1) the optimal mix of _____ and (2) the cost of _____.

6. The theory of asset selection by individual investors, or _____ management, was developed in the 1960s and 1970s and contributed to the merging of investments and _____ _____.

7. Sole proprietorships are easily formed, but they often have difficulty raising _____, they subject proprietors to unlimited _____, and they have a limited _____.

8. Partnership profits are taxed as _____ income in proportion to each partner's proportionate ownership.

9. A partnership is dissolved upon the _____ or _____ of any one of the partners. In addition, the difficulty of _____ _____ is a major disadvantage of the partnership form of business organization.

10. A _____ is a legal entity created by a state, and it is separate from its _____ and managers.

11. The concept of _____ _____ means that a firm's stockholders are not personally liable for the debts of the business.

12. Modern financial theory operates on the assumption that the goal of management is the _____ of shareholder _____. This goal is accomplished if the firm's _____ _____ is maximized.

13. Socially responsible activities that increase a firm's costs will be most difficult in those industries where _____ is most intense.

14. Even firms with above-average profit levels will find social actions _____ by capital market factors.

15. An _____ relationship exists when one or more persons (the principals) hire another person (the agent) to act on their behalf.

16. Potential agency problems exist between a firm's shareholders and its _____ and also between shareholders and _____.

17. A firm's stock price depends on several factors. Among the most important of these are the level of projected _____ _____ _____ as well as the _____ of those projections.

CONCEPTUAL QUESTIONS

18. The primary objective of the firm is to maximize EPS.

    a. True   b. False

19. Which of the following factors affect stock price?

    a. Level of projected earnings per share
    b. Riskiness of projected earnings per share
    c. Timing of the earnings stream
    d. The manner of financing the firm
    e. All of the above factors

20. Which of the following factors tend to encourage management to pursue stock price maximization as a goal?

    a. Shareholders link management's compensation to company performance.
    b. Managers' reaction to the threat of tender offers and proxy fights.
    c. Managers do not have goals other than stock price maximization.
    d. Statements a and b are both correct.
    e. Statements a, b, and c are all correct.

21. The types of actions that help a firm maximize stock price are generally not directly beneficial to society at large.

    a. True   b. False

22. There are factors that influence stock price over which managers have virtually no control.

    a. True   b. False

ANSWERS

1. legalistic

2. depression; governmental

3. 1950s; models

4. liabilities; asset

5. securities; capital

6. portfolio; corporate finance

7. capital; liability; life

8. personal

9. withdrawal; death; transferring ownership (or raising capital)

10. corporation; owners

11. limited liability

12. maximization; wealth; stock price

13. competition

14. constrained

15. agency

16. managers; bondholders

17. earnings per share; riskiness

18. b. An increase in earnings per share will not necessarily increase stock price. For example, if the increase in earnings per share is accompanied by an increase in the riskiness of the firm, stock price might fall. *The primary objective is the maximization of stock price.*

19. e.

20. d.

21. b. The actions that maximize stock price generally also benefit society by promoting efficient, low-cost operations; encouraging the development of new technology, products and jobs; and requiring efficient and courteous service.

22. a. Managers have no control over factors such as (1) external constraints (for example, antitrust laws and environmental regulations), (2) the general level of economic activity, (3) taxes, and (4) conditions in the stock market, all of which affect the price of the firm's stock.

CHAPTER 2
FINANCIAL STATEMENTS, TAXES,
AND CASH FLOWS

OVERVIEW

All businesses, regardless of organizational form, must have assets in order to operate. The capital needed to acquire these assets can be raised either from creditors as debt capital or from stockholders as equity capital. Investors supplying debt capital have a fixed claim on the firm's earnings, while investors supplying equity capital (common stockholders) have a claim on all earnings after payments to debtholders (residual earnings). Because interest paid is a tax-deductible expense but dividends are not, the tax system favors debt financing over equity financing.

In the United States, income to both individuals and businesses is taxed by the federal government. Individuals pay taxes on ordinary income at rates that go up to 28 percent, while corporations are taxed at a rate up to 34 percent. However, 80 percent of income received as dividends by a corporation is excluded from its taxable income. Some small businesses that meet certain restrictions, called S corporations, may be set up as corporations, yet they may elect to be taxed as proprietorships or partnerships. Depreciation, which is a tax-deductible expense to a business to recognize the wear, tear, and obsolescence of fixed assets, is calculated for tax purposes using the Accelerated Cost Recovery System (ACRS). Tax depreciation rules have a major impact on the profitability of capital investments.

OUTLINE

I. **Any business, irrespective of its organizational form, must have assets to operate. The capital raised to acquire these assets comes in two basic forms.**

A. Creditors supply debt capital to the firm.
   1. Debt capital is obtained mainly by buying on credit from suppliers or by borrowing from banks and other institutions.
   2. Creditors have first claim against the firm's income, but the claim is limited to a fixed interest charge. Also, creditors have first claim on the proceeds from the sale of assets if a firm goes bankrupt and must be liquidated.

B. Equity capital is supplied by preferred stockholders and common stockholders.
   1. Preferred stockholders have a fixed claim on the firm's income. Preferred dividends must be paid before any dividends can be paid on common stock, and preferred has a claim ahead of common in the event of bankruptcy. However, nonpayment of preferred dividends cannot force a firm into bankruptcy.
   2. Common stockholders have a claim on the residual income remaining after creditors' and preferred stockholders' claims have been met. Common equity funds are obtained (1) by retaining earnings within the firm and (2) by the sale of new common stock to investors.

II. **Income taxes in the United States are progressive; that is, the higher the income, the larger the percentage paid in taxes.**

    A. Individuals pay income taxes on wages and salaries, on investment income (dividends and interest), and on the profits from proprietorships and partnerships.

        1. Under current rules (1986), Federal income marginal tax rates for individuals will go up to 28 percent in 1988, and they may approach 40 percent when state and city taxes are included.

        2. During an inflationary period such as the 1970s, a progressive tax structure can result in a decline in real after-tax income because a higher percentage of income is paid out in taxes. This is known as "bracket creep," and it can be reduced by periodic adjustments to the tax rates.

        3. Since dividends are paid from corporate income that has already been taxed (at rates going up to 34 percent), there is double taxation of corporate income.

        4. Interest on most state and local government securities, which are often called "municipals," is not subject to federal income taxes. This is a strong incentive for individuals in high tax brackets to purchase such securities.

    B. Gains and losses on the sale of capital assets such as stocks, bonds, and real estate have historically received special tax treatment.

        1. An asset sold within 6 months of purchase produces a *short-term capital gain or loss*.

        2. An asset held for more than 6 months, and then sold, produces a *long-term capital gain or loss*.

        3. Short-term gains are taxed as ordinary income.

        4. Long-term gains are currently taxed as ordinary income, but prior to 1986 only 40 percent of the gain was taxed as ordinary income. The other 60 percent of the gain was excluded from taxable income. Congress may in the future reinstate a differential treatment for capital gains.

    C. Corporations pay taxes on profits.

        1. Corporate tax rates for 1988 and thereafter (under 1986 rules) are as follows:

            a. 15 percent on the first $50,000 of taxable income.

            b. 25 percent on the next $25,000.

            c. 34 percent on the next $25,000.

            d. 39 percent on income between $100,000 and $335,000.

            e. For income greater than $335,000, the tax rate is 34 percent.

        2. Interest and dividends received by a corporation are taxed.

            a. Interest is taxed as ordinary income at regular corporate tax rates.

            b. 80 percent of the dividends received by one corporation from another is excluded from taxable income. The remaining 20 percent is taxed at the ordinary rate. Thus, the effective tax rate on dividends received by a 34 percent tax bracket corporation is 0.2 X 34% = 6.8%.

        3. The tax system favors debt financing over equity financing.

            a. Interest paid is a tax-deductible business expense.

            b. Dividends on common and preferred stock are not deductible. Thus, a 34 percent tax bracket corporation must earn $1/(1.0 - 0.34) = $1/0.66 = $1.52 before taxes to pay $1 of dividends.

        4. Long-term corporate capital gains are at times taxed at lower rates than ordinary income. However, at present long-term capital gains are taxed as ordinary income.

5. Ordinary operating losses may first be carried back 3 years and then forward 15 years to offset taxable income, thus reducing taxes in those years. This procedure is particularly helpful to firms with widely fluctuating income.
6. The Internal Revenue Code imposes a penalty on corporations that improperly accumulate earnings if the purpose of the accumulation is to enable stockholders to avoid personal income tax on dividends.
7. If a corporation owns 80 percent or more of another corporation's stock, it can aggregate profits and losses and file a consolidated tax return. Thus, losses in one area can offset profits in another.

III. **Under the Internal Revenue Code, small businesses that meet certain restrictions may be set up as corporations (and receive the benefits of this type of organization), yet they may elect to be taxed as proprietorships or partnerships. These corporations are called S corporations. S corporation status has several advantages over filing as an ordinary corporation.**

A. Business income is reported on a pro rata basis as taxable income to its stockholders, who may then withdraw funds without the payment of further taxes. This avoids double taxation of dividends. Also, with the top corporate rate of 34 percent versus a top personal rate of 28 percent, S corporation status is advantageous even if funds are to be left in a business.

B. Operating losses may be claimed on a pro rata basis by stockholders and deducted against their other personal income, provided the owners are active in the business.

IV. **Capital investment, or the purchase of fixed assets such as plant and equipment, has a significant impact on a corporation's taxable income.**

A. The cost of goods produced by plant and equipment must include a charge for the wear and tear, and the obsolescence, of fixed assets. This charge, called **depreciation**, reduces profits, but it also reduces taxable income.
1. Depreciation is usually calculated by the straight line method when reporting income to investors, but for tax purposes, depreciation is calculated using the Accelerated Cost Recovery System (ACRS, which is pronounced "acres").
2. ACRS created several classes of assets, each class with a more-or-less arbitrarily prescribed life called a *recovery period* or *class life*. The actual economic life of an asset is ignored by ACRS. Each asset falls into a particular ACRS class. Research equipment falls into the 3-year class life; motor vehicles, computers, and certain tools into the 5-year class; industrial equipment and office furniture into the 7-year class; most other equipment into the 10-year class; and buildings into the 31.5 year class life.
3. Once the class life of an asset is determined, ACRS specifies the percentage of the asset's depreciable basis that can be deducted each year as depreciation expense. For example, the recovery percentages for a 3-year asset are 34%, 33%, and 33%, while they are 20%, 32%, 20%, 14%, and 14% for a 5-year class asset.
4. Under ACRS, the depreciable basis is the asset's cost; salvage value is not deducted when calculating tax depreciation.

B. An investment tax credit (ITC), which is designed to stimulate investment, is a direct reduction of taxes. It is calculated by multiplying the applicable ITC percentage times the capitalized cost of the asset. The ITC is taken in and out of the Tax Code depending on the mood of the Congress. The ITC was eliminated by the tax revision of 1986, but it will be reinstated if Congress deems it to be needed to stimulate business investment and hence economic growth.

DEFINITIONAL QUESTIONS

1. Capital is raised by a firm in two basic forms, _____ and _____.

2. _____ have first claim against a firm's income.

3. Common equity capital is obtained by a firm through the _____ of common stock, and by _____ earnings within the firm.

4. A _____ tax system is one in which tax rates are higher at higher levels of income.

5. A progressive tax structure, combined with _____, can _____ the government's share of GNP without any change in tax rates. This is called _____ _____.

6. The marginal tax rate on the largest corporations is ____ percent, while that on the wealthiest individuals is ____ percent.

7. Interest received on _____ bonds is generally not subject to federal income taxes. This feature makes them particularly attractive to investors in _____ tax brackets.

8. In order to qualify as a long-term capital gain or loss, an asset must be held for more than _____ months.

9. Gains or losses on assets held less than 6 months are referred to as _____ transactions.

10. *Interest income* received by a corporation is taxed as _____ income. However, only ____ percent of *dividends received* from another corporation is subject to taxation.

11. Another important distinction is that between interest and dividends paid by a corporation. Interest payments are _____, while dividend payments are not.

12. Ordinary corporate operating losses can first be carried back ____ years and then forward ____ years.

13. A firm that refuses to pay dividends in order to help stockholders avoid personal income taxes may be subject to a penalty for _____ _____ of earnings.

14. A corporation that owns 80 percent or more of another corporation's stock may choose to file _____ tax returns.

15. When Congress permits it, the _____ _____ credit, which is calculated as a percentage of the cost of _____ _____, reduces the effective cost of fixed assets and thus serves to stimulate _____.

16. The Tax Code permits a corporation (that meets certain restrictions) to be taxed by the owners personal tax rates and also avoids the impact of _____ _____ of dividends. This type of corporation is called an _____ corporation.

17. The wear, tear, and obsolescence of fixed assets used for business is deducted from taxable income as _____. The current system for calculating this expense for tax purposes is called _____.

CONCEPTUAL QUESTIONS

18. The fact that 80 percent of the dividends received by a corporation is excluded from taxable income has encouraged debt financing over equity financing.

    a. True   b. False

19. An individual with substantial personal wealth and income is considering the possibility of opening a new business. The business will have a relatively high degree of risk, and losses may be incurred for the first several years. Which legal form of business organization would probably be best?

    a. Proprietorship
    b. Corporation
    c. Partnership
    d. S corporation
    e. Limited partnership

PROBLEMS

20. In 1988, Wayne Corporation had income from operations of $385,000, it received interest payments of $15,000, it paid interest of $20,000, it received dividends from another corporation of $10,000, and it paid $40,000 in dividends to its common stockholders. What is Wayne's 1988 federal income tax?

    a. $122,760
    b. $129,880
    c. $141,700
    d. $155,200
    e. $163,500

21. A firm purchases $10 million of corporate bonds which paid a 16 percent interest rate, or $1.6 million in interest. If the firm's marginal tax rate is 34 percent, what is the after-tax interest yield?

a. 7.36%
b. 8.64%
c. 10.56%
d. 13.89%
e. 14.72%

22. Refer to Problem 21. The firm also invests in the common stock of another company having a 16 percent before-tax dividend yield. What is the after-tax dividend yield?

a. 7.36%
b. 8.64%
c. 10.56%
d. 13.89%
e. 14.91%

23. The Carter Company's taxable income and income tax payments are shown below for 1985 through 1988:

Year	Taxable Income	Tax Payment
1985	$10,000	$1,700
1986	5,000	850
1987	10,000	1,700
1988	5,000	850

Assume that Carter's tax rate for all 4 years was a flat 17 percent; that is, each dollar of taxable income was taxed at 17 percent. In 1989, Carter incurred a loss of $17,000. Using corporate loss carry-back, what is Carter's adjusted tax payment for 1988?

a. $850
b. $750
c. $610
d. $550
e. $510

24. A firm can undertake a new project which will generate a before-tax return of 20 percent or it can invest the same funds in the preferred stock of another company which yields 13 percent before taxes. If the only consideration is which alternative provides the highest relevant (after-tax) return, and the applicable tax rate is 34 percent, should the firm invest in the project or the preferred stock?

a. Preferred stock; its relevant return is 12 percent.
b. Project; its relevant return is 1.08 percentage points higher.
c. Preferred stock; its relevant return is 0.22 percentage points higher.
d. Project; its before-tax return is 20 percent.
e. Either alternative can be chosen; they have the same relevant return.

25. Wharton Wholesalers purchased an asset in 1987 for $100,000 which falls into the ACRS 5-year class life. What is the ACRS depreciation expense in Year 3 (1989)?

    a. $18,950
    b. $20,000
    c. $19,990
    d. $20,900
    e. $22,950

ANSWERS AND SOLUTIONS

1. debt; equity (or stock and bonds)

2. Creditors (or debtholders)

3. sale; retaining

4. progressive

5. inflation; increase; bracket creep

6. 34, 28

7. municipal; high

8. 6

9. short-term

10. ordinary; 20

11. tax-deductible

12. 3; 15

13. improper accumulation

14. consolidated

15. investment tax; new assets; investment

16. double taxation; S

17. depreciation; ACRS

18. b. Debt financing is encouraged by the fact that interest payments are tax deductible while dividend payments are not.

19. d. The S corporation limits the liability of the individual, but permits losses to be deducted against personal income.

20. b. The first step is to determine taxable income:

Income from operations	$385,000
Interest income (fully taxable)	15,000
Interest expense (fully deductible)	(20,000)
Dividend income (20% taxable)	2,000
Total	$382,000

(Note that dividends are paid from after-tax income and do not affect taxable income.)

Based on the 1988 corporate tax table, the tax calculation is as follows:

15% of first $50,000	$ 7,500
25% of next $25,000	6,250
34% of next $25,000	8,500
39% of next $235,000	91,650
34% of $47,000	15,980
Total tax	$129,880

21. c. The after-tax yield (or dollar return) equals the before-tax yield (or dollar return) multiplied by one minus the effective tax rate, or

$$AT = BT(1 - \text{Effective T}).$$

Therefore,

$$AT = 16\%(1 - 34\%) = 16\%(1 - 0.34) = 16\%(0.66) = 10.56\%.$$

22. e. Since the dividends are received by a corporation, only 20 percent are taxable, and the Effective T = Tax rate x 20 percent:

$$
\begin{aligned}
AT &= BT(1 - \text{Effective T}) \\
&= 16\%[1 - 34\%(20\%)] \\
&= 16\%(1 - 0.068) \\
&= 16\%(0.932) \\
&= 14.91\%.
\end{aligned}
$$

23. e.

Year	Taxable Income	Tax Payment	Adjusted Taxable Income	Adjusted Tax Payment
1985	$10,000	$1,700	$10,000	$1,700
1986	5,000	850	0	0
1987	10,000	1,700	0	0
1988	5,000	850	3,000	510

The carry-back can only go back 3 years. Thus, there was no adjustment made in 1985. After $5,000 of adjustment in 1986 and $10,000 in 1987, there was a $2,000 loss remaining to apply to 1988. The 1988 adjusted tax payment is $3,000(0.17) = $510. Thus, Carter received a total of $2,890 in tax refunds after the adjustment.

$$AT = 13\%[(1 - 0.34(0.20)]$$
$$= 13\%(1 - 0.068) = 13\%(0.932) = 12.12\%.$$

Therefore, the new project should be chosen since its after-tax return is 1.08 percentage points higher.

24. b. The project is fully taxable, thus its after-tax return is as follows:

$$AT = 20\%(1 - 0.34) = 20\%(0.66) = 13.2\%.$$

But only 20 percent of the preferred stock dividends are taxable, thus its after-tax yield is

$$AT = 13\%[(1 - 0.34(0.20)]$$
$$= 13\%(1 - 0.068) = 13\%(0.932) = 12.12\%.$$

Therefore, the new project should be chosen since its after-tax return is 1.08 percentage points higher.

25. b. First, note that the depreciable basis is the cost of $100,000.

Then, apply the ACRS recovery percentages for each year:

Year	Recovery Percentage	Depreciation Expense
1	20	$ 20,000
2	32	32,000
3	20	20,000
4	14	14,000
		$100,000

CHAPTER 3
FINANCIAL MARKETS AND INTEREST RATES

OVERVIEW

A developed economy relies on financial markets and institutions for efficient transfers of funds from savers to borrowers. In the United States, our stock markets include the organized exchanges, such as the New York Stock Exchange, (NYSE), and the over-the-counter (OTC) market, which provides for all security transactions not conducted on the organized exchanges.

One of the most important factors affecting the transfer of funds from savers to borrowers is interest rates. The interest rate is the price paid for the use of money, and it is determined by the combination of producers' expected rates of return on invested capital and consumers' time preferences for consumption. Many factors go into making up the actual interest rate. It is composed of the real, or risk-free rate, plus premiums to compensate investors for expected inflation, default risk, lack of liquidity, and maturity risk.

The term structure of interest rates is the relationship between long and short-term interest rates, and this relationship, when plotted, produces a yield curve. The slope of the yield curve is important to corporate treasurers, who must make decisions regarding long-term and short-term borrowing. Since interest rates are very difficult to predict, sound financial policy calls for using a mix of securities that will enable a firm to survive in any interest rate environment.

OUTLINE

I. **Financial markets bring together lenders and borrowers of money.**

   A. There are many different financial markets in a developed economy, each dealing with a different type of security, serving a different set of customers, or operating in a different part of the country.

   B. The following markets are of most interest to financial managers.
      1. *Money markets* are the markets for short-term debt securities, those securities that mature in less than one year.
      2. *Capital markets* are the markets for long-term debt and corporate stocks.
      3. *Primary markets* are the markets in which newly issued securities are sold for the first time.
      4. *Secondary markets* are the markets in which existing, outstanding securities are bought and sold.

II. **Transfer of capital between savers and borrowers take place in three different ways.**

   A. *Direct transfer* occurs when money passes directly from the investor to the firm issuing the security.

B. Transfer through an *investment banking house* occurs when a brokerage firm, such as Merrill Lynch, serves as a middleman. These middlemen help corporations design securities that will be attractive to investors, buy these securities from the corporations, and then resell them to savers in the primary markets.

C. Transfer through a *financial intermediary* occurs when a bank or mutual fund obtains funds from savers, issues its own securities in exchange, and then uses these funds to purchase other securities. In the past, regulation of intermediaries has tended to impede the free flow of capital. Recent changes in Congress, intended to increase the efficiency of the capital markets, have resulted in a trend toward huge financial service corporations.

III. **The stock market is one of the most important markets to financial managers, because it is here that the price of each stock, hence the value of all publicly-owned firms, is established. There are two basic types of stock markets:**

    A. The *organized exchanges*, which are typified by the New York Stock Exchange (NYSE) and the American Stock Exchange (AMEX), are tangible, physical entities.

    B. The *over-the-counter* (OTC) *market* is, basically, all the dealers, brokers, and communications facilities that provide for security transactions not conducted on the organized exchanges.

IV. **Capital in a free economy is allocated through the price system. The interest rate is the price paid to borrow capital.**

    A. The level of interest rates is determined by the supply of, and demand for, investment capital.
        1. The demand for investment capital is determined by production opportunities available, and the rates of return producers can expect to earn on invested capital.
        2. The supply of investment capital depends on consumers' time preferences for current versus future consumption.

    B. The *real, or pure, rate of interest (k^*)* is the equilibrium level of interest on a totally riskless debt security if there is zero inflation. The real rate is often associated with the rate of interest on short-term U.S. Treasury securities in an inflation-free world.

    C. The *actual, or nominal, rate of interest* is the real rate of interest plus premiums to compensate investors for inflation and risk.
        1. The *inflation premium (IP)*, which is the average inflation rate expected over the life of the security, compensates investors for the expected loss of purchasing power.
        2. The *default risk premium (DP)* compensates investors for the risk that a borrower will default, or not pay the interest or principal on a loan.
        3. A security which can be sold and quickly converted into cash at a fair price is said to be *liquid*. A *liquidity premium (LP)* is also added to the real rate for securities that are not liquid.

4. Long-term securities are more price sensitive to interest rate changes than are short-term securities. Therefore, a *maturity risk premium* (MP) is added to longer-term securities to compensate investors for interest rate risk.

D. The nominal rate of interest can be expressed as $k = k^* + IP + DP + LP + MP$, where the values of the various premiums vary among debt securities.

V. The term structure of interest rates is the relationship between yield to maturity and term to maturity for bonds of a given default risk class.

A. When plotted, this relationship produces a *yield curve*.

B. Yield curves have different shapes depending on expected inflation rates and supply and demand conditions.
  1. The "normal" yield curve is upward sloping, generally signifying that investors expect inflation to remain steady or increase in the future.
  2. An "inverted," or downward sloping, yield curve signifies that investors expect inflation to decrease.

VI. Three theories have been proposed to explain the shape of the yield curve, or the term structure of interest rates.

A. The *market segmentation theory* states that the slope of the yield curve depends on supply and demand conditions in the long-term and short-term markets. The curve could, at any time, be either upward or downward sloping.

B. The *liquidity preference theory* states that the yield curve tends to be upward sloping because investors prefer short-term to long-term securities due to risk factors associated with long-term securities.

C. The *expectations theory* states that the yield curve depends upon expectations about future inflation rates. If the rate of inflation is expected to decline, the curve will be downward sloping, and if the rate of inflation is expected to increase, the curve will be upward sloping.

D. All three theories have merit; that is, actual yield curves are determined by all three sets of factors.

VII. The level of interest rates also has a significant effect on stock prices.

A. Interest rates, since interest is the cost of borrowed capital, have a direct effect on corporate profits.

B. Additionally, stocks and bonds compete in the marketplace for investor's capital. A rise in interest rates will increase the rate of return on bonds, causing investors to transfer funds from the stock market to the bond market. The resultant selling of stocks lowers stock prices.

VIII. Interest rate movements have a significant impact on business decisions.

    A. Wrong decisions, such as using short-term debt to finance long-term projects just before interest rates rise, can be very costly.

    B. However, it is extremely difficult, if not impossible, to predict future interest rate levels.

    C. Sound financial policy therefore calls for using a mix of long-term and short-term debt, and equity, so that the firm can survive in almost any interest rate environment.

DEFINITIONAL QUESTIONS

1. Markets for short-term debt securities are called _____ markets, while markets for long-term debt and equity are called _____ markets.

2. Newly issued securities are initially sold in the _____ markets, while existing, outstanding securities are traded in the _____ market.

3. An institution which issues its own securities in exchange for funds and then uses these funds to purchase other securities is called a _____ _____.

4. An _____ _____ _____ facilitates the transfer of capital between savers and borrows by acting as a middleman.

5. The two basic types of stock markets are the _____ _____ such as the NYSE, and the _____ markets.

6. The risk that a borrower will not pay the interest or principal on a loan is _____ risk.

7. _____ bonds have zero default risk.

8. An _____ premium is added to the real rate to protect investors against loss of purchasing power.

9. The nominal rate of interest is determined by adding a _____ premium plus a _____ risk premium plus a _____ premium plus a _____ risk premium to the real riskless rate of return.

10. The relationship between yield to maturity and term to maturity for bonds in a given default risk class is called the _____ _____ of interest rates, while the resulting plotted curve is the _____ curve.

11. The "normal" yield curve has an _____ slope.

12. Three theories have been proposed to explain the term structure of interest rates. They are the market _____ theory, the _____ preference theory and the _____ theory.

13. Because interest rates fluctuate, a sound financial policy calls for using a mix of _____ and _____ _____ debt, and _____.

CONCEPTUAL QUESTIONS

14. If the economy is about to enter a recession, and a firm needs to borrow money, it should probably use short-term rather than long-term debt.

    a. True   b. False

15. Long-term interest rates reflect expectations about future inflation. Inflation has varied greatly from year to year over the last 10 years, and, as a result, long-term rates have fluctuated more than short-term rates.

    a. True   b. False

PROBLEMS

16. You have determined the following data:

    Real riskless rate (k^*)   = 3%
    Inflation premium   = 8%
    Default risk premium   = 2%
    Liquidity premium   = 1%
    Maturity risk premium   = 1%

    The rate of inflation is expected to be constant and a liquid market exists only for very short-term Treasury securities. What is the nominal risk-free rate?

    a. 10%
    b. 11%
    c. 12%
    d. 13%
    e. 14%

17. Refer to Problem 16. What is the interest rate on long-term Treasury securities, or T-bonds?

    a. 10%
    b. 11%
    c. 12%
    d. 13%
    e. 14%

18. Assume that a 3-year Treasury note has no maturity risk premium or liquidity premium and that the real rate of interest (real riskless rate) is 2 percent. A T-note carries a yield to maturity of 12 percent. If the expected inflation rate is 12 percent next year and 10 percent the year after, what is the implied expected inflation rate for the third year?

    a. 8%
    b. 9%
    c. 10%
    d. 11%
    e. 12%

ANSWERS AND SOLUTIONS

1. money; capital

2. primary; secondary

3. financial intermediary

4. investment banking house

5. organized exchanges; over-the-counter (OTC)

6. default

7. U.S. Treasury

8. inflation

9. inflation; default; liquidity; maturity

10. term structure; yield

11. upward

12. segmentation; liquidity; expectations

13. short; long-term; equity

14. a. The firm should borrow short-term until interest rates drop due to the recession, then go long-term.

15. b. Fluctuations in long-term rates are smaller because the long-term inflation premium is an average of inflation expectations over many years.

16. b.
$$k = k^* + IP + DP + LP + MP$$
$$= 3\% + 8\% + 0 + 0 + 0$$
$$= 11\%.$$

17. d.

$$k = k^* + IP + DP + LP + MP$$
$$= 3\% + 8\% + 0\% + 1\% + 1\%$$
$$= 13\%.$$

There is virtually no risk of default on a federal government Treasury security.

18. a.

$$k = k^* + IP + DP + LP + MP$$
$$12\% = 2\% + X\% + 0\% + 0\% + 0\%$$
$$X\% = 10\%, \text{ average expected inflation rate over next three years.}$$

The average expected inflation rate over the next three years is 10%. The implied expected inflation rate for the third year can be found by solving the equation that sets the two known plus the one unknown expected inflation rates, equal to 10%:

$$\frac{12\% + 10\% + X\%}{3} = 10\%$$

$$X = 8\%.$$

CHAPTER 4
DISCOUNTED CASH FLOW ANALYSIS

OVERVIEW

A dollar in the hand today is worth more than a dollar to be received in the future because, if you had it now, you could invest that dollar and earn interest. A knowledge of compound value, or future value, and present value techniques is essential to an understanding of many aspects of finance, such as security valuation and capital budgeting. Future value and present value techniques can be applied to lump sums, ordinary annuities, annuities due, and irregular cash flow streams. Future and present values can be calculated using interest factor tables, a regular calculator, or a calculator with financial functions. When compounding occurs more frequently than once a year the effective rate is greater than the stated rate of interest, and future and present value calculations must be based on the effective rate.

OUTLINE

I. Future value (FV_n) is defined as the value to which a beginning lump sum or present value (PV) will grow in a certain number of periods, n, at a specified rate of interest, k. (On a financial calculator, the term i is frequently used rather than k.) The amount of interest earned in each period is designated as I. The concept of finding a future value is known as compounding.

    A. The formula for the future value after one period is

$$FV_n = PV + I = PV + PV(k) = PV(1 + k).$$

    B. However, for more than one period the formula is

$$FV_n = PV(1 + k)^n.$$

    C. In the above equation, $(1 + k)^n$ is known as the future value interest factor, or $FVIF_{k,n}$. Therefore,

$$FV_n = PV(FVIF_{k,n}).$$

    D. These factors have been calculated for various interest rates and time periods and organized into tables to simplify future value calculations. FVIFs may be found in text Table A-3 in the back of the text.

        1. Select the appropriate $FVIF_{k,n}$ for the specified interest rate and the given number of periods.

2. Multiply the initial amount, PV, by the interest factor to determine the future value, or ending amount.

E. For example, the future value of $1,000 at 6 percent for 5 years is $FV_5 = \$1,000(1.3382) = \$1,338.20$.

F. The same calculation can be made using a calculator.
   1. Using the exponential function, simply raise 1.06 to the 5th power, $1.06^5 = 1.3382$, then multiply by $1,000 to get $1,338.20.
   2. When using a financial calculator, you need only enter $n = 5$, $i = 6$, and $PV = \$1,000$. Then press the FV key and $1,338.23 is displayed. (Please note that some calculators require that the $1,000 be entered as -$1,000.)
   3. The differences between the tabular and calculator solutions are caused by rounding errors.

II. **The concept of present value is the reverse of compounding and is often referred to as discounting.**

A. Discounting determines the present value of a sum to be received at a future point in time.

B. The formula for present value is

$$PV = FV_n/(1 + k)^n = FV_n(1/1 + k)^n.$$

C. The term $(1/1+k)^n$ is known as the present value interest factor, $PVIF_{k,n}$, and also has been determined for a wide range of interest rates and time periods. PVIFs may be found in text Table A-1. Therefore,

$$PV = FV_n(PVIF_{k,n}).$$

D. The present value of $1,338.20 to be received in 5 years discounted at an interest rate of 6 percent is $1,338.20(0.7473) = $1,000.04. This result can be compared with the future value calculation to confirm that these are reciprocal processes. The slight difference in values is due to the fact that the interest factors are only carried to four places.

E. The present value interest factor is the reciprocal of the future value interest factor:

$$PVIF_{k,n} = 1/FVIF_{k,n}$$

F. Present value calculations can be made using a calculator.
   1. The exponential function and reciprocal key can be used to calculate the $PVIF_{k,n}$. Multiplying the number obtained by $1,338.20 would give a value of $999.98.
   2. Using the financial functions, you need only enter $n = 5$, $i = 6$, and $FV = \$1,338.20$. Then hit the PV key and $999.98 is displayed. If you used $FV = \$1,338.23$ (the future value obtained using the financial function) the PV would be $1,000. (Again note that some calculators require the $1,338.23 to be entered as -$1,338.23.)

III. **An annuity is defined as a series of payments of constant amount for a specified number of periods. If the payments occur at the end of each period, as they typically do, the annuity is an ordinary, or deferred, annuity. If the payments occur at the beginning of each period, the annuity is an annuity due.**

A. The future value of an annuity is the total amount one would have at the end of the annuity period if each payment were invested at a given periodic interest rate and held to the end of the annuity period.
   1. Defining FVA_n as the compound sum of an ordinary annuity of n years and PMT as the periodic payment, we can write

$$FVA_n = PMT(FVIFA_{k,n}).$$

   2. $FVIFA_{k,n}$ is the future value interest factor for an ordinary annuity. FVIFAs may be found in Table A-4 of the text.
   3. For example, the future value of a 10-year, 7 percent ordinary annuity of $200 per year would be $200(13.8164) = $2,763.28.
   4. The same calculation can be made using the financial functions of a calculator. First, check to insure that the calculator is set for an ordinary annuity. Now, enter n = 10, i = 7, and PMT = $200. Then, hit the FV key and $2,763.29 is displayed.
   5. For an annuity due, the compound sum is

$$FVA_n(\text{annuity due}) = PMT(FVIFA_{k,n})(1 + k).$$

   6. The future value of a 10-year, 7 percent annuity due of $200 per year is $200(13.8164)(1.07) = $2956.71.
   7. Most calculators with financial functions have an annuity due switch. Merely repeat the procedure in subparagraph 3 above with the calculator in the annuity due mode. Then $2,956.72 is displayed.

B. The present value of an annuity is the lump-sum payment required today that would be equivalent to the annuity payments spread over the annuity period. It is the amount today that would permit withdrawals of equal amount (PMT) at the end (or beginning for an annuity due) of each period for n periods.
   1. Defining PVA_n as the present value of an ordinary annuity of n years and PMT as the periodic payment, we can write

$$PVA_n = PMT(PVIFA_{k,n}).$$

   2. $PVIFA_{k,n}$ is the present value interest factor for an ordinary annuity. PVIFAs may be found in text Table A-2.
   3. For example, an annuity of $1,200 per year for 10 years at 8 percent would have a present value of $1,200(6.7101) = $8,052.12.
   4. The $PVIFA_{k,n}$ is always smaller than the number of years the annuity runs, whereas the $FVIFA_{k,n}$ for the sum of an annuity is larger than the number of years, assuming k is greater than zero.

5. The same calculation can be made using the financial functions of a calculator. First, check to insure that the calculator is set for an ordinary annuity. Now, enter n = 10, i = 8, and PMT = $1,200. Then, hit the PV key and $8,052.10 is displayed.
6. The present value for an annuity due is

$$PVA_n(\text{annuity due}) = PMT(PVIFA_{k,n})(1 + k).$$

7. The present value of a 10-year, 8 percent annuity due of $1,200 is $1,200(6.7101)(1.08) = $8,696.29.
8. To use a calculator, repeat the steps in subparagraph 5 using the annuity due mode. Then $8,696.27 is displayed.

IV. **An annuity that goes on indefinitely is called a perpetuity. The payments of a perpetuity constitute an infinite series.**

A. The present value of a perpetuity is

$$PV \text{ of a perpetuity} = \text{Payment/Discount rate} = PMT/k.$$

B.   For example, if the discount rate were 12 percent, a perpetuity of $1,000 a year would have a present value of $1,000/0.12 = $8,333.33.

V. **Many financial decisions require the analysis of irregular cash flows rather than a stream of fixed payments such as an annuity. The present value of an uneven stream of income is the sum of the PVs of the individual cash flow components. Similarly, the future value of an uneven stream of income is the sum of the FVs of the individual cash flow components.**

VI. **If one knows the relevant cash flows, the effective interest rate can be calculated.**

A. For example, if one borrows $2,000 today and agrees to repay $2,805.20 at the end of 5 years, what is the interest rate?

$$FV_n = PV(FVIF_{k,n})$$

$$FVIF_{k,5} = FV_n/PV = \$2,805.20/\$2,000 = 1.4026.$$

Looking at the Period 5 row of Table A-3, 1.4026 is the FVIF for 7 percent.

B. To solve this problem using a calculator's financial functions, simply enter n = 5, PV = 2,000, and FV = $2,805.20. Then, hit the i key and 7.00 percent is displayed.

C. Similar procedures can be used to solve for the effective interest rate if the cash flow stream is an annuity.

VII. Semiannual, quarterly, and other compounding period more frequent than annual compounding are often used in financial transactions. Compounding on a non-annual basis requires an adjustment in the way in which the interest factors are determined.

    A. *The effective annual percentage rate (EAR) is the rate that would have produced the* final compound value under annual compounding. The effective annual percentage rate is given by the following formula:

$$EAR = (1 + k_{Nom}/m)^m - 1 \; ,$$

where k_{Nom} is the stated annual rate and m is the number of compounding periods per year.

    B. Divide the nominal, or stated, interest rate by the number of times compounding occurs each year.

    C. Use these adjusted values for k and n in the computations and when looking up interest factors in the tables.

    D. For example, the EAR for 12 percent, compounded quarterly, is as follows:

$$EAR = (1 + 0.12/4)^4 - 1 = 12.55\%.$$

    E. For annual compounding use the formula:

$$FV_n = PV(1 + k)^n$$

to find the future value of a lump sum. But when compounding occurs more frequently than once a year, use the formula:

$$FV_n = PV(1 + k_{Nom}/m)^{mn}$$

where m is the number of times per year compounding occurs and n is the number of years.

    F. For example, the amount to which $1,000 will grow after 5 years if quarterly compounding is applied to a stated 8 percent interest rate is as follows:

$$FV_n = \$1,000(1 + 0.08/4)^{(4)(5)} = \$1,000(1.02)^{20} = \$1,485.95.$$

VIII. An amortized loan is a loan that is paid off in equal, periodic installments over time.

    A. The amount of each payment, PMT is found as follows:

$$\text{PV of annuity} = PMT(PVIFA_{k,n}).$$

$$PMT = PV \text{ of annuity}/PVIFA_{k,n}.$$

B. Each payment consists partly of interest and partly of a repayment of principal. This breakdown is often depicted in a loan amortization schedule.
   1. The interest component is largest in the first period and declines subsequently.
   2. The repayment of principal is smallest in the first period and increases thereafter.

IX. Appendix 4A discusses continuous compounding and discounting.

   A. The future value of a present lump sum, when compounded continuously, is given by $FV_n = PVe^{kn}$ where k is the stated interest rate, and n is the number of years of continuous compounding, and e is the value 2.7183.

   B. For example, the future value of $100 compounded continuously for 5 year at 10 percent is $FV_5 = \$100(2.7183)^{(0.1)(5)} = \$100(2.7183)^{0.5} = \$100(1.64873) = \$164.87$. The value of $e^{0.5}$ can be obtained by using the antilog (e^X) function on a calculator, or by using the exponential function and the known value of e.

   C. The present value of a future lump sum, when discounted continuously, is given by $PV = FV_n e^{-kn}$.

DEFINITIONAL QUESTIONS

1. The beginning value of an account or investment in a project is known as its _____ _____.

2. Using a savings account as an example, the difference between the account's _____ value and its _____ value at the end of a period is due to _____ earned during the period.

3. The equation $FV_n = PV(1 + k)^n$ determines the future value of a sum at the end of n periods. The factor $(1 + k)^n$ is known as the _____ _____ _____ _____.

4. The process of finding present values is often referred to as _____ and is the reverse of the _____ process.

5. The $PVIF_{k,n}$ for a 5-year, 5 percent investment is 0.7835. This value is the _____ of the $FVIF_{k,n}$ for 5 years at 5 percent.

6. For a given number of time periods, the $PVIF_{k,n}$ will decline as the _____ _____ increases.

7. A series of payments of a constant amount for a specified number of periods is an _____. If the payments occur at the end of each period it is an _____ annuity, while if the payments occur at the beginning of each period it is an annuity _____.

8. The present value of an uneven stream of future payments is the _____ of the PVs of the individual payments.

9. Since different types of investments use different compounding periods, it is important to distinguish between the stated, or _____, rate and the _____ annual interest rate.

10. To use the interest factor tables when compounding occurs more than once a year, divide the _____ _____ by the number of times compounding occurs and multiply the years by the number of _____ _____ per year.

11. When the number of compounding periods becomes _____, we have the special case of _____ compounding.

CONCEPTUAL QUESTIONS

12. You have determined the profitability of a planned project by finding the present value of all the cash flows from that project. Which of the following would cause the project to look less appealing, that is, have a lower present value?

    a. The discount rate decreases.
    b. The cash flows are extended over a longer period of time.
    c. The discount rate increases.
    d. b and c are both correct.
    e. a and b are both correct.

13. If a bank uses quarterly compounding for savings accounts, the nominal rate will be greater than the effective annual percentage rate (EAR).

    a. True   b. False

14. If money has time value, the future value of some amount of money will always be more than the amount invested. The present value of some amount to be received in the future is always less than the amount to be received.

    a. True   b. False

PROBLEMS

(Note: In working these problems, you may get an answer which differs from ours by a few cents due to differences in rounding. This should not concern you; just pick the closest answer.)

15. Assume that you purchase a 6 year, 8 percent savings certificate for $1,000. If interest is compounded annually, what will be the value of the certificate when it matures?

    a. $630.17
    b. $1,469.33
    c. $1,677.10
    d. $1,586.90
    e. $1,766.33

16. A savings certificate similar to the one in Problem 15 is available with the exception that interest is compounded semiannually. What is the difference between the ending value of the savings certificate compounding semiannually and the one compounded annually?

    a. The semiannual is worth $14.10 more than the annual.
    b. The semiannual is worth $14.10 less than the annual.
    c. The semiannual is worth $21.54 more than the annual.
    d. The semiannual is worth $21.54 less than the annual.
    e. The semiannual is worth the same as the annual.

17. A friend promises to pay you $600 two years from now if you loan him $500 today. What annual interest rate is your friend offering?

    a. 7.5%
    b. 8.5%
    c. 9.5%
    d. 10.5%
    e. 11.5%

18. You are offered an investment opportunity with the "guarantee" that your investment will double in 5 years. Assuming annual compounding, what annual rate of return would this investment provide?

    a. 40.00%
    b. 100.00%
    c. 14.87%
    d. 20.00%
    e. 18.74%

19. You decide to begin saving toward the purchase of a new car in 5 years. If you put $1,000 in a savings account paying 6 percent compounded annually at the end of each of the next 5 years, how much will you accumulate after 5 years?

    a. $6,691.13
    b. $5,637.10
    c. $1,338.23
    d. $5,975.33
    e. $5,731.95

20. Refer to Problem 19. What would be the ending amount if the payments were made at the beginning of each year?

    a. $6.691.13
    b. $5,637.10
    c. $1,338.23
    d. $5,975.33
    e. $5,731.95

21. Refer to Problem 19. What would be the ending amount if $500 payments were made at the end of each 6 month period for 5 years and the account paid 6 percent compounded semiannually?

    a. $6.691.13
    b. $5,637.10
    c. $1,338.23
    d. $5,975.33
    e. $5,731.95

22. Calculate the present value of $1,000 to be received at the end of 8 years. Assume an interest rate of 7 percent.

    a. $582.00
    b. $1,718.19
    c. $531.82
    d. $5,971.30
    e. $649.37

23. How much would you be willing to pay today for an investment that would return $800 each year at the end of each of the next 6 years? Assume a discount rate of 5 percent.

    a. $5,441.53
    b. $4,800.00
    c. $3,369.89
    d. $4,060.56
    e. $4,632.37

24. You have applied for a mortgage of $60,000 to finance the purchase of a new home. The bank will require you to make annual payments of $7,047.55 at the end of each of the next 20 years. Determine the interest rate in effect on this mortgage.

    a. 8.0%
    b. 9.8%
    c. 10.0%
    d. 51.0%
    e. 11.2%

25. If you would like to accumulate $7,500 over the next 5 years, how much must you deposit each six months, starting six months from now, given a 6 percent interest rate and semiannual compounding?

    a. $1,330.47
    b. $879.23
    c. $654.23
    d. $569.00
    e. $732.67

26. A company is offering bonds which pay $100 per year indefinitely. If you require a 12 percent return on these bonds--that is, the discount rate is 12 percent--what is the value of each bond?

a. $1,000.00
b. $962.00
c. $904.67
d. $866.67
e. $833.33

27. What is the present value (t = 0) of the following cash flows if the discount rate is 12 percent?

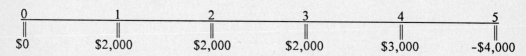

a. $4,782.43
b. $4,440.50
c. $4,221.79
d. $4,041.23
e. $3,997.98

28. What is the effective annual percentage rate (EAR) of 12 percent compounded monthly?

a. 12.00%
b. 12.55%
c. 12.68%
d. 12.75%
e. 13.00%

29. Problem 24 refers to a 20-year mortgage of $60,000. This is an amortized loan. How much principal will be repaid in the second year.

a. $1,152.30
b. $1,725.70
c. $5,895.25
d. $7,047.55
e. $1,047.55

30. You have $1,000 invested in an account which pays 16 percent compounded annually. A commission agent (called a "finder") can locate for you an equally safe deposit which will pay 16 percent, compounded quarterly, for 2 years. What is the maximum amount you should be willing to pay him now as a fee for locating the new account?

   a. $10.92
   b. $13.78
   c. $16.14
   d. $16.80
   e. $21.13

31. The present value (t = 0) of the following cash flow stream is $11,958.20 when discounted at 12 percent annually. What is the value of the missing t = 2 cash flow?

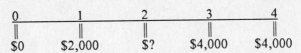

   a. $4,000.00
   b. $4,500.00
   c. $5,000.00
   d. $5,500.00
   e. $6,000.00

32. Today is your birthday and you decide to start saving for your college education. You will begin college on your 18th birthday and will need $4,000 per year at the end of each of the next 4 years. You will make a deposit 1 year from today in an account paying 12 percent annually, and continue to make an identical deposit each year up to and including the year you begin college. If a deposit amount of $2,542.05 will allow you to reach your goal, what birthday are you celebrating today?

   a. 13
   b. 14
   c. 15
   d. 16
   e. 17

(The next problem relates to Appendix 4A)

33. You invest $500 for 12 years in an account that pays 9 percent interest, compounded continuously. What is the ending amount?

   a. $1,298.18
   b. $1,376.48
   c. $1,472.35
   d. $1,503.72
   e. $1,591.83

ANSWERS AND SOLUTIONS

1. present value

2. present; future; interest (I)

3. future value interest factor

4. discounting; compounding

5. reciprocal

6. interest rate

7. annuity; ordinary (deferred); due

8. sum

9. nominal; effective

10. nominal rate; compounding periods

11. infinite; continuous

12. d. The slower the cash flows come in and the higher the interest rate, the lower the present value.

13. b. The EAR is always greater than or equal to the nominal rate.

14. a.

15. d. $FV_n = PV(FVIF_{k,n}) = \$1,000(FVIF_{8\%,6}) = \$1,000(1.5869) = \$1,586.90$.

    Calculator solution = $1,586.87.

16. a. $FVIF_{k,n}$ is now $FVIF_{4\%,12}$ or 1.6010. Thus $FV_n = \$1,000(1.6010) = \$1,601.00$. The difference, $1,601.00 - $1,586.90 = $14.10, is the additional interest.
    Calculator solution = $14.16.

17. c. $FV_n = PV(FVIF_{k,n})$
        $\$600 = \$500(FVIF_{k,2})$
     $FVIF_{k,2} = 1.2000$.

    Looking across the Period 2 row in Table A-3, we see $FVIF_{9\%,2} = 1.1881$ and $FVIF_{10\%,2} = 1.2100$. Therefore, the annual interest rate is between 9% and 10%. Calculator solution = 9.54%.

18. c. Assume any value for the present value and double it:

$$FV_n = PV(FVIF_{k,n})$$
$$\$2 = \$1(FVIF_{k,5})$$
$$FVIF_{k,5} = 2.0000.$$

Looking across the Period 5 row in Table A-3, we see that 2.0000 occurs between 14% and 15%. Calculator solution = 14.87%.

19. b. $FVA_5 = PMT(FVIFA_{6\%,5}) = \$1,000(5.6371) = \$5,637.10.$
Calculator solution = \$5,637.09.

20. d.

$$FVA_5(\text{Annuity due}) = PMT(FVIFA_{6\%,5})(1 + k)$$

$$= \$1,000(5.6371)(1.06) = \$5975.33.$$

Calculator solution = \$5,975.32.

21. e.

$$FVA_{10} = PMT(FVIFA_{3\%,10})$$
$$= \$500(11.4639) = \$5,731.95.$$

Calculator solution = \$5,731.94.

(Note that to use the annuity tables the compounding period and payment period <u>must be the same</u>, in this case both are semiannual. If this is not the case, each cash flow must be treated individually.)

22. a.

$$PV = FV_8(PVIF_{7\%,8})$$
$$= \$1,000(0.5820) = \$582.00.$$

Calculator solution = \$582.01.

(Note that annual compounding is assumed if not otherwise specified.)

23. d.

$$PVA_6 = PMT(PVIFA_{5\%,6})$$
$$= \$800(5.0757) = \$4,060.56.$$

Calculator solution = \$4,060.55.

24. c. The amount of mortgage (\$60,000) is the present value of a 20-year ordinary annuity with payments of \$7,047.55. Therefore,

$$PVA_{20} = PMT(PVIFA_{k,20})$$
$$\$60,000 = \$7,047.55(PVIFA_{k,20})$$
$$PVIFA_{k,20} = 8.5136$$
$$k = 10.00\% \text{ exactly.}$$

25. c.

$$FVA_{10} = PMT(FVIFA_{3\%,10})$$
$$\$7,500 = PMT(11.4639)$$
$$PMT = \$654.23.$$

26. e. $PV = PMT/k = \$100/0.12 = \$833.33.$

27. b.

$$PV = \$2,000(PVIFA_{12\%,3}) + \$3,000(PVIF_{12\%,4})$$
$$+ \$4,000(PVIF_{12\%,5})$$
$$= \$2,000(2.4018) + \$3,000(0.6355) - \$4,000(0.5674)$$
$$= \$4,440.50.$$

Calculator solution = $4,440.51.

28. c. $EAR = (1 + k_{nom}m/m) - 1.0 = (1 + 0.12/12)^{12} - 1.0 = (1.01)^{12} - 1.0 = 1.1268 - 1.0$

$$= 0.1268 = 12.68\%$$

29. a.

Year	Payment	Interest	Repayment on Principal	Remaining Principal Balance
1	$7,047.55	$6,000.00	$1,047.55	$58,952.45
2	7,047.55	5,895.25	1,152.30	57,800.15

30. d.

Currently: $FV_n = \$1,000(FVIF_{16\%,2}) = \$1,000(1.3456)$
$$= \$1,345.60.$$

New account:
$$FV_n = \$1,000 (1 + k_{Nom}/m)mn = \$1,000(1.3686) = \$1,368.60.$$

Thus, the new account will be worth $23.00 more after 2 years.

$$PV \text{ of difference} = \$23(PVIF_{4\%,8})$$
$$= \$23(0.7307) = \$16.80.$$

Calculator solution = $16.80.

Therefore, the most you should be willing to pay the finder for locating the new account is $16.80.

31. e.

$$\$11,958.20 = \$2,000(PVIF_{12\%,1}) + X(PVIF_{12\%,2})$$
$$+ \$4,000(PVIF_{12\%,3}) + \$4,000(PVIF_{12\%,4})$$
$$\$11,958.20 = \$2,000(0.8929) + X(0.7972)$$
$$+ \$4,000(0.7118) + \$4,000(0.6355)$$
$$\$11,958.20 = \$7,175.00 + 0.7972X$$
$$0.7972X = \$4,783.20$$
$$X = \$6,000.00$$

Calculator solution = $6,000.16.

4-14

32. b. First, how much must you accumulate on your 18th birthday?

$$PVA_n = \$4,000(PVIFA_{12\%,4}) = \$4,000(3.0373) = \$12,149.20.$$

Using a financial calculator (with the calculator set for an ordinary annuity), enter:

PMT = \$4,000
   i = 12
   n = 4

and solve by pushing the PV key. \$12,149.40 is displayed. This is the amo it (or lump sum) that must be present in your bank account on your 18th birthday i rder for you to be able to withdraw \$4,000 at the end of each year for the next 4 year

Now, how many payments must you make to accumulate \$12,149.20?

$$FVA_n = \$12,149.20 = \$2,542.05(FVIFA_{12\%,n}).$$
$$FVIFA_{12\%,n} = 4.7793$$
$$n = 4.$$

Using a financial calculator, enter:

 FV = -\$12,149.20
PMT = \$2,542.05
  i = 12

Solve for n by pushing the n key. 4 will be displayed.

Therefore, if you make payments at 18, 17, 16, and 15, you are now 14.

33. c.

$$FV = PVe^{kn}$$
$$= \$500(2.7183)^{(12)(0.09)}$$
$$= \$500(2.7183)^{1.08}$$
$$= \$500(2.9447)$$
$$= \$1,472.35.$$

Calculator solution = \$1,472.34.

CHAPTER 5
VALUATION MODELS

OVERVIEW

This chapter uses the time value of money concept to determine the values of bonds and stocks. The value of any financial asset is the present value of the cash flows expected from that asset. Therefore, once the cash flows have been estimated, and a discount rate determined, the value of the financial asset can be calculated. A bond is valued as the present value of the stream of interest payments (an annuity) plus the present value of the par value which is received by the investor on the bond's maturity date. Depending on the relationship between the current interest rate and the bond's coupon rate, a bond can sell at its par value, at a discount, or at a premium. The total rate of return on a bond is comprised of two components: interest yield and capital gains yield.

The value of a share of preferred stock which is expected to pay a constant dividend forever is found as the dividend divided by the discount rate. A common stock is valued as the present value of the expected future dividend stream. The total rate of return on a stock is comprised of a dividend yield plus a capital gains yield. For both stocks and bonds, the total expected return must equal the average investor's required rate of return.

OUTLINE

I. **Capital is raised in two primary forms--debt and equity. A bond is the primary type of long-term debt.**

   A. A *bond* is a long-term promissory note.

   B. The *par value* is the stated face value of a bond, usually $1,000. This is the amount of money that the firm borrows and promises to repay at some specified future date.

   C. The *maturity date* is the date when the par value is repaid to bondholders.

   D. The *coupon interest payment* is the dollar amount that is paid yearly to a bondholder by the issuer for use of the $1,000 loan. This payment is a fixed amount, established at the time the bond is issued. The coupon interest rate is obtained by dividing the coupon payment by the par value of the bond.

   E. A *new issue* is the term applied to a bond that has just been issued. At the time of issue, the coupon payment is generally set at a level that will force the market price of the bond to equal its par value. Once the bond has been on the market for a while, it is classified as an outstanding, or *seasoned*, bond.

II. Using these definitions, a basic bond valuation model can be constructed.

A. Bonds with annual coupon payments represent an annuity of I dollars (the coupon interest payment) per year for n years, plus a final payment of M dollars (the par value) at the end of n years.

B. The present value of this payment stream determines the value of the bond.

C. As an example, consider a 3-year, $1,000 bond paying $50 annually, when the appropriate interest rate, k_d, is 7 percent:

$$V_B = PV = \sum_{t=1}^{n} \frac{I}{(1+k_d)^t} + \frac{M}{(1+k_d)^n}$$

$$= I(PVIFA_{k,n}) + M(PVIF_{k,n})$$

$$= \$50(2.6243) + \$1,000(0.8163) = \$947.52.$$

D. Financial calculators have a bond valuation capability. The known parameters are entered, and the calculator then displays the unknown value.

E. Bond prices and interest rates are inversely related, that is, they tend to move in the opposite direction from one another.
   1. A bond will sell at par when its coupon interest rate is equal to the going rate of interest, k_d.
   2. When the going rate of interest is above the coupon rate, the bond will sell at a "discount" from its par value, as in the example above.
   3. If current interest rates are below the coupon rate, the bond will sell at a "premium" above its par value.
   4. The discount is equal to the present value of the amount of interest payment one sacrifices to buy a low-coupon old bond rather than a high-coupon new bond. The premium is equal to the present value of the additional interest payment one receives by buying a high-coupon old bond rather than a low-coupon new bond. The exact amount can be obtained by using the formula:

$$\begin{matrix}\text{Discount} \\ \text{or premium}\end{matrix} = \left(\begin{matrix}\text{(Interest payment} \\ \text{on old bond)}\end{matrix} - \begin{matrix}\text{(Interest payment)} \\ \text{on new bond)}\end{matrix}\right)(PVIFA_{kd,n})$$

F. *The longer a bond's maturity, the larger the price change in response to a given movement in market interest rates.* This means that the prices of long-term bonds are more sensitive to interest rate changes than are short-term bond prices.

G. The rate of interest earned on a bond if it is held until redeemed by the issuer is known as the *yield to maturity (YTM)*. The YTM for a bond that sells at par consists entirely of an interest yield, but if the bond sells at a price other than its par value, the YTM consists of the interest yield plus a positive or negative capital gains yield.

H. The bond valuation model must be adjusted when interest is paid semiannually:

$$V = (I/2)(PVIFA_{k/2,2n}) + M(PVIF_{k/2,2n}).$$

I. Interest rates fluctuate over time, and people or firms who invest in bonds are exposed to risk from changing interest rates, or *interest rate risk*. The longer the maturity of the bond, the greater the exposure to interest rate risk. However, the shorter the maturity of the bond, the greater the exposure to *reinvestment rate risk*.

III. Equity capital is usually raised by selling common stock, but it also can be raised through the sale of preferred stock.

    A. *Preferred stock* is stock which pays a constant, stated dividend each year, usually forever. Thus, preferred stock is normally a type of annuity.

    B. The value of any perpetuity is found as the income to be received each year divided by the discount rate:

$$V_{ps} = D_{ps}/k_{ps}$$

Here D_{ps} is the dividend to be received in each year and k_{ps} is the required rate of return on the preferred stock.

IV. Common stocks are also valued by finding the present value of the expected future cash flow stream.

    A. People typically buy common stock expecting to earn *dividends* plus a *capital gain* when they sell their shares at the end of some holding period. The capital gain may or may not be realized, but most people expect a gain or else they would not buy stocks.

    B. The expected dividend yield on a stock during the coming year is equal to the expected dividend, D_1, divided by the current stock price, P_0. The term $(P_1 - P_0)/P_0$ is the expected capital gains yield. The expected dividend yield plus the expected capital gains yield equals the expected total return.

    C. The value of the stock today is calculated as the present value of an infinite stream of dividends. For any investor, cash flows consist of dividends plus the expected future sales price of the stock. This sales price, however, is dependent upon dividends expected by future investors:

$$\hat{P}_0 = \frac{D_1}{(1 + k_s)^1} + \frac{D_2}{(1 + k_s)^2} + \cdots + \frac{D}{(1 + k_s)^n}$$

$$= \sum_{t=1}^{n} \frac{D_t}{(1 + k_s)^t}.$$

Here k_s is the discount rate used to find the present value of the dividends.

D. Dividends are not expected to remain constant in the future, and dividends are harder to predict than bond interest payments. Thus, stock valuation is a more complex task than bond valuation.

E. If expected dividend growth is zero ($g = 0$), the value of the stock is found as follows: $P_0 = D/k_s$. Since a zero growth stock is expected to pay a constant dividend, it can be thought of as a perpetuity. The expected rate of return is simply the dividend yield: $k_s = D/P_0$.

F. For many companies, earnings and dividends are expected to grow at some "normal" or constant rate. Dividends in any future Year t may be forecast as $D_t = D_0(1 + g)^t$, where D_0 is the last dividend paid and g is the expected rate of growth. For a company which last paid a $2.00 dividend and which has an expected 6 percent growth rate, the estimated dividend 1 year from now would be $D_1 = \$2.00(1.06) = \$2.12$; D_2 would be $\$2.00(1.06)^2 = \$2.25$, and the estimated dividend 4 years hence would be $D_t = D_0(1 + g)^t = \$2.00(1.06)^4 = \$2.525$. Using this method of estimating future dividends, the current price, P_0, is determined as follows:

$$P_0 = \frac{D_1}{(1 + k_s)^1} + \frac{D_2}{(1 + k_s)^2} + \frac{D_3}{(1 + k_s)^3} + \cdots$$

$$= \frac{D_0(1 + g)^1}{(1 + k_s)^1} + \frac{D_0(1 + g)^2}{(1 + k_s)^2} + \frac{D_0(1 + g)^3}{(1 + k_s)^3} + \cdots$$

$$= \sum_{t=1}^{n} \frac{D_0(1 + g)^t}{(1 + k_s)^t}.$$

If g is constant, and if k_s is greater than g, this equation simplifies as follows:

$$P_0 = \frac{D_1}{k_s - g}.$$

This equation for valuing a constant growth stock is often called the "Gordon model," after Myron J. Gordon, who developed it.

G. For all stocks,

$$\hat{k}_s = \text{Dividend yield} + \text{Capital gains yield}$$

$$= D_1/P_0 \qquad + \qquad g.$$

Thus, the total expected return is composed of an expected dividend yield plus an expected capital gains yield. For a constant growth stock, both the dividend yield and the capital gains yield remain constant over time.

H. The Gordon model can also be used to estimate a stock's expected rate of return, given its price. Rearranging terms, we obtain

$$\hat{k}_s = \frac{D_1}{P_0} + g .$$

I. Firms typically go through periods of nonconstant growth, after which time their growth rate settles to a rate close to that of the economy as a whole. The value of such a firm is equal to the present value of its expected future dividends. To find the value of such a stock, we proceed in three steps:

   1. Find the present value of the dividends during the period of nonconstant growth.
   2. Find the price of the stock at the end of the nonconstant growth period, at which point it has become a constant growth stock, and then discount this price back to the present at the rate k_s.
   3. Add these two components to find the present value of the stock, P_0.

J. A declining firm's return consists of a relatively high dividend yield combined with a capital loss yield; a no-growth firm's total return equals its dividend yield; a normal-growth firm provides both a dividend and a capital gains yield; and a firm experiencing a period of supernormal growth has a relatively low dividend yield and a relatively high capital gains yield expectation.

V. Anyone who has ever invested in the stock market knows that there can be, and generally are, large differences between expected and realized prices and returns.

   A. Investors always expect positive returns from stock investments or else they would not buy them.

   B. However, in some years negative returns are actually earned.

   C. Even in bad years, some individual stocks do well, and the "name of the game" in security analysis is to pick the winners. Financial managers are trying to take those actions that will help put their companies in the winner's column.

DEFINITIONAL QUESTIONS

1. A _____ is a long-term promissory note issued by a business firm or governmental unit.

2. The stated face value of a bond is referred to as its _____ value and is usually set at $_____.

3. The "coupon interest rate" on a bond is determined by dividing the _____ _____ by the _____ _____ of the bond.

4. The date at which the par value of a bond is repaid to each bondholder is known as the _____ _____.

5. A bond with annual coupon payments represents an annuity of I dollars per year for n years, plus a lump sum of M dollars at the end of n years, and its value, V, is the _____ _____ of this payment stream.

6. At the time a bond is issued, the coupon interest rate is generally set at a level that will cause the _____ _____ and the _____ _____ of the bond to be approximately equal.

7. Market interest rates and bond prices move in _____ directions from one another.

8. The rate of interest earned by purchasing a bond and holding it until maturity is known as the bond's _____ _____ _____ .

9. To adjust the bond valuation formula for semiannual coupon payments, the _____ _____ and _____ _____ must be divided by 2, and the number of _____ must be multiplied by 2.

10. Like other financial assets, the value of common stock is the _____ value of a future stream of income.

11. The income stream expected from a common stock consists of a _____ ield and a _____ _____ yield.

12. If ι e future growth rate of dividends is expected to be _____, the rate of return is simp. the _____ yield.

13. Investor. always expect a _____ return on stock investments, but in some years _____ returns may actually be earned.

CONCEPTUAL QUESTIONS

14. Changes in economic conditions cause interest rates and bond prices to vary over time.

    a. True   b. False

15. If the appropriate rate of interest on a bond is greater than its coupon rate, the market value of that bond will be above par value.

    a. True   b. False

16. A 20-year bond with 1 year left to maturity has the same interest rate risk as a 10-year bond with 1 year left to maturity. Both bonds have the same coupon rate.

    a. True   b. False

17. According to the valuation model developed in this chapter, the value that an investor assigns to a share of stock is independent of the length of time the investor plans to hold the stock.

    a. True   b. False

18. Which of the following assumptions would cause the constant growth stock valuation model to be invalid?

$$P_0 = \frac{D_0(1 + g)}{k_s - g}$$

a. The growth rate is negative.
b. The growth rate is zero.
c. The growth rate is less than the required rate of return.
d. The required rate of return is above 30 percent.
e. None of the above assumptions would invalidate the model.

PROBLEMS

19. Delta Corporation has a bond issue outstanding with a coupon rate of 7 percent per year and 4 years remaining until maturity. The par value of the bond is $1,000. Determine the current value of the bond if present market conditions justify a 14 percent required rate of return. The bond pays interest annually.

a. $1,126.42
b. $1,000.00
c. $796.06
d. $791.00
e. $536.42

20. Refer to Problem 19. Suppose the bond had a semiannual coupon. Now what would be the current value?

a. $1,126.42
b. $1,000.00
c. $796.06
d. $791.00
e. $536.42

21. Refer to Problem 19. Assume an annual coupon, but 20 years remaining to maturity. What is the current value under these conditions?

a. $1,126.42
b. $1,000.00
c. $796.06
d. $791.00
e. $536.42

22. Acme Products has a bond issue outstanding with 8 years remaining to maturity, a coupon rate of 10 percent with interest paid annually, and a par value of $1,000. If the current market price of the bond issue is $814.45, what is the yield to maturity, k_d?

    a. 12%
    b. 13%
    c. 14%
    d. 15%
    e. 16%

23. Stability, Inc., has maintained a dividend rate of $4 per share for many years. The same rate is expected to be paid in future years. If investors require a 12 percent rate of return on similar investments, determine the present value of the company's stock.

    a. $15.00
    b. $30.00
    c. $33.33
    d. $35.00
    e. $40.00

24. Your sister-in-law, a stockbroker at Invest, Inc., is trying to sell you a stock with a current market price of $25. The stock's last dividend (D_0) was $2.00, and earnings and dividends are expected to increase at a constant growth rate of 10 percent. Your required return on this stock is 20 percent. From a strict valuation standpoint, you should:

    a. Buy the stock; it is fairly valued.
    b. Buy the stock; it is undervalued by $3.00.
    c. Buy the stock; it is undervalued by $2.00.
    d. Not buy the stock; it is overvalued by $2.00.
    e. Not buy the stock; it is overvalued by $3.00.

25. Lucas Laboratories' last dividend was $1.50. Its current equilibrium stock price is $15.75, and its expected growth rate is a constant 5 percent. If the stockholders' required rate of return is 15 percent, what is the expected dividend yield and expected capital gains yield for the coming year?

    a. 0%; 15%
    b. 5%; 10%
    c. 10%; 5%
    d. 15%; 0%
    e. 15%; 15%

22. Acme Products has a bond issue outstanding with 8 years remaining to maturity, a coupon rate of 10 percent with interest paid annually, and a par value of $1,000. If the current market price of the bond issue is $814.45, what is the yield to maturity, k_d?

    a. 12%
    b. 13%
    c. 14%
    d. 15%
    e. 16%

23. Stability, Inc., has maintained a dividend rate of $4 per share for many years. The same rate is expected to be paid in future years. If investors require a 12 percent rate of return on similar investments, determine the present value of the company's stock.

    a. $15.00
    b. $30.00
    c. $33.33
    d. $35.00
    e. $40.00

24. Your sister-in-law, a stockbroker at Invest, Inc., is trying to sell you a stock with a current market price of $25. The stock's last dividend (D_0) was $2.00, and earnings and dividends are expected to increase at a constant growth rate of 10 percent. Your required return on this stock is 20 percent. From a strict valuation standpoint, you should:

    a. Buy the stock; it is fairly valued.
    b. Buy the stock; it is undervalued by $3.00.
    c. Buy the stock; it is undervalued by $2.00.
    d. Not buy the stock; it is overvalued by $2.00.
    e. Not buy the stock; it is overvalued by $3.00.

25. Lucas Laboratories' last dividend was $1.50. Its current equilibrium stock price is $15.75, and its expected growth rate is a constant 5 percent. If the stockholders' required rate of return is 15 percent, what is the expected dividend yield and expected capital gains yield for the coming year?

    a. 0%; 15%
    b. 5%; 10%
    c. 10%; 5%
    d. 15%; 0%
    e. 15%; 15%

26. The Canning Company has been hard hit by increased competition. Analysts predict that earnings (and dividends) will decline at a rate of 5 percent annually into the foreseeable future. If Canning's last dividend (D_0) was $2.00, and investors' required rate of return is 15 percent, what will be Canning's stock price *in 3 years*?

   a. $8.15
   b. $9.50
   c. $10.00
   d. $10.42
   e. $10.96

(The following data are applied in Problems 27 through 29.)

The Club Auto Parts Company has just recently been organized. It is expected to experience no growth for the next 2 years as it identifies its market and acquires its inventory. However, Club will grow at an annual rate of 5 percent in the third year, and, beginning with the fourth year, should attain a 10 percent growth rate which it will sustain thereafter. The first dividend (D_1) to be paid at the end of the first year is expected to be $0.50 per share. Investors require a 15 percent rate of return on Club's stock.

27. What is the current equilibrium stock price?

   a. $5.00
   b. $8.75
   c. $9.57
   d. $12.43
   e. $15.00

28. What will Club's stock price be at the end of the first year (P_1)?

   a. $5.00
   b. $8.76
   c. $9.56
   d. $12.43
   e. $15.00

29. What dividend yield and capital gains yield should an investor in Club expect for the first year?

   a. 0%; 15%
   b. 3%; 12%
   c. 6%; 9%
   d. 10%; 5%
   e. 12%; 3%

30. You have just been offered a bond for $863.731. The coupon rate is 8 percent, payable annually, and interest rates on new issues with the same degree of risk are 10 percent. You want to know how many more interest payments you will receive, but the party selling the bond cannot remember. If the par value is $1,000, how many interest payments remain?

    a. 10
    b. 11
    c. 12
    d. 13
    e. 14

31. Johnson Corporation's stock is currently selling at $45.83 per share. The last dividend paid (D_0) was $2.50. Johnson is a constant growth firm. If investors require a return of 16 percent on Johnson's stock, what do they think Johnson's growth rate will be?

    a. 6%
    b. 7%
    c. 8%
    d. 9%
    e. 10%

ANSWERS AND SOLUTIONS

1. bond

2. par; 1,000

3. coupon payment; par value

4. maturity date

5. present value

6. market price; par value

7. opposite

8. yield to maturity

9. coupon payment; interest rate; years

10. present

11. dividend; capital gains

12. zero; dividend

13. positive; negative

14. a. For example, if inflation increases, the required return will increase, resulting in a decline in price.

15. b. It will sell at a discount.

16. a. Both bonds are valued as 1-year bonds regardless of their original issue dates, and since they have the same coupon rate, their prices must be equal. Therefore, the interest rate risk is the same.

17. a. The model considers all future dividends. This produces a current value which is appropriate for all investors independent of their expected holding period.

18. e. The model would be invalid, however, if the growth rate *exceeded* the required rate of return.

19. c.

$$V = I(PVIFA_{k,n}) + M(PVIF_{k,n})$$

$$= \$70(PVIFA_{14\%,4}) + \$1,000(PVIF_{14\%,4})$$

$$= \$70(2.9137) + \$1,000(0.5921) = \$796.06.$$

Calculator solution = $796.04.

20. d.

$$V = (I/2)(PVIFA_{k/2,2n}) + M(PVIF_{k/2,2n})$$

$$= \$35(PVIFA_{7\%,8}) + \$1,000(PVIF_{7\%,8})$$

$$= \$35(5.9713) + \$1,000(0.5820) = \$791.00.$$

Calculator solution = $791.00.

21. e.

$$V = I(PVIFA_{k,n}) + M(PVIF_{k,n})$$

$$= \$70(PVIFA_{14\%,20}) + \$1,000(PVIF_{14\%,20})$$

$$= \$70(6.6231) + \$1,000(0.0728) = \$536.42.$$

Calculator solution = $536.38.

22. c.
$$V = I(PVIFA_{k,n}) + M(PVIF_{k,n})$$

$$\$814.45 = \$100(PVIFA_{k,8}) + \$1,000(PVIF_{k,8}).$$

Now use trial and error techniques. Try $k = 12\%$:

$$\$814.45 = \$100(4.9676) + \$1,000(0.4039) = \$900.66.$$

Since $\$814.45 \neq \$900.66$, the yield to maturity is not 12 percent. The calculated value is too large. Therefore, increase the value of k to 14 percent to lower the calculated value:

$$\$814.45 = \$100(4.6389) + \$1,000(0.3506) = \$814.49.$$

This is close enough to conclude that k_d = yield to maturity = 14%. Calculator solution = 14.00%.

23. c. This is a zero-growth stock, or perpetuity:

$$P_0 = D/k_s = \$4.00/0.12 = \$33.33.$$

24. a.
$$P_0 = \frac{D_0(1 + g)}{k_s - g} = \frac{\$2.00(1.10)}{0.20 - 0.10} = \$22.00.$$

Since the stock is currently selling for $25.00, the stock is not in equilibrium and is overvalued by $3.00.

25. c.
$$\text{Dividend yield} = \frac{D_1}{P_0} = \frac{D_0(1 + g)}{P_0} = \frac{\$1.50(1.05)}{\$15.75}$$

$$= 0.10 = 10\%.$$

$$\text{Capital gains yield} = \frac{P_1 - P_0}{P_0} = \frac{P_0(1 + g) - P_0}{P_0}$$

$$= \frac{\$16.54 - \$15.75}{\$15.75} = g = 5\%.$$

For a constant growth stock the capital gains yield is equal to g.

26. a. $P_0 = \dfrac{D_0(1 + g)}{k_s - g} = \dfrac{\$2.00(0.95)}{0.15 - (-0.05)} = \dfrac{\$1.90}{0.20} = \$9.50.$

$P_3 = P_0(1 + g)^3 = \$9.50(0.95)^3 = \$9.50(0.8574)$

$\quad = \$8.15.$

The Gordon model can also be used:

$P_3 = \dfrac{D_4}{k_s - g} = \dfrac{D_0(1 + g)^4}{0.15 - (-0.05)} = \dfrac{\$2.00(.95)^4}{0.20} = \dfrac{\$2.00(.8145)}{0.20}$

$\quad = \$8.15.$

27. b. To calculate the current value of a nonconstant growth stock, follow these steps:

(1) Determine the expected stream of dividends during the nonconstant growth period. Also calculate the expected dividend at the end of the first year of constant growth that will be used later to calculate stock price.

$D_1 = \$0.50$

$D_2 = D_1(1 + g)$

$\quad = \$0.50(1 + 0.0)$

$\quad = \$0.50.$

$D_3 = D_2(1 + g)$

$\quad = \$0.50(1.05)$

$\quad = \$0.525.$

$D_4 = D_3(1 + g)$

$\quad = \$0.525(1.10)$

$\quad = \$0.5775.$

(2) Discount the expected dividends during the nonconstant growth period at the investor's required rate of return to find their present value.

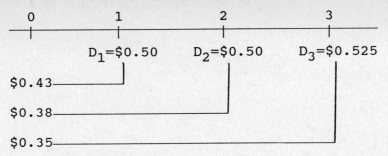

(3) Calculate the expected stock at the end of the final year of nonconstant growth. This occurs at the end of Year 3. Use the Gordon model for this calculation.

$$P_3 = D_4/k_s - g = \$0.5775/0.15 - 0.10 = \$11.55.$$

Then discount this stock price 3 periods at the investor's required rate of return to find its present value.

$$PV = \$11.55(PVIF_{15\%,3})$$

$$= \$11.55(0.6575)$$

$$= \$7.59.$$

(4) Add the present value of the stock price expected at the end of Year 3 plus the dividends expected in Years 1, 2 and 3 to find the present value of the stock, P_0.

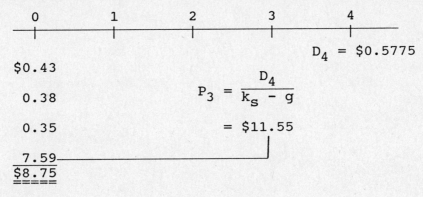

28. c. To calculate the expected stock price at the end of Year 1, P_1, follow the same procedure you would to find the value of a nonconstant growth stock. However, discount values to Year 1 instead of Year 0. Also, remember that the dividend in Year 1, D_1, is not included in the valuation because it has already been paid and therefore adds nothing to the wealth of the investor buying the stock at the end of Year 1.

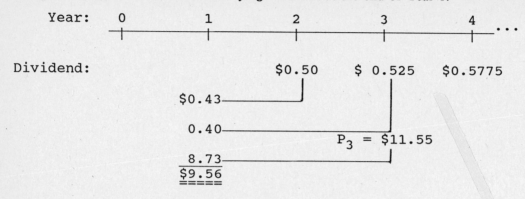

29. c.

$$\text{Dividend yield} = D_1/P_0 = \$0.50/\$8.75 = 0.057 \approx 6\%.$$

$$\text{Capital gains yield} = P_1 - P_0/P_0 = \$9.56 - \$8.75/\$8.75 = 0.093 \approx 9\%.$$

The total yield = dividend yield + capital gains yield = 6% + 9% = 15%. The total yield must equal the required rate of return. Also, the capital gains yield is not equal the growth rate during the nonconstant growth phase of a nonconstant growth stock. Finally, the dividend and capital gains yields are not constant until the constant growth phase is reached.

30. c.

$$V = I(PVIFA_{k,n}) + M(PVIF_{k,n})$$

$$\$863.731 = \$80(PVIFA_{10\%,n}) + \$1,000(PVIF_{10\%,n})$$

Now use trial and error to find the value of n for which the equality holds. For n = 12, $\$863.731 = \$80(6.8137) + \$1,000(0.3186) = \$863.70$. Or using a financial calculator, enter:

$$FV = \$1,000$$

$$PV = -\$863.731$$

$$PMT = \$80$$

$$i = 10\%$$

Solve for n, which equals 12.

31.

$$P_0 = D_0(1 + g)/k_s - g$$

$$\$45.83 = \$2.50(1 + g)/0.16 - g$$

$$\$7.33 - \$45.83g = \$2.50 + \$2.50g$$

$$\$48.33g = \$4.83$$

$$g = 0.0999 \approx 10\%.$$

III. The relevant riskiness of an individual stock is its contribution to the riskiness of a well-diversified portfolio. Different stocks will affect a portfolio differently; thus, they have different degrees of relevant risk. This risk can be measured by the relationship of the individual stock's movements to overall market movements. This measurement is called the stock's beta coefficient.

    A. The beta coefficient of an individual stock measures that stock's volatility relative to an average stock.

    B. An "average stock" by definition has a beta coefficient of 1.0.

    C. A stock that is twice as volatile as the market will have a beta of 2.0, while a stock that is half as volatile as the market will have a beta coefficient of 0.5.

    D. The beta coefficient of a portfolio of securities is the weighted average of the betas of the individual stocks:

$$b_p = \sum_{i=1}^{n} w_i b_i.$$

IV. The Capital Asset Pricing Model (CAPM) employs the concept of beta, which measures risk as the relationship between a particular stock's movements and the movements of the overall stock market. The CAPM uses a stock's beta in conjunction with the average degree of risk aversion of investors to calculate the return that an investor requires, k_s, on that particular stock.

    A. The CAPM is a useful tool for investment analysis because it specifies how risk should be measured (by beta) and how risk should be incorporated into required rates of return.

    B. The Capital Asset Pricing Model states that the required return on the ith stock, k_i, is found as follows:

$$k_i = k_{RF} + b_i(k_M - k_{RF}).$$

Here k_{RF} is the rate of interest on risk free securities, b_i is the ith stock's beta, and k_M is the return on the market or, alternatively, on an average stock.

    1. The term, $k_M - k_{RF}$, is the market risk premium, RP_M. This is a measure of the additional return over the risk-free rate that is required to compensate investors for assuming an average amount of risk. It is dependent upon the degree of aversion that investors in the aggregate have to risk--the higher investors' risk aversion, the larger RP_M.

    2. In the CAPM the *market risk premium*, $k_M - k_{RF}$, is multiplied by the stock's beta to determine the additional premium over the risk-free rate that is required to compensate investors for the risk inherent in a particular stock.

    3. This premium may be larger or smaller than the premium required on an average stock, depending on the riskiness of that stock in relation to the overall market as measured by the stock's beta.

4. The risk premium calculated by $b_i(k_M - k_{RF})$ is added to the risk free rate, k_{RF} (the rate on Treasury securities), to determine the total rate of return required by investors on a particular stock, k_s.

C. A graph of the CAPM equation can be used to visualize the relationship between risk and rate of return. The equation in a CAPM graph is called the *Security Market Line (SML)*.

D. The risk-free rate of interest consists of two parts: (1) a real or inflation-free rate and (2) an inflation premium equal to the anticipated rate of inflation.
   1. The real rate on risk-free government bonds has, historically, ranged from 2 to 4 percent.
   2. As inflation increases, a higher premium must be added to the real rate of return to compensate for the loss of purchasing power.
   3. An increase in the risk-free rate will cause an upward shift in the SML.
   4. The risk-free rate usually changes because of a change in expectations about future inflation. However, it could also change as a result of a change in the real rate, k^*.

E. The slope of the SML reflects the extent to which investors are averse to risk--the steeper the slope of the line, the greater the average investors' aversion to risk.

V. **The relationship between a stock's required and expected rates of return determines the equilibrium price level where buying and selling pressures will just offset each other.**

A. If the expected rate of return is less than the required rate, investors will desire to sell the stock, and there will be a tendency for the price to decline.

B. When the expected rate of return is greater than the required rate, investors will try to purchase shares of the stock, and this will drive the price upward.

C. Only at the equilibrium price, where the expected and required rates are equal, will the stock be stable.

D. Equilibrium will generally exist for a given stock, because security prices adjust rapidly to new developments.

E. Changes in the equilibrium price can be brought about (1) by a change in risk aversion, (2) by a change in the risk-free rate, (3) by a change in the stock's beta coefficient, or (4) by a change in the stock's expected rate of growth.

F. The *Efficient Markets Hypothesis (EMH)* hypothesizes that stocks are always in equilibrium, and that it is impossible for an investor to consistently "beat the market."
   1. The *weak form* of the EMH states that past trends in stock prices can not be used to predict future prices. Empirical tests support weak form efficiency.
   2. The *semi-strong form* of the EMH states that all publicly announced information is reflected in stock prices. This form is supported by empirical tests to a reasonable extent, especially for large NYSE companies.
   3. *Strong form* efficiency states that all information is reflected in stock prices. This is not true, because people with inside information can make (illegal) profits.

VI. Although logical in its development, the CAPM is not without deficiencies.

    A. Betas are generally calculated for some past period, and the assumption is made that the relative volatility of a stock will remain constant in the future. However, conditions may change and alter a stock's future volatility, which is the item of real concern to investors.

    B. The CAPM should use only expected data, yet only historic data are generally available.

    C. The CAPM assumes no brokerage costs, yet such costs exist and hinder full diversification as required by the model.

DEFINITIONAL QUESTIONS

1. Investment risk is association with the _____ of low or negative returns; the greater the chance of loss, the _____ the investment.

2. A listing of all possible _____, with a probability assigned to each, is known as a _____ _____.

3. Weighting each possible outcome of a distribution by its _____ of occurrence and summing the results give the _____ _____ of the distribution.

4. One measure of the tightness of a probability distribution is the _____ _____.

5. Investors who prefer outcomes with a high degree of certainty to those that are less certain are described as being _____ _____.

6. Owning a _____ of securities enables investors to benefit from _____.

7. Diversification of a portfolio can result in lower _____ for the same level of _____.

8. Diversification of a portfolio is achieved by selecting securities that are not perfectly _____ correlated with each other.

9. That part of a stock's risk that can be reduced by _____ is known as _____ risk, while the portion that cannot be eliminated is called _____ risk.

10. The _____ _____ measures a stock's relative volatility as compared with a stock market index.

11. A stock that is twice as volatile as the market in general would have a beta coefficient of _____, while a stock with a beta of 0.5 would be only _____ as volatile as the market.

12. The beta coefficient of a portfolio is the _____ _____ of the _____ of the individual stocks.

13. The expected value of a probability distribution of future returns is known as the _____ rate of return. The minimum expected return that will induce investors to buy a particular security is the _____ rate of return.

14. The security used to measure the risk-free rate is the return available on _____ securities.

15. The difference between the _____ rate of return on a risky asset and the _____ rate is referred to as a _____ _____ .

16. The risk premium for a stock may be calculated by multiplying the stock's _____ _____ times the _____ risk premium.

17. A stock's required rate of return is equal to the _____ rate plus the stock's _____ _____ .

18. The risk-free rate is made up of two parts: An inflation-free or _____ rate of return plus an _____ premium.

19. Changes in investors' _____ _____ alter the _____ of Security Market Line.

20. The price at which a stock's expected and _____ rates of return are equal is known as the _____ price.

21. Among the factors that may cause a stock's equilibrium price to change are (1) the _____ rate, (2) the stock's _____ coefficient, and (3) the stock's _____ rate of growth.

CONCEPTUAL QUESTIONS

22. The Y axis intercept of the Security Market Line (SML) indicates the required rate of return on an individual stock with a beta of 1.0.

    a. True   b. False

23. If a stock has a beta of zero, it will be riskless when held in isolation.

    a. True   b. False

24. Which is the best measure of risk for an asset held in a well-diversified portfolio?

    a. Variance
    b. Standard deviation
    c. Beta
    d. Semi-variance
    e. Expected value

25. In a portfolio of three different stocks, which of the following could <u>not</u> be true?

   a. The riskiness of the portfolio is less than the riskiness of each stock held in isolation.
   b. The riskiness of the portfolio is greater than the riskiness of one or two of the stocks.
   c. The beta of the portfolio is less than the beta of each of the individual stocks.
   d. The beta of the portfolio is greater than the beta of one or two of the individual stocks.
   e. The beta of the portfolio is equal to the beta of one of the individual stocks.

26. If investors expected inflation to increase in the future, and they also became more risk averse, what could be said about the change in the Security Market Line (SML)?

   a. The SML would shift up and the slope would increase.
   b. The SML would shift up and the slope would decrease.
   c. The SML would shift down and the slope would increase.
   d. The SML would shift down and the slope would decrease.
   e. The SML would remain unchanged.

PROBLEMS

27. Stock A has the following probability distribution of expected returns:

Probability	Rate of Return
0.1	-15%
0.2	0
0.4	5
0.2	10
0.1	25

What is Stock A's expected rate of return and standard deviation?

   a. 8.0%; 9.5%
   b. 8.0%; 6.5%
   c. 5.0%; 3.5%
   d. 5.0%; 6.5%
   e. 5.0%; 9.5%

28. If $k_{RF} = 5\%$, $k_M = 11\%$ and $b = 1.3$ for Stock X, what is k_X, the required rate of return for Stock X?

   a. 18.7%

   e. 11.9%

29. Refer to Problem 28. What would k_X be if investors expected the inflation rate to increase by 2 percentage points?

   a. 18.7%
   b. 16.7%
   c. 14.8%
   d. 12.8%
   e. 11.9%

30. Refer to Problem 28. What would k_X be if investors' risk aversion increased by 3 percentage points?

   a. 18.7%
   b. 16.7%
   c. 14.8%
   d. 12.8%
   e. 11.9%

31. Refer to Problem 28. What would k_X be if investors expected the inflation rate to increase by 2 percentage points *and* their risk aversion increased by 3 percentage points.

   a. 18.7%
   b. 16.7%
   c. 14.8%
   d. 12.8%
   e. 11.9%

32. Land Corporation's stock has a beta of 1.5, and a constant growth of 6 percent. Its next expected dividend (D_1) is $2.00. If the risk free rate of return is 10 percent, and the required rate of return on the market is 15 percent, what is the stock's equilibrium price?

   a. $15.93
   b. $16.52
   c. $17.39
   d. $18.21
   e. $19.76

33. The Apple Investment Fund has a total investment of $450 million in five stocks.

Stock	Investment (millions)	Beta
1	$130	0.4
2	110	1.5
3	70	3.0
4	90	2.0
5	50	1.0

What is the fund's overall, or weighted average, beta?

a. 1.14
b. 1.22
c. 1.35
d. 1.46
e. 1.53

34. Refer to Problem 33. If the risk-free rate is 12 percent, and the market risk premium is 6 percent, what is the required rate of return on the Apple Fund?

a. 20.76%
b. 19.92%
c. 18.81%
d. 17.62%
e. 15.77%

35. Browne, Inc., a constant-growth firm, has just paid a dividend (D_0) of $2.00 per share. Its stock is now selling for $88.00 per share. The firm's stock is half as volatile as the market. The expected rate of return on the market is 14 percent, and the yield on U.S. Treasury securities is 11 percent. If the stock is in equilibrium, what rate of growth is expected?

a. 7%
b. 8%
c. 9%
d. 10%
e. 11%

36. You are managing a portfolio of 10 stocks which are held in equal dollar amounts. The current beta of the portfolio is 1.8, and the beta of Stock A is 2.0. If Stock A is sold, ~~and replacement stock~~ what does the beta of the ~~...~~

a. 1.4
b. 1.3
c. 1.2
d. 1.1
e. 1.0

37. Rollins Company's stock is in equilibrium. The following data reflect current conditions:

P_0 = $10.00; D_0 = $1.50; g = constant = 6%; k_{RF} = 10%; k_M = 15%.

What is the beta of Rollins' stock?

a. 2.50
b. 2.38
c. 2.14
d. 1.96
e. 1.75

ANSWERS AND SOLUTIONS

1. probability; riskier

2. outcomes; probability distribution

3. probability; expected return

4. standard deviation

5. risk averse

6. portfolio; diversification

7. risk; return

8. positively

9. diversification; company-specific; market

10. beta coefficient

11. 2.0; half

12. weighted average; betas

13. expected; required

14. U.S. Treasury

15. required; risk-free; risk premium

16. beta coefficient; market

17. risk-free; risk premium

18. real; inflation

19. risk aversion; slope

20. required; equilibrium

21. risk-free; beta; expected

22. b. The Y axis intercept of the SML is k_{RF}, which is the required rate of return of an individual stock with a beta of zero.

23. b. A zero beta stock is riskless from a market risk viewpoint but still has company-specific risk and will be risky when held in isolation.

24. c.

25. c.

26. a.

27. e. $\hat{k}_A = 0.1(-15\%) + 0.2(0\%) + 0.4(5\%) + 0.2(10\%) + 0.1(25\%) = 5.0\%$.

Variance $= 0.1(-0.15 - 0.05)^2 + 0.2(0.0 - 0.05)^2 + 0.4(0.05 - 0.05)^2$

$\qquad + 0.2(0.10 - 0.05)^2 + 0.2(0.0 - 0.05)^2 + 0.4(0.05 - 0.05)^2$

$\qquad = 0.009$.

Standard deviation $= \sqrt{0.009} = 0.0949 \approx 9.5\%$.

28. d. $k_X = k_{RF} + b_X(k_M - k_{RF}) = 5\% + 1.3(11\% - 5\%) = 12.8\%$.

29. c. $k_X = k_{RF} + b_X(k_M - k_{RF}) = 7\% \quad 1.3(13\% - 7\%) = 14.8\%$.

A change in the inflation premium does *not* change the mark   risk premium $(k_M - k_{RF})$ since both k_M and k_{RF} are affected.

30. b. $k_X = k_{RF} + b_X(k_M - k_{RF}) = 5\% + 1.3(14 \quad - 5\%) = 16.7\%$.

31. a. $k_X = k_{RF} + b_X(k_M - k_{RF}) = 7\% + 1.5(10\% - 7\%) = 10.7\%.$

32. c. $k_L = k_{RF} + b_L(k_M - k_{RF}) = 10\% + 1.5(15\% - 10\% \quad = 17.5\%$.

$$P_0 = \frac{D_1}{k_s \quad y} = \frac{\$2.00}{0.175 \quad 0.000} = \$17.39.$$

33. d.

$$b_p = \sum_{i=1}^{5} w_i b_i$$

$= (130/450)(0.4) + (110/450)(1.5) + (70/450)(3.0)$

$+ (90/450)(2.0) + (50/450)(1.0)$

$= 1.46$.

34. a. $k_p = k_{RF} + b_p(k_M - k_{RF}) = 12\% + 1.46(6\%) = 20.76\%$.

35. d. $k_B = k_{RF} + b_B(k_M - k_{RF}) = 11\% + 0.5(14\% - 11\%) = 12.5\%$.

$$P_0 = \frac{D_0(1 + g)}{k_s - g}$$

$$\$88 = \frac{\$2(1 + g)}{0.125 - g}$$

$$11 - 88g = 2 + 2g$$

$$90g = 9$$

$$g = 0.10 = 10\%.$$

36. e. First find the beta of the remaining 9 stocks:

$$1.8 = 0.9(b_R) + 0.1(b_A)$$

$$1.8 = 0.9(b_R) + 0.1(2.0)$$

$$1.8 = 0.9(b_R) + .2$$

$$1.6 = 0.9(b_R)$$

$$b_R = 1.78.$$

Now find the beta of the new stock that produces $b_p = 1.7$.

$$1.7 = 0.9(1.78) + 0.1(b_N)$$

$$1.7 = 1.6 + 0.1(b_N)$$

$$0.1 = 0.1(b_N)$$

$$b_N = 1.0.$$

37. b.

$$\hat{k}_R = \frac{D_0(1 + g)}{P_0} + g \quad \text{and} \quad k_R = k_{RF} + b_R(k_M - k_{RF}).$$

In equilibrium, $\hat{k}_R = k_R$: Thus,

$$\frac{\$1.50(1.06)}{\$10.00} + 0.06 = 0.10 + b_R(0.15 - 0.10)$$

$$0.159 + 0.06 = 0.10 + 0.05b_R$$

$$b_R = 2.38.$$

CHAPTER 7
FINANCIAL ANALYSIS

OVERVIEW

Financial analysis is d_ gned to determine the relative strengths and weaknesses of a company. Investors need this _ _ormation to estimate both future cash flows from the firm and the riskiness of those fl_ _s. Financial managers need the information provided by analysis both to evaluate the firm's _ist performance and to map future plans. Financial analysis concentrates on *financial stat_ _ent analysis*, which highlights the key aspects of a firm's operation. Financial stateme_ _analysis involves a study of the relationships between income statement and balance sheet a_ _unts, how these relationships change over time (or trend analysis), and how a particular fi_ _compares with other firms in its industry. Although financial analysis has limitations, _ _en used with care and judgment, it can provide some very useful insights into the operat_ _s of a company.

OUTLINE

I. A firm's *annual report* to shareholders presents two important types of information. The first is a *verbal statement* of the company's recent operations and its expectations for the coming year. The second is a set of *financial statements* which report what actually happened.

A. The *income statement* reports the results of operations for the past year. Earnings per share (EPS) is generally considered to be the most important item shown on this statement--EPS is "the bottom line."

B. The *balance sheet* shows the firm's assets and the claims against those assets. It portrays the financial condition at a point in time.
  1. Assets, found on the left-hand side of the balance sheet, are typically shown in the order of their liquidity. Claims, found on the right-hand side, are generally listed in the order in which they must be paid.
  2. Only cash is available to pay current claims. Noncash assets are expected to produce cash over time through the normal operations of the business.
  3. Claims against the assets consist of liabilities and stockholders' ownership, called stockholders' equity.
  4. Assets - Liabilities = Net worth, or Stockholders' equity.
  5. The equity section of the balance sheet is divided into four accounts: preferred stock, common stock, paid-in capital, and retained earnings. The latter three accounts total to the firm's common equity.
  6. Retained earnings are built up from undistributed earnings over time, but these earnings are not kept in the form of cash--they are normally reinvested in various types of operating assets as the business grows.
  7. The common stock and paid-in capital accounts arise from the sale of stock by the firm.

8. Different methods, such as FIFO and LIFO, can be used to determine the value of inventory. These methods, in turn, affect the reported cost of goods sold, profits, and EPS.

9. ACRS depreciation can be used for stockholder reporting as well as for tax purposes. Use of a rapid depreciation method causes reported profits, EPS, and retained earnings to be lower than if straight line depreciation were used.

10. If a slower depreciation method (straight line) is used for stockholder reporting, the reported tax liability will generally exceed the actual tax liability. The difference is called *deferred taxes*.

C. The statement of retained earnings reports changes in the equity accounts between balance sheet dates.

1. The balance sheet account "retained earnings" represents a part of the stockholders' claim against assets.

2. Retained earnings do not represent cash, and the amount reported in this balance sheet account is not available for the payment of dividends or anything else. However, if the firm expects to pay out less than 100 percent of its earnings for the current year, then the retained earnings for the year (an income statement item) will be available for investment in assets.

3. Visualize retained earnings on a personal level. Suppose you expect to make $30,000 and to spend $20,000 during 1988. Therefore, you expect to have $10,000 of "retained earnings" for 1988. You can invest this $10,000 in new assets, and your net worth will rise by $10,000. If that same situation holds for 5 years, your net worth will (if you started with zero) be $50,000, your retained earnings will also be $50,000, and you will have $50,000 of assets bought with the retained earnings. But your assets will not include $50,000 of cash unless you invested only in a bank account.

D. The *sources and uses of funds statement*, or *statement of changes in financial position*, reports how funds were obtained by the firm, how they were used, and how the firm's liquidity position changed during the year. Normally, funds from operations are the most significant source of funds, but external financing can also be important.

1. In financial analysis, depreciation is considered to be a source of funds. Depreciation is a noncash charge against income made to recognize the cost of fixed assets used in the production process.

2. The change in the firm's cash and marketable securities is used to measure whether a firm's liquidity position has improved or not.

3. A *decrease in an asset account* or *an increase in a liability account* is a *source of funds*.

4. An *increase in an asset account* or a *decrease in a liability account* is a *use of funds*.

5. In the sources and uses of funds statement, net income is reported as a source of funds, while dividends are reported as a use. The change in retained earnings is not shown.

II. **Dividends represent the basic cash flow stream passed from the firm to its stockholders.**

A. Normally, dividends are smaller than earnings, although in any given year the opposite can be true.

B. The percentage of earnings paid out as dividends is called the *dividend payout ratio*.

III. **Financial analysis is made difficult by two factors: (1) differing accounting treatments and (2) the fact that cash expenditures do not produce immediate cash inflows.**

    A. Firms may use different inventory valuation and depreciation methods which will cause differences in reported profits for otherwise similar firms.

    B. Cash flows are generally more important in financial analysis than the level of profits.
        1. A firm's net cash flow is the net cash that flows into or out of the firm during a specified period.
        2. The firm's transactions will cause changes in the cash account, but sometimes an action will produce an immediate (or soon) cash outflow and a much later cash inflow. This can lead to cash shortages.
        3. Even a profitable firm can experience cash shortages because it must spend cash to purchase materials to produce goods before it collects cash from the sale of those goods.

IV. **Financial statements can be analyzed from different points of view. (1) Investors are interested in past events primarily as an aid in predicting future success or failure. (2) Management analyzes the data in order to anticipate future events and to help identify actions which will improve operations. Financial ratios are a useful tool in the analysis of financial statements.**

    A. Financial ratios are designed to show relationships among financial statement accounts.
        1. *Liquidity ratios* are used to measure a firm's ability to meet its current obligations as they come due.
            a. The *current ratio* measures the extent to which the claims of short-term creditors are covered by short-term assets. It is determined by dividing current assets by current liabilities.
            b. The *quick, or acid-test, ratio* is calculated by deducting inventories from current assets and then dividing the remainder by current liabilities. Inventories are excluded because it may be difficult to liquidate them at their full book value.
        2. *Asset management ratios* measure how effectively a firm is managing its assets, and whether or not the level of those assets is properly related to the level of operations as measured by sales.
            a. The *inventory turnover ratio*, or inventory utilization ratio, is defined as sales divided by inventory. It is often necessary to use the average inventory figure rather than the year-end figure, especially for seasonal business.
            b. The *average collection period (ACP)* represents the average length of time that a firm must wait after making a sale before receiving cash. Annual sales are divided by 360 to get average daily sales, which are then divided into accounts receivable to find the number of days' sales tied up in receivables.
            c. The *fixed assets turnover*, or fixed assets utilization ratio, is the ratio of sales to net fixed assets. It measures the utilization of plant and equipment.
            d. The *total assets turnover*, or total assets utilization ratio, is calculated by dividing sales by total assets. It measures the utilization of all the firm's assets.

3. *Debt management ratios* measure the extent to which a firm is using debt, or *financial leverage*, and the degree of safety afforded to creditors.
   a. The *debt ratio*, or ratio of total debt to total assets, measures the proportion of funds provided by creditors. The lower the ratio, the greater the protection afforded creditors in the event of liquidation.
   b. The *times-interest-earned ratio (TIE)* is calculated by dividing earnings before interest and taxes (EBIT) by the interest charges. The TIE shows the degree to which earnings can decline yet still be sufficient to meet fixed interest charges.
   c. The *fixed charge coverage ratio* is similar to the time-interest-earned ratio, but it recognizes that lease payments, which are similar to interest payments, must be made in a timely manner to avoid possible bankruptcy.
   d. The *cash flow coverage ratio* shows the margin by which operating cash flows cover financial requirements.
4. *Profitability ratios* show the combined effects of liquidity, asset management, and debt management on the overall operating results of the firm.
   a. The *profit margin* on sales is calculated by dividing net income after taxes by sales.
   b. The *basic earnings power* of assets is calculated by dividing the earnings before interest and taxes (EBIT) by total assets.
   c. The *return on assets (ROA)* is the ratio of net income after taxes to total assets.
   d. The *return on common equity (ROE)* measures the rate of return on the common stockholders' investment. It is equal to net income after taxes divided by common stockholders' equity.
5. *Market value ratios* relate investors' expectations about the company's future to its present performance and financial condition.
   a. The *price/earnings ratio (P/E)*, or price per share divided by earnings per share, shows the amount that investors are currently willing to pay per dollar of current earnings. The P/E is positively related to a firm's growth prospects, and inversely related to risk.
   b. Another indicator of investors' feelings is the *market/book ratio*, defined as market value per share divided by book value per share. Higher ratios are generally associated with firms that have a high rate of return on common equity.

B. Ratio analysis of financial statements can provide meaningful information; however, individual ratios based on one year's data may be misleading. The *trend* of a particular ratio over a period of time is useful in determining the firm's actual financial condition.

C. A *Du Pont chart* shows how debt, asset turnover, and profit margin combine to determine the return on equity.
   1. The profit margin times the total assets turnover is called the Du Pont equation. This equation gives the rate of return on assets (ROA):

   ROA = Profit margin x Total asset turnover.

2. The rate of return on assets times the equity multiplier (assets divided by common equity) yields the return on equity (ROE).
   a. Profit margin reflects expense control.
   b. Total assets turnover reflects asset utilization.
   c. The equity multiplier reflects debt utilization.
   d. ROE = Profit margin x Total assets turnover x Equity multiplier.

D. Comparative ratio analysis can be performed using information from financial sources such as Dun & Bradstreet, Robert Morris Associates, and the Federal Trade Commission.

E. There are a number of limitations to ratio analysis.
   1. Ratios are often not useful for analyzing the operations of conglomerate firms which operate in many different industries because comparative ratios are not meaningful.
   2. The use of industry averages may not provide a very challenging target for high-level performance.
   3. Inflation affects depreciation charges, inventory costs, and therefore the value of both balance sheet items and net income. For this reason, the analysis of a firm over time, or a comparative analysis of firms of different ages, can be misleading.
   4. Ratios may be distorted by seasonal factors, or manipulated by management to give the impression of a sound financial condition (window dressing).
   5. Different operating policies, such as the decision to lease rather than to buy equipment, may have an impact on financial ratios.
   6. Many ratios can be interpreted in different ways, and whether a particular ratio is good or bad should be based upon a complete financial analysis rather than the level of a single ratio at a single point in time.

DEFINITIONAL QUESTIONS

1. Of all its communications with shareholders, a firm's _____ _____ is generally the most important.

2. The _____ statement reports the results of operations during the past year, the most important item being _____ _____ _____.

3. The _____ _____ lists the firm's assets as well as _____ against those assets.

4. Typically, assets are listed in order of their _____, while _____ are listed in the order in which they must be paid.

5. Assets - Liabilities = _____ worth, or _____ equity.

6. The three accounts which normally make up the common equity section of the balance sheet are _____ stock, _____ capital, and _____ _____.

7. _____ _____ as reported on the balance sheet represent income earned by the firm in past years that has not been paid out as _____.

8. Retained earnings are generally reinvested in _____ _____ and are not held in the form of _____.

9. An _____ in a claim against assets or a decrease in an _____ account is a source of funds.

10. A decrease in a _____ account or an _____ in an asset account is a use of funds.

11. The current ratio and acid-test ratio are examples of _____ ratios. They measure a firm's ability to meet its _____ obligations.

12. The average collection period is found by dividing _____ _____ by _____, and then dividing average sales per day into accounts _____. The average collection period (ACP) is the length of time that a firm must wait after making a sale before it receives _____.

13. Debt management ratios are used to evaluate a firm's use of financial _____.

14. The debt ratio, which is the ratio of _____ _____ to _____ _____, measures the proportion of funds supplied by _____.

15. The _____ ratio is calculated by dividing earnings before interest and taxes by the amount of _____ charges.

16. The combined effects of liquidity, asset management, and debt management are measured by _____ ratios.

17. Dividing net profit after taxes by sales gives the _____ _____ on sales.

18. The _____ ratio measures how much investors are willing to pay for each dollar of a firm's current income.

19. Firms with higher rates of return on stockholders' equity tend to sell at relatively high ratios of _____ _____ to _____ _____.

20. Individual ratios are of little value in analyzing a company's financial condition. More important are the _____ of a ratio over time and the comparison of the company's ratios to _____ _____ ratios.

21. A _____ chart shows the relationships among debt, asset turnover, and profit margin, and how they combine to produce return on _____.

22. Return on assets is a function of two variables, the profit _____ and _____ _____ turnover.

23. The _____ of a particular ratio over time or a _____ ratio analysis gives a good indication of a firm's actual financial situation with regard to that ratio.

CONCEPTUAL QUESTIONS

24. The equity multiplier can be expressed as 1 - (Debt/Assets).

    a. True   b. False

25. International Appliances, Inc., has a current ratio of 0.5. Which of the following actions would improve (increase) this ratio?

    a. Use cash to pay off current liabilities.
    b. Collect some of the current accounts receivable.
    c. Use cash to pay off some long-term debt.
    d. Purchase additional inventory on credit (accounts receivable).
    e. Sell some of the existing inventory at cost.

26. Which of the following account changes would be classified as a use of funds?

    a. An increase in accounts payable
    b. A decrease in cash
    c. A decrease in accounts receivable
    d. An increase in retained earnings
    e. A decrease in mortgage bonds

27. A high quick ratio is *always* a good indication of a well-managed liquidity position.

    a. True   b. False

PROBLEMS

(The following financial statements apply to the next six problems.)

Roberts Manufacturing
Balance Sheet
December 31, 1986
(Dollars in Thousands)

Cash	$ 200	Accounts payable	$ 205
Receivables	245	Notes payable	425
Inventory	625	Other current liabilities	115
Total current assets	$1,070	Total current liabilities	$ 745
Net fixed assets	1,200	Long-term debt	420
		Common equity	1,105
Total assets	$2,270	Total liabilities and equity	$2,270

Roberts Manufacturing
Income Statement for Year Ended December 31, 1986
(Dollars in Thousands)

Sales		$2,400
Cost of goods sold:		
Materials	$1,000	
Labor	600	
Heat, light, and power	89	
Indirect labor	65	
Depreciation	80	1,834
Gross profit		$ 566
Selling expenses		175
General and administrative expenses		216
Earnings before interest and taxes		$ 175
Less interest expense		(35)
Net profit before taxes		$ 140
Less taxes (at 40%)		(56)
Net income		$ 84

28. Calculate the liquidity ratios, that is, the current ratio and the quick ratio.

   a. 1.20; 0.60
   b. 1.20; 0.80
   c. 1.44; 0.60
   d. 1.44; 0.80
   e. 1.60; 0.60

29. Calculate the asset management ratios, that is, the inventory turnover ratio, fixed assets turnover, total assets turnover, and average collection period.

   a. 3.84; 2.00; 1.06; 36.75 days
   b. 3.84; 2.00; 1.06; 35.25 days
   c. 3.84; 2.00; 1.06; 34.10 days
   d. 3.84; 2.00; 1.24; 34.10 days
   e. 3.84; 2.20; 1.48; 34.10 days

30. Calculate the debt management ratios, that is, the debt ratio and times-interest-earned ratios.

   a. 0.39; 3.16
   b. 0.39; 5.00
   c. 0.51; 3.16
   d. 0.51; 5.00
   e. 0.73; 3.16

31. Calculate the profitability ratios, that is, the profit margin on sales, return on total assets, return on common equity, and basic earning power of assets.

   a. 3.50%; 4.25%; 7.60%; 8.00%
   b. 3.50%; 3.70%; 7.60%; 7.71%
   c. 3.70%; 3.50%; 7.60%; 7.71%
   d. 3.70%; 3.50%; 8.00%; 8.00%
   e. 4.25%; 3.70%; 7.60%; 8.00%

32. Calculate the market value ratios, that is, the price-earnings ratio and the market/book value ratio. Samson had an average of 10,000 shares outstanding during 1986, and the stock price on December 31, 1986, was $40.00.

   a. 4.21; 0.36
   b. 3.20; 1.54
   c. 3.20; 0.36
   d. 4.76; 1.54
   e. 4.76; 0.36

33. Use the Du Pont equation with the equity multiplier to determine Roberts' return on equity.

   a. 6.90%
   b. 7.24%
   c. 7.47%
   d. 7.60%
   e. 8.41%

American Products Corporation
Balance Sheets
(Dollars in Millions)

	December 31, 1986	December 31, 1987
Cash	$ 45	$ 21
Marketable securities	33	0
Net receivables	66	90
Inventories	159	225
Total current assets	$303	$336
Gross fixed assets	225	450
Less accumulated depreciation	(78)	(123)
Net fixed assets	147	327
Total assets	$450	$663
Accounts payable	$ 45	$ 54
Notes payable	45	9
Other current liabilities	21	45
Long-term debt	24	78
Common stock	114	192
Retained earnings	201	285
Total liabilities and equity	$450	$663

During 1987, the company earned $114 million after taxes, of which $30 million were paid out as dividends.

34. Looking only at the balance sheet accounts, what are the total sources of funds (which must equal the total uses of funds) for 1987?

   a. $213 million
   b. $286 million
   c. $351 million
   d. $428 million
   e. $531 million

35. What are the total sources and total uses of funds from operations for 1987?

   a. $225 million; $225 million
   b. $225 million; $159 million
   c. $159 million; $225 million
   d. $159 million; $351 million
   e. $225 million; $351 million

36. Lewis, Inc., has sales of $2 million per year, all of which are credit sales. Its average collection period is 42 days. What is its average accounts receivable balance?

    a. $233,333
    b. $266,667
    c. $333,333
    d. $350,000
    e. $366,667

37. A firm has total interest charges of $20,000 per year, sales of $2 million, a tax rate of 40 percent, and a profit margin of 6 percent. What is the firm's times-interest-earned ratio?

    a. 10
    b. 11
    c. 12
    d. 13
    e. 14

38. A fire has destroyed many of the financial records at Anderson Associates. You are assigned to piece together information to prepare a financial report. You have found the return on equity to be 12 percent, and the debt ratio was 0.40. What was the return on assets?

    a. 4.90%
    b. 5.35%
    c. 6.60%
    d. 7.20%
    e. 8.40%

39. Rowe and Company has a debt ratio of 0.50, a total assets turnover of 0.25, and a profit margin of 10 percent. The president is unhappy with the current return on equity, and he thinks it could be doubled. This could be accomplished (1) by increasing the profit margin to 14 percent and (2) by increasing debt utilization. Total assets turnover will not change. What new debt ratio, along with the 14 percent profit margin, is required to double the return on equity?

    a. 0.55
    b. 0.60
    c. 0.65
    d. 0.70
    e. 0.75

ANSWERS AND SOLUTIONS

1. annual report

2. income; earnings per share

3. balance sheet; claims

4. liquidity; liabilities

5. Net; Stockholders'

6. common; paid-in; retained earnings

7. Retained earnings; dividends

8. operating assets; cash

9. increase; asset

10. liability; increase

11. liquidity; short-term (or current)

12. annual sales; 360; receivable; cash

13. leverage

14. total debt; total assets; creditors

15. times-interest-earned (TIE); interest

16. profitability

17. profit margin

18. price/earnings

19. market price; book value

20. trend; industry average

21. Du Pont; equity

22. margin; total assets

23. trend; comparative

24. b. The equity multiplier is assets/equity.

25. d. This question is best analyzed using numbers. For example, assume current assets = $50 and current liabilities = $100; thus, the current ratio = 0.5. For Answer a, assume $5 in cash is used to pay off $5 in current liabilities. The new current ratio would be $45/$95 = 0.47. For Answer d, assume a $10 purchase of inventory on credit (accounts receivable). The new current ratio would be $60/$110 = 0.55, which is an increase over the old current ratio of 0.5.

26. e. A use of funds is a decrease in a liability or equity account, or an increase in an asset account. Therefore, only a decrease in mortgage bonds qualifies as a use of funds.

27. b. Excess cash resulting from poor management could produce a high quick ratio. Similarly, if accounts receivable are not collected promptly, this could also lead to a high quick ratio.

28. c.

$$\text{Current ratio} = \text{Current assets/Current liabilities}$$
$$= \$1,070/\$745 = 1.44.$$
$$\text{Quick ratio} = (\text{Current assets - Inventory})/\text{Current liabilities}$$
$$= (\$1,070 - \$625)/\$745$$
$$= \$445/\$745 = 0.60.$$

29. a.

$$\text{Inventory turnover} = \text{Sales/Inventories}$$
$$= \$2,400/\$625 = 3.84.$$
$$\text{Fixed assets turnover} = \text{Sales/Fixed assets}$$
$$= \$2,400/\$1,200 = 2.00.$$
$$\text{Total assets turnover} = \text{Sales/Total assets}$$
$$= \$2,400/\$2,270 = 1.06.$$
$$\text{ACP} = \text{Accounts receivable/(Sales/360)}$$
$$= \$245/(\$2,400/360) = 36.75 \text{ days.}$$

30. d. Debt ratio = Total debt/Total assets = $1,165/$2,270 = 0.51.

TIE ratio = EBIT/I = $175/$35 = 5.00.

31. b. Profit margin = Net profit (income)/Sales = $84/$2,400 = 0.0350 = 3.50%.

ROA = Net profit/Total assets = $84/$2,270 = 0.0370 = 3.70%.

ROE = Net profit/Common equity = $84/$1,105 = 0.0760 = 7.60%.

BEP = EBIT/Total assets = $175/$2,270 = 0.0771 = 7.71%.

32. e. EPS = Net profit/Number of shares outstanding = $84,000/10,000 = $8.40.

P/E ratio = Price/EPS = $40.00/$8.40 = 4.76.

Market/book value = Market value/Book value = $40(10,000)/$1,105,000 = 0.36.

33. d. ROE = (Profit margin)(Total assets turnover)(Equity multiplier)

$$= \frac{\$84}{(\$2,400)} \frac{\$2,400}{(\$2,270)} \frac{\$2,270}{(\$1,105)}$$

$$= (0.035)(1.057)(2.054) = 0.0760 = 7.60\%.$$

34. c.

	Sources	Uses
Cash	$ 24	
Marketable securities	33	
Net receivables		$ 24
Inventories		66
Gross fixed assets		225
Accumulated depreciation		45
Accounts payable	9	
Notes payable		36
Other current liabilities		24
Long-term debt	54	
Common stock	78	
Retained earnings	84	
	$351	$351

Note that accumulated depreciation is a contra-asset account, and an increase is a source of funds. Also note that no total lines such as total current assets can be used to determine sources and uses since to do so would be to "double count."

35. c. Sources of funds:

Net income after taxes	$114
Depreciation	45
Total sources	$159

Uses of funds:

Increase in gross fixed assets	$225
Total uses	$225
Net funds from operations	$(66)

36. a.

$$ACP = \text{Accounts receivable}/(\text{Sales}/360)$$
$$42 \text{ days} = AR/(\$2,000,000/360)$$
$$AR = \$233,333.$$

37. b.

$$\text{Net profit} = \$2,000,000(0.06) = \$120,000.$$
$$\text{Net profit before taxes} = \$120,000/0.6 = \$200,000.$$
$$EBIT = \$200,000 + \$20,000 = \$220,000.$$
$$TIE = EBIT/I = \$220,000/\$20,000 = 11.$$

38. d. If Total debt/Total assets = 0.40, then Total equity/Total assets = 0.60, and the equity multiplier (Assets/Equity) = 1/0.60 = 1.667.

$$\frac{NI}{E} = \frac{NI}{A} \times \frac{A}{E}$$

```
ROE = (ROA)(EM)
12% = (ROA)(1.667)
ROA = 7.20%.
```

39. c. If Total debt/Total assets = 0.50, then Total equity/Total assets = 0.50, and the equity multiplier (assets/equity) = 1/0.50 = 2.0.

$$ROE = \frac{NI}{S} \times \frac{S}{A} \times \frac{A}{E}$$

```
ROE = (PM)(Total assets turnover)(EM).
Before:    ROE = (10%)(0.25)(2.00)  = 5.00%.
After:   10.00% = (14%)(0.25)(EM)
              EM = 2.86.
```

$$\text{Equity multiplier} = \frac{\text{Assets}}{\text{Equity}}$$

$$2.86 = \frac{1}{\text{Equity}}$$

$$0.35 = \text{Equity}$$

```
Assets - Equity = Debt
       1 - 35% = Debt
           65% = Debt
```

CHAPTER 8
FINANCIAL FORECASTING

OVERVIEW

Managers are vitally concerned with *future financial statements* and with the effects of alternative assumptions and policies on these *projected*, or *pro forma*, statements. The construction of pro forma statements begins with a *sales forecast*. Based on the sales forecast, the amount of assets necessary to support this sales level are determined. Although some liabilities will increase *spontaneously* with increased sales, if the sales growth rate is rapid, then external capital will be required to support the growth in sales. Pro forma statements are important for two reasons. First, if projected operating results look poor, management can reformulate its plans for the coming year. Second, it is desirable to plan the acquisition of funds well in advance to insure that funds will be available when they are needed.

OUTLINE

I. Both managers and investors are concerned about the impact of future operations and alternative financial plans on the future financial condition of the firm. *Pro forma*, or *projected*, statements are useful in forecasting the results of different courses of action.

    A. The most important element in financial planning is the *sales forecast*.
       1. Sales forecasts generally start with a review of sales over the past five to ten years.
       2. Companies must project the state of the national economy, economic conditions within their own geographic areas, and conditions in the product markets they serve.

    B. Several methods are used to forecast financial statements. We concentrate on the percentage of sales method.

II. The *percentage of sales method* is a simple but practical method of forecasting financial statement variables.

    A. The first step in the percentage of sales method of forecasting is to *isolate those balance sheet items that vary directly with sales*.
       1. All asset accounts can be assumed to vary directly with sales unless the firm is operating at less than full capacity. If the firm is not operating at full capacity, then fixed assets will not vary directly with sales, but the cash, receivables, and inventory accounts will increase in proportion to the increase in sales.
       2. Liabilities, equity, or both must also increase if assets increase--asset expansions must be financed in some manner.
       3. Certain liability accounts, such as accounts payable and accruals, will increase *spontaneously* with sales. Retained earnings will increase, but not proportionately with sales.

4. Other financing accounts, such as short-term debt, long-term debt, and common stock, are not directly related to sales. Changes in these accounts result from managerial decisions; they do not increase spontaneously and automatically as sales increase.

B. The second step is to express each account that varies with sales as a percentage of sales by dividing the amount in the account by sales for the preceding period. Then this percentage is multiplied by the sales level forecasted for the next period.
   1. Accounts that do not vary directly with sales are initially held constant at current levels.
   2. The addition to retained earnings is estimated by multiplying the profit margin minus the payout ratio by the projected sales.

C. The difference between projected total assets and projected liabilities and capital is the amount of external financing required.

D. The specific form of financing is then chosen by management. Sometimes contractual agreements, such as a limit on the debt ratio, will restrict the firm's financing decisions.

III. Although a forecast of capital requirements can be made by constructing pro forma financial statements, it is often easier to use a simple forecasting formula. In addition, the formula can be used to show the relationship between sales growth and financing requirements.

A. The formula is as follows:

Additional funds needed = Required increase in assets - Spontaneous increase in liabilities - Increase in retained earnings

$$AFN = A/S(\Delta S) \ - \ L/S(\Delta S) \ - \ MS_1(1 - d).$$

Here,

A/S = assets that increase spontaneously with sales as a percentage of sales, or required dollar increase in assets per $1 increase in sales.

L/S = liabilities that increase spontaneously with sales as a percentage of sales, or spontaneously generated financing per $1 increase in sales.

S_1 = total expected sales for the year in question (note that S_0 = last year's sales).

ΔS = change in sales = $S_1 - S_0$

M = profit margin, or rate of profits after taxes per $1 of sales.

d = the percentage of earnings paid out in dividends.

B. The equation must be used with caution if excess capacity exists in any of the asset accounts. Excess capacity is most likely to exist in fixed assets. When excess capacity exists, first determine how large ΔS can be before capacity is reached, and then base additional fixed assets needed on sales *beyond* capacity sales.

C. The equation can also be used to calculate the maximum growth rate that can be financed without external funds. This is done by setting the additional funds requirement equal to zero and solving for the growth rate in sales.

D. If management cannot (or does not wish to) use external financing, it may have to limit potential growth and turn away sales beyond some specified amount.

IV. Dividend policy is a major factor in determining a corporation's financial needs.

A. Dividends paid to stockholders will reduce the amount of earnings retained by the firm. This will increase the amount of additional financing required for a given level of sales.

B. Dividend policy may be changed to satisfy internal financing requirements, but this may have a negative impact on stock prices and may be met with resistance from investors. This is discussed later in the book (Chapter 19).

V. The amount of assets required per dollar of sales, A/S, is often called the capital intensity ratio. This factor has a major effect on capital requirements per unit of sales growth. If the capital intensity ratio is low, then sales can grow rapidly without much outside capital. However, if a firm is capital intensive, even a small growth in output will require a great deal of outside capital.

VI. Profit margin, M, also has an effect on capital requirements. The higher the margin, the lower the funds requirement, and the lower the margin, the higher the requirement. Thus, highly profitable firms such as IBM can raise most of their capital internally-- IBM rarely finds it necessary to issue stock or bonds, even though its growth rate is high.

VII. The forecasting process is greatly complicated if the ratios of balance sheet items to sales are not constant at all levels of sales.

A. Where economies of scale occur in asset use, the ratio of that asset to sales will change as the size of the firm increases.

B. Technological considerations sometimes dictate that fixed assets be added in discrete or "lumpy" amounts. This automatically creates excess capacity immediately after a plant expansion.

VIII. To determine the future optimal level of an asset not currently being used to full capacity, first determine full capacity sales (divide actual sales by the utilization rate) and then use this figure in the calculation of additional requirements.

IX. Larger, well-managed firms have computerized financial planning models. These models automatically generate pro forma statements based on a set of assumptions and input parameters.

DEFINITIONAL QUESTIONS

1. The most important element in financial planning is the forecast of _____.

2. Those asset items that typically increase proportionately with higher sales are _____, _____, and _____. _____ assets are frequently not used to full capacity and hence do not increase in proportion to sales.

3. If various asset categories increase, _____ and/or _____ must also increase.

4. Typically, certain liabilities will rise _____ with sales. These include accounts _____ and _____.

5. _____ and _____ _____ are examples of accounts that do not increase automatically with higher levels of sales.

6. As the dividend _____ _____ is increased, the amount of earnings available to finance new assets is _____.

7. Retained earnings depend not only on next year's sales level and dividend payout ratio but also on the _____ _____.

8. The amount of assets required per dollar of sales, A/S is often called the _____ _____ _____.

9. A capital intensive industry will require large amounts of _____ capital to finance increased growth.

10. The percentage of sales method assumes that the _____ of balance sheet items to _____ is _____ at all levels of sales.

11. The assumption of constant percentage of sales ratios may not be accurate when assets must be added in discrete amounts, called "_____" assets, or when _____ of scale are considered.

CONCEPTUAL QUESTIONS

12. An increase in a firm's inventories will call for additional financing unless the increase is offset by an equal or larger *decrease* in some other asset account.

    a. True   b. False

13. If the capital intensity ratio of a firm actually decreases as sales increase, use of the percentage of sales method will typically *overstate* the amount of additional funds required, other things held constant.

    a. True   b. False

14. If the dividend payout ratio is 100 percent, all ratios are held constant, and the firm is operating at full capacity, then any increase in sales will require additional financing.

    a. True   b. False

15. Which of the following would *reduce* the additional funds required if all other things are held constant?

    a. An increase in the dividend payout ratio
    b. A decrease in the profit margin
    c. An increase in the capital intensity ratio
    d. An increase in the expected sales growth rate
    e. A decrease in the firm's tax rate

16. One of the first steps in the percentage of sales method of forecasting is to identify those asset and liability accounts which increase spontaneously with retained earnings.

    a. True   b. False

PROBLEMS

17. United Products, Inc., has the following balance sheet:

Current assets	$ 5,000	Accounts payable	$ 1,000
Net fixed assets	5,000	Notes payable	1,000
		Long-term debt	4,000
		Common equity	4,000
Total assets	$10,000	Total claims	$10,000

Business has been slow, therefore, fixed assets are vastly underutilized. Management believes it can double sales next year with the introduction of a new product. No new fixed assets will be required, and management expects that there will be no earnings retained next year. What is next year's additional funding requirement?

    a. $0
    b. $4,000
    c. $6,000
    d. $13,000
    e. $19,000

18. The 1986 balance sheet for American Pulp and Paper is shown below (millions of dollars):

Cash	$ 3.0	Accounts payable	$ 2.0
Accounts receivable	3.0	Notes payable	1.5
Inventory	5.0	Long-term debt	3.0
Current assets	$11.0	Common equity	7.5
Fixed assets	3.0		
Total assets	$14.0	Total claims	$14.0

In 1986, sales were $60 million. In 1987, management believes that sales will increase by 20 percent to a total of $72 million. The profit margin is expected to be 5 percent, and the dividend payout ratio is targeted at 40 percent. The firm has excess capacity and no increase in fixed assets will be required. What is the additional funding requirement for 1987?

a. $0.36 million
b. $0.24 million
c. $0 million
d. -$0.24 million
e. -$0.36 million

19. Refer to Problem 18. Assume no excess capacity exists. How much can sales grow above the 1986 level of $60 million without requiring any additional funds?

a. 12.28%
b. 14.63%
c. 15.75%
d. 17.65%
e. 18.14%

20. Smith Machines, Inc., has a net income this year of $500 on sales of $2,000 and is operating its fixed assets at full capacity. Management expects sales to increase by 25 percent next year and is forecasting a dividend payout ratio of 30 percent. The profit margin is not expected to change. If spontaneous liabilities are $500 this year, and no excess funds are expected next year, what is Smith's total assets this year?

a. $1,000
b. $1,500
c. $2,250
d. $3,000
e. $3,500

ANSWERS AND SOLUTIONS

1. sales

2. cash; receivables; inventories; Fixed

3. liabilities; equity

4. spontaneously; payable; accruals

5. Bonds; common stock (or preferred stock, or retained earnings)

6. payout ratio; decreased

7. profit margin

8. capital intensity ratio

9. external

10. ratio; sales; constant

11. "lumpy"; economies

12. a. When an increase in one asset account is not offset by a equivalent decrease in another asset account, then financing is needed to reesta lish equilibrium on the balance sheet. Note, though, that this additional finai ing may come from a spontaneous increase in accounts payable or from retained ear ngs.

13. a. A decreasing capital intensity ratio, A/S, means that l s assets are required, proportionately, as sales increase. Thus, the external nding requirement is overstated. Always keep in mind that the percentage of sales hethod assumes that the asset/sales ratios are constant regardless of the level of sales.

14. a. With a 100% payout ratio, there will be no retained earnings. When operating at full capacity, all assets are spontaneous, but all liabilities cannot be spontaneous since a firm must have common equity. Thus, the growth in assets nnot be matched by a growth in spontaneous liabilities, so additional financing will e required in order to keep the financial ratios (the debt ratio in particular) constant.

15. e. Answers a through d would increase the additional funds requ red, but a decrease in the tax rate would raise the profit margin and thus increase t e amount of available retained earnings.

16. b. The first step is to identify those accounts which increase sponta eously with sales.

17. b. Look at next year's balance sheet:

Current assets	$10,000	Accounts payable	$ 2,000
Net fixed assets	5,000	Notes payable	1,000
		Long-term debt	4,000
		Common equity	4,000
	$15,000		$11,000

With no retained earnings next year, the common equity account remains at $4,000. Thus, the additional financing requirement is $15,000 - $11,000 = $4,000.

18. e. Since fixed assets are sufficient to absorb the increase in sales, this item is not included in the computation. Therefore, only $11 million of the $14 million in total assets will increase spontaneously with sales. None of the items on the right side of the balance sheet rises spontaneously with sales except accounts payable. Therefore,

$$AFN = (A/S)(\text{ }S) - (L/S)(\text{ }S) - MS_1(1 - d)$$

$$= (\$11/\$60)(\$12) - (\$2/\$60)(\$12) - (0.05)(\$72)(0.6)$$

$$= \$2.2 - \$0.4 - \$2.16 = -\$0.36 \text{ million.}$$

This means that the increased profits and spontaneously generated liabilities are sufficient to support the additional assets required. Thus, no additional funds will be required. In fact, there will be an internally generated surplus of funds of $360,000.

19. d. Note that g = sales growth = S/S, and $S_1 = S_0(1 + g)$. Then,

$$AFN = Ag - Lg - M[(S_0)(1 + g)](1 - d) = 0$$

$$\$14g - \$2g - 0.05[(\$60)(1 + g)](0.6) = 0$$

$$\$12g - 1(\$3 + \$3g)(0.60) = 0$$

$$\$12g - \$1.8 - \$1.8g = 0$$

$$\$10.20g = \$1.80$$

$$g = 0.1765 = 17.65\%.$$

20. c.

$$0 = (A/S)(\Delta S) - (L/S)(\Delta S) - MS_1(1 - d)$$

$$0 = (A/\$2,000)(\$500) - (\$500/\$2,000)(\$500) - (\$500/\$2,000)(\$2,500)(1 - 0.3)$$

$$0 = (\$500A/\$2,000) - \$125 - \$437.50$$

$$0 = (\$500A/\$2,000) - \$562.50$$

$$\$562.50 = 0.25A$$

$$A = \$2,250.$$

CHAPTER 9
FINANCIAL PLANNING AND CONTROL

OVERVIEW

Chapter 8 discussed methods of forecasting financial requirements. Now we go on, in this chapter, to consider planning and control. We begin by examining the relationship between sales volume and profitability under different operating conditions, with an emphasis on breakeven analysis. Next, cash budgeting is discussed as a tool to help managers forecast their funds requirements. Finally, we examine the ROA control process, which is used by firms to insure that plans are executed properly and modified when needed.

OUTLINE

I. **Both financial planning and financial control are needed to insure that funds are available when needed and that plans are executed properly.**

   A. *Financial planning* involves making and then analyzing projections of future financial statements.

   B. *Financial controls* involve procedures for comparing projections to actual results, and then adjusting operations if deviations occur.

   C. A *budget system* encompasses both planning and control.
      1. Budgets analyze costs for every major area of a firm's activities.
      2. Part of the budget system calls for forecasting income statements, balance sheets, and other financial statements for the firm.
      3. The projected statements can then be analyzed (1) to see if all constraints, such as maintaining a minimum current ratio, are maintained, and (2) to see if projected earnings and rates of return are at satisfactory levels. If not, management will examine projected operations to see if a better plan can be devised.
      4. Projections of financing requirements give a firm the lead time necessary to arrange for required financing.
      5. Comparisons of projected and actual financial statements help the firm to pinpoint reasons for deviations from the plan and to correct problems. Thus, the planning and control process helps a firm improve its performance and profitability.

II. **Breakeven analysis is an important tool in profit planning.**

   A. The relationship between fixed costs, variable costs, and profits can be studied using an analytical technique called cost-volume-profit planning, or *breakeven analysis*.
      1. Breakeven analysis provides information on the volume of sales at which total revenues just cover total costs.

2. Breakeven analysis guides the manager in the comparison of prices, expected sales volume, and the sales volume required to cover total costs.

B. A firm's breakeven point can be calculated algebraically in terms of units or of total dollar sales.
   1. The breakeven quantity in units is defined as the units of output at which revenues are just equal to total costs (fixed costs plus variable costs).
      a. Let:

      P = Sales price per unit.
      F = Total fixed costs.
      V = Variable costs per unit.

      The breakeven quantity, Q_{BE}, is that quantity which solves the following equation and forces total revenues to equal total costs:

      $$PQ = VQ + F.$$

      b. The equation can be solved for Q_{BE}:

      $$Q_{BE} = \frac{F}{P-V} .$$

   2. The breakeven sales volume, S_{BE}, can be calculated as $Q_{BE}(P)$.

C. Although breakeven analysis is useful in financial planning, it does have limitations:
   1. Any linear breakeven chart is based on the assumption of constant sales price. Profit possibilities under different prices require a whole series of breakeven charts.
   2. Breakeven analysis assumes that total fixed costs, and also variable cost per unit, are constant for all quantities of output. Variable costs per unit may rise as capacity limits are approached, as increasing levels of output may require additional fixed investments in plant and equipment.

D. Used appropriately, breakeven analysis is applicable to three important types of business decisions:
   1. *New product decisions.* Breakeven analysis helps identify the sales volume required on a new product to just recover costs or to realize a target profit level. Then management can ask, "How likely is it that we can achieve the target sales level?"
   2. *General expansion of operations.* Breakeven points are calculated on the basis of total sales (in dollar amounts rather than in units of output) and total costs.
   3. *Automation and modernization decisions.* Breakeven analysis helps determine the consequences of substituting fixed costs for variable costs, and the effects of volume changes on profitability with different mixes of fixed and variable costs.

III. **Operating leverage is defined as the extent to which fixed costs are used in operations. High fixed costs arise from employing larger amounts of capital, thus permitting the firm to operate with reduced labor and smaller variable costs.**

A. A high *degree of operating leverage* implies a situation where a relatively small change in sales results in a large change in net operating income.

1. The breakeven point is higher with higher operating leverage because fixed costs are greater.
2. Once sales exceed the breakeven point, profits rise at a faster rate with higher operating leverage.

B. The degree of operating leverage (DOL) is defined as the percentage change in operating income divided by a given percentage change in units sold.

1. The degree of operating leverage can be expressed as:

$$\text{DOL} = \frac{\text{Percentage change in EBIT}}{\text{Percentage change in sales}}$$

$$= \frac{\dfrac{\Delta\ \text{EBIT}}{\text{EBIT}}}{\dfrac{\Delta Q}{Q}}.$$

The degree of operating leverage can also be calculated as:

$$\text{DOL} = \frac{Q(P - V)}{Q(P - V) - F}.$$

2. The degree of operating leverage of a firm has a number of important implications:
   a. A high degree of operating leverage suggests that a firm might be able to profit from increasing its sales volume even if it had to lower its price to do so.
   b. On the other hand, a high degree of operating leverage indicates that a firm is subject to large swings in profit if its volume fluctuates.

IV. Cash breakeven analysis can be used to analyze the firm's situation on a cash basis. It allows the firm to calculate a breakeven point considering only cash inflows and outflows.

A. The formulas for breakeven quantity and sales level must be adjusted for noncash outlays:

$$Q_{BE} = \frac{F - \text{Noncash outlays}}{P - V}.$$

B. Cash breakeven analysis provides a picture of the flow of funds from operations.
   1. A firm may utilize a higher degree of operating leverage (high fixed costs) to achieve higher profits if its risk of insolvency (in the sense of being unable to meet cash obligations) is low. Thus, a low cash breakeven point allows a firm to use more operating leverage.
   2. If cash outlays are low, such a firm will be able to continue to operate during periods of loss, as long as its contribution margin remains above the cash breakeven point.

V. The cash budget is an important aspect of financial planning.

  A. A cash budget reflects the effects of future operations on the firm's cash flow.

  B. It indicates not only the total amount of financing required but its timing as well.

  C. The methodology is quite logical.
   1. If a firm sells on credit, there is a lag between sales and cash collections.
   2. Similarly, a firm buying on credit benefits from a waiting period before having to disburse cash.
   3. The cash budget recognizes that some cash payments are made in "lumps" at uneven intervals, while other expenses occur on a uniform monthly basis.
   4. It is important to take into account interest and principal repayment as cash outflows.

  D. The cash budget projects cash inflows and outflows over some specified period of time.
   1. The cash budget is useful in determining when cash surpluses or shortages will occur. Plans can then be made to borrow to cover shortages or to invest surpluses.
   2. Improved forecasts of cash inflows and outflows permit a firm to hold a smaller cash balance.

VI. The Du Pont system of financial analysis is a form of control used in multidivisional companies.

  A. The Du Pont system reveals how activity ratios and profit margins on sales interact to determine the profitability of assets.

  B. A modified Du Pont control chart illustrates, among other things, that profits and return on investment in assets depend upon control of costs and investment. If investment is not controlled, the asset turnover ratio (sales to total assets) declines.

  C. Profit planning depends to a great extent upon the control of costs and the proper utilization of assets.
   1. Cost control requires detailed study of the operations of the individual business firm to determine the nature of the costs inherent to the firm's industry.
   2. Firms which have low asset turnover ratios should have correspondingly higher profit margins than firms with high turnover ratios.
   3. The profit margin times the total asset turnover, which gives the return on asset investment (ROA), is called the Du Pont equation:

$$\text{ROA} = \frac{\text{Profit}}{\text{Sales}} \times \frac{\text{Sales}}{\text{Assets}} \ .$$

  D. When the Du Pont system is used for divisional control, it is often called ROA control.
   1. Each division is defined as a profit center with its own assets, and each is expected to earn an appropriate return on its investment.
   2. If a division's ROA falls below a target figure, the centralized corporate staff traces back through the Du Pont system to locate the cause.

3. Division managers are judged by their division's ROA, and therefore are motivated to keep the ROA up to target level.
4. ROA may be influenced by factors other than managerial competence. These factors include:
   a. Depreciation policy.
   b. Book value versus current value of assets.
   c. Transfer pricing methods.
   d. Short-term versus long-term perspectives.
   e. Industry conditions.
5. These factors necessitate supplementing the performance evaluation with other criteria, including the following:
   a. The division's growth rate in sales.
   b. The division's equipment modernization and replacement policies.
   c. The division's market share as compared with other firms in the industry.

DEFINITIONAL QUESTIONS

1. A _____ _____ compares projected financial statements with actual statements and helps the firm to pinpoint reasons for _____.

2. _____ analysis allows managers to study the relationships between fixed costs, _____ _____, and profits.

3. The _____ _____ is that volume of sales at which _____ just equal total costs.

4. The breakeven sales volume can be expressed as the ratio of total fixed costs to the _____ _____.

5. Breakeven analysis assumes that the _____ _____ and costs are _____ for all quantities of output.

6. _____ _____ is defined as the extent to which fixed costs are used in the firm's operations.

7. The _____ of operating leverage is defined as the percentage change in _____ _____ that result from a given _____ change in units sold.

8. A high degree of operating leverage subjects the firm to _____ changes in net income in response to relatively small changes in _____.

9. Cash breakeven analysis allows a firm to calculate a _____ _____ for _____ inflows and outflows.

10. The cash breakeven volume is equal to fixed _____ outlays divided by the _____ _____ per unit.

11. A cash budget reflects the effects of future operations on the firm's _____ _____.

12. A good cash budgeting system improves _____ of cash inflows and outflows and permits firms to hold _____ cash balances.

13. The _____ _____ reveals how activity ratios and profit margins on sales interact to determine the _____ of assets.

14. The Du Pont equation is equal to the _____ _____ on sales times the _____ _____ turnover ratio.

CONCEPTUAL QUESTIONS

15. The goal of financial planning and control is to:

    a. Project financial statements.
    b. Analyze costs in each of the firm's divisions.
    c. Help the firm improve its performance and profitability.
    d. Project costs based on standards of performance.
    e. Reward managers for adhering to budgets.

16. A high degree of operating leverage lowers risk by stabilizing a firm's earnings stream.

    a. True   b. False

17. Which of the following assumptions is not a limitation of breakeven analysis?

    a. Constant price for all levels of sales.
    b. Constant variable cost per unit for all levels of output.
    c. Constant total fixed costs over the range of output being evaluated.
    d. Constant product mix over time.
    e. Constant sales volume over time.

18. A relatively low ROA is always an indicator of managerial incompetence.

    a. True   b. False

PROBLEMS

19. Aquarium Suppliers, Inc., produces 10-gallon aquariums. The firm's variable costs equal 40 percent of dollar sales, while fixed costs total $150,000. The firm plans to sell the aquariums for $10 each. What is Aquarium Suppliers' breakeven quantity of sales.

    a. 22,000
    b. 25,000
    c. 28,000
    d. 30,000
    e. 40,000

20. Refer to Problem 19. What is Aquarium Suppliers' breakeven sales volume?

    a. $100,000
    b. $150,000
    c. $200,000
    d. $250,000
    e. $300,000

21. Refer to Problem 19. What price must Aquarium Suppliers charge to break even at sales of 40,000 units.

    a. $5.28
    b. $5.60
    c. $5.95
    d. $6.25
    e. $7.00

22. The Spade Company has identified two methods of producing playing cards. One method involves using a machine having a fixed cost of $20,000 and variable costs of $1.00 per deck. The other method would use a less expensive machine having a fixed cost of $5,000, but it would require variable costs of $2.00 per deck. If the selling price will be the same under each method, at what level of output would the two methods produce the same earnings before interest and taxes (EBIT)?

    a. 5,000
    b. 10,000
    c. 15,000
    d. 20,000
    e. 25,000

23. Outfitters, Inc., is a new firm just starting operations. The firm will produce backpacks which will sell for $22.00 apiece. Fixed costs are $300,000 per year, and variable costs are $2.00 per unit of production. The company expects to sell 50,000 backpacks per year, and its marginal tax rate is 40 percent. What is Outfitters' degree of operating leverage at the expected level of sales?

    a. 1.00
    b. 1.08
    c. 2.00
    d. 2.16
    e. 3.00

24. Refer to Problem 23. What is Outfitters' breakeven quantity of sales?

    a. 5,000
    b. 10,000
    c. 15,000
    d. 20,000
    e. 25,000

25. Refer to Problem 24. If Outfitters has $120,000 in noncash expenses, what is the firm's cash breakeven quantity of sales?

    a. 27,000
    b. 25,000
    c. 23,000
    d. 21,000
    e. 19,000

26. Robinson and Company has a total assets turnover of 0.30 and a profit margin of 10 percent. The president is unhappy with the current return on assets, and he thinks it could be doubled. This could be accomplished (1) by increasing the profit margin to 15 percent and (2) by increasing the total assets turnover. What new total assets turnover ratio, along with the 15 percent profit margin, is required to double the return on assets?

    a. 30%
    b. 35%
    c. 40%
    d. 45%
    e. 50%

27. Matthew and Sarah Weisner recently leased space in the Plaza Shopping Center and opened a new business, Weisner's Ice Cream Shop. Business has been good but the Weisners frequently run out of cash. This has necessitated late payment on certain ice cream orders, which in turn is beginning to cause a problem with suppliers. The Weisners plan to borrow from a bank to have cash ready as needed, but first they need to forecast how much cash will be needed. Therefore, they have decided to prepare a cash budget for June, July, and August to determine their cash needs.

    Ice cream sales are made on a cash basis only. The Weisners must pay for their ice cream orders 1 month after the purchase. Rent is $1,000 per month, and they pay themselves a combined salary of $2,400 per month. In addition, they must make a tax payment of $6,000 in June. The current cash on hand (June 1) is $200, but the Weisners have decided to maintain an average balance of $3,000. Estimated ice cream sales and purchases for June, July and August are given below. May purchases amounted to $70,000.

	Sales	Purchases
June	$80,000	$ 20,000
July	20,000	20,000
August	30,000	20,000

    What amount of money must be borrowed or have in surplus in each of the months in the budget period (June, July, and August)?

    a. $2,200; $5,600; ($1,000)*
    b. $2,700; $5,600; ($1,000)*
    c. $2,200; $9,400; ($1,000)*
    d. ($1,000)*; $4,700; $500
    e. $2,200; $5,600; $2,000

    *The firm projects a cash surplus in this month.

ANSWERS AND SOLUTIONS

1. budget system; deviations

2. Breakeven; variable costs

3. breakeven quantity (or point); revenues

4. contribution margin (or P-VC)

5. sales price; constant

6. Operating leverage

7. degree; operating income (or EBIT); percentage

8. large; sales

9. breakeven point; cash

10. cash; contribution margin

11. cash flows

12. forecasts; smaller

13. Du Pont system; profitability

14. profit margin; total asset

15 c.

16. b.   A high degree of operating leverage increases a firm's risk by causing earnings fluctuate more with changes in sales.

17. e.   Breakeven analysis does not assume a constant level of sales.

18. b.   A division's ROA is influenced by factors other than managerial competence, such as the firm's depreciation policy, transfer pricing methods, and industry conditions.

19. b.

$$P - V = \$10.00 - (0.40)(\$10.00)$$
$$= \$10.00 - \$4.00$$
$$= \$6.00.$$

$$Q_{BE} = \frac{F}{P - V}$$

$$= \$150,000/\$6.00$$
$$= 25,000.$$

20. d.

$$S_{BE} = (P)(Q_{BE})$$
$$= (\$10)(25,000)$$
$$= \$250,000.$$

21. d.

$$Q_{BE} = \frac{F}{P - V}$$

$$40,000 = \frac{\$150,000}{P - V}$$

$$V = 0.40P$$

$$40,000 = \frac{\$150,000}{P - 0.40P}$$

$$40,000 = \frac{\$150,000}{0.60P}$$

$$24,000P = \$150,000$$

$$P = \$6.25.$$

22. c.

First method: EBIT $= PQ - \$1.00Q - \$20,000.$
Second method: EBIT $= PQ - \$2.00Q - \$ 5,000.$

Now, equate the EBITs:

$$PQ - \$1.00Q - \$20,000 = PQ - \$2.00Q - \$5,000$$
$$\$1.00Q = \$15,000$$
$$Q = 15,000.$$

23. The DOL at 50,000 units can be calculated as follows:

$$DOL_{50,000} = \frac{Q(P - V)}{Q(P - V) - F}$$

$$= \frac{50,000(\$22 - \$2)}{50,000(\$22 - \$2) - \$500,000}$$

$$= \frac{\$1,000,000}{\$1,000,000 - \$500,000}$$

$$= 2.0.$$

24. e.

$$Q_{BE} = \frac{F}{P - V}$$

$$= \frac{\$500,000}{\$22 - \$2}$$

$$= \frac{\$500,000}{\$20}$$

$$= 25,000.$$

25. e.

$$Q_{BE} = \frac{F - noncash\ outlays}{P - V}$$

$$= \frac{\$500,000 - \$120,000}{\$22 - \$2}$$

$$= \frac{\$380,000}{\$20}$$

$$= 19,000.$$

26. c.

ROA	=	(Profit margin)(Total assets turnover)
Before: ROA	=	(10%)(0.30) = 3.00%.
After: 6%	=	(15%)(Total assets turnover)
Total assets turnover	=	0.40 = 40%.

27. a.

Worksheet	June	July	August
Sales	$80,000	$20,000	$30,000
Purchases	20,000	20,000	20,000
Payments for purchases	70,000	20,000	20,000
Cash budget:			
Receipts from sales	$80,000	$20,000	$30,000
Payments:			
Purchases	$70,000	$20,000	$20,000
Salaries	2,400	2,400	2,400
Rent	1,000	1,000	1,000
Taxes	6,000		
Total payments	$79,400	$23,400	$23,400
Net cash gain (loss)	$ 600	($ 3,400)	$ 6,600
Cash at start of month	200	800	(2,600)
Cash at end of month	$ 800	($ 2,600)	$ 4,000
Less: Target cash balance	$ 3,000	$ 3,000	$ 3,000
Total loans to maintain $3,000 target cash balance	($2,200)	($ 5,600)	
Surplus cash	----	----	$1,000

CHAPTER 10
WORKING CAPITAL POLICY

OVERVIEW

Typically, 40 percent of industrial firms' assets consist of working capital, or current assets. Thus, working capital policy and management is vitally important to both the firm and its shareholders. This chapter focuses on working capital policy, which involves (1) setting working capital levels and (2) deciding how to finance working capital acquisitions. Because short-term credit can be obtained quicker and on more flexible terms, and often at a lower cost, most firms use at least some current debt in spite of the fact that such debt increases the firm's risk.

OUTLINE

I. **Working capital policy and management is concerned with current assets, including decisions about how these assets will be financed.**

   A. *Gross working capital* is defined as total current assets, while *net working capital* is current assets minus current liabilities.

   B. The *current ratio*, which is current assets divided by current liabilities, is a common measure of the firm's liquidity.

   C. The *quick ratio*, which also measures liquidity, is current assets less inventories, divided by current liabilities.

II. **The cash flow cycle of a firm influences the amount of growth which can be financed without causing cash flow problems.**

   A. Working capital management involves providing financing for increases in current asset requirements caused by growth, by cyclical and seasonal variations in sales levels, and by random fluctuations in sales.

   B. Firms need assets in order to make sales, and if sales are to increase, assets must also grow.

   C. The *cash flow cycle* is the length of time required to convert raw materials into finished goods, inventories into receivables, and then receivables into cash.
      1. Raw material purchases are financed by trade credit, giving rise to accounts payable.
      2. Funds are paid to labor to begin processing the raw materials.
      3. Before goods are completed, they represent work-in-process inventories. The firm's cash has declined, and current liabilities in the form of accounts payable and accrued wages payable are in existence.

4. Goods are finished and go from work-in-process inventories to finished goods inventories. The firm is more liquid at this point because finished goods can be sold to raise cash, while work-in-process inventories cannot be sold.
5. When goods are sold on credit, accounts receivable are created.
6. The collection of accounts receivable generates cash to complete a cycle.
7. The firm orders raw materials, and the cash cycle begins again.

III. **Managing the cash flow cycle is the crux of working capital management.**

A. Working capital management requires a consideration of three separate factors, the *inventory conversion period*, the *receivables conversion period*, and the *payables deferral period*, which combine to form the *cash conversion cycle*.
1. The *inventory conversion period* is an indicator of the average time it takes a firm to convert its raw materials into finished goods.
2. The *receivables conversion period* is an indicator of the average time it takes a firm to convert its accounts receivables into cash.
3. The *payables deferral period* measures the average time that a firm can delay cash payments for raw materials by purchasing goods on credit.
4. The *cash conversion cycle* is the net time interval between cash expenditures for raw materials and cash receipts on accounts receivables.

B. The cash conversion cycle is influenced by expansion or contraction of any of the three liquidity flow measures just discussed.
1. The length of the cash conversion period is equal to the inventory conversion period plus the receivables conversion period, minus the payables deferral period.
2. An increase in either the inventory conversion period or the receivables conversion period, without an offsetting increase in the payables deferral period, leads to an increase in the cash conversion period.
3. A decline in the cash conversion cycle indicates a reduction in required non-spontaneous financing.

C. The cash conversion cycle concept gives a useful picture of a firm's liquidity position over time.

IV. **A firm's working capital requirements rise and fall with both business cycles and seasonal trends.**

A. At the peak of such cycles, businesses carry the maximum amounts of working capital.

B. However, even at the troughs of these cycles, the working capital accounts do not fall to zero.

V. **Working capital policy involves two basic decisions.**

A. The first decision involves the *level of investment* in current assets.
1. The firm must set its working capital level based on sales.
2. A *loose working capital policy* would result in a relatively high level of current assets.
3. A *tight working capital policy* would result in a relatively low level of working capital.

4. Generally, the decision on working capital level involves a risk/return tradeoff. The loose policy minimizes risk, but it also has the lowest expected return. On the other hand, the tight policy offers the highest expected return coupled with the highest risk.

5. The minimum level of working capital held over the cycle is called the *permanent working capital*, or permanent current assets.

6. The minimum level of total assets held over the cycle is called *permanent assets.*

B. The second working capital policy decision involves the *manner of financing* working capital.

1. The *maturity matching approach* calls for the use of permanent financing (long-term debt and equity) to finance permanent assets, and then the use of short-term financing to cover seasonal and/or cyclical temporary assets. This is referred to as a *moderate* approach.

2. On the other hand, a firm could use temporary (short-term) financing to cover a portion of its permanent assets. Here, permanent capital is less than permanent assets. This is an *aggressive approach.*

3. A *conservative approach* would be to use permanent capital to finance all permanent assets and also to meet some of the cyclical demand, and then to hold temporary surplus funds as marketable securities at the trough of the cycle. Here, the amount of permanent capital exceeds the level of permanent assets.

4. The working capital financing decision also involves a risk/return tradeoff. Since short-term financing generally costs less than long-term capital, the aggressive approach has the highest expected return, but short-term financing brings with it the greatest risk. Conversely, the conservative approach offers the lowest expected return but also the lowest risk.

VI. **There are advantages and disadvantages to the use of short-term credit.**

A. One advantage is *speed*--a short-term loan can be obtained much more quickly than a long-term loan.

B. Another advantage is *flexibility*--short-term debt may be repaid if the firm's financing requirements decline. Long-term debt can be refunded, but this will generally involve a prepayment penalty.

C. *Cost* is another advantage--short-term interest rates are normally lower than long-term rates. Therefore, financing with short-term credit usually results in lower interest expenses.

D. The primary disadvantage of short-term debt is that it is generally more risky than long-term debt.

1. Short-term interest rates fluctuate widely, so if a company finances with short-term debt, its interest expenses will also fluctuate. However, if it uses long-term debt, interests costs will be "locked in" and hence its profits will be more stable.

2. Short-term debt comes due every few months. If a firm does not have the cash to repay debt when it comes due, and if its business is temporally depressed, then it may be unable to refinance the loan, and it may be forced into bankruptcy.

DEFINITIONAL QUESTIONS

1. Working capital management involves decisions relating to _____ assets and liabilities.

2. _____ working capital is defined as _____ assets minus current _____.

3. The cash conversion cycle is the _____ time interval between cash _____ for raw materials and cash receipts on _____ _____.

4. A _____ in the cash conversion cycle reduces the need for _____ financing.

5. In the maturity matching approach to working capital financing, permanent assets should be financed with _____-_____ capital, while _____ assets should be financed with short-term credit.

6. Some firms use short-term debt to finance permanent assets. This approach maximizes the firm's _____ _____, but it also involves the greatest _____.

7. Short-term debt provides more _____ for firms that are uncertain about their _____ borrowing needs.

8. Short-term debt will be less expensive than long-term debt if the yield curve is _____ sloping.

9. Short-term interest rates fluctuate _____ than long-term rates.

CONCEPTUAL QUESTIONS

10. The matching of asset and liability maturities is considered desirable because this strategy minimizes interest rate risk.

    a. True   b. False

11. Other things held constant, an increase in the payables deferral period will lead to a reduction in the need for nonspontaneous funding.

    a. True   b. False

12. A firm should always use short-term debt, rather than long-term financing, to minimize its interest expense.

    a. True   b. False

PROBLEMS

13. Schnell Industries, Inc., has an inventory conversion period of 60 days, a receivables conversion period of 35 days, and a payments cycle of 28 days. What is the length of the firm's cash conversion cycle?

   a. 67 days
   b. 82 days
   c. 95 days
   d. 104 days
   e. 117 days

14. Refer to Problem 13. If Schnell's sales are $972,000 annually, what is the firm's investment in accounts receivables?

   a. $72,450
   b. $79,600
   c. $85,300
   d. $94,500
   e. $100,000

ANSWERS AND SOLUTIONS

1. current

2. Net; current; liabilities

3. net; expenditures; accounts receivables

4. decline; nonspontaneous

5. long-term; temporary

6. expected return; risk

7. flexibility; future

8. upward

9. more

10. b. The matching of maturities lowers *default risk*, or the risk that the firm will be unable to pay off its maturing obligations.

11. a.

12. a. Generally, the yield curve slopes up, making the statement true. Even when the curve slopes down, this suggests that rates are likely to fall, in which case interest expenses will fall if the firm uses short-term debt, but rates will be locked in (at a high level) if it uses long-term debt. Of course, if interest rates rise, the firm which financed with short-term debt may end up paying far more interest than a firm which obtained long-term funds when rates were lower.

13. a. Cash conversion cycle = Inventory conversion period + Receivables conversion period

- Payables deferral period = 60 days + 35 days - 28 days = 67 days.

14. d. Average sales per day = $972,000/360 = $2,700.

Average investment in receivables = $2,700(35) = $94,500.

CHAPTER 11
CASH AND MARKETABLE SECURITIES MANAGEMENT

OVERVIEW

This chapter begins with a discussion of cash management, then covers the various types of marketable securities in which firms can invest temporary cash surpluses, and ends with a discussion of the Baumol model for determining the optimal cash balance. Many factors contribute to good cash management. For example, it is possible to influence the timing of cash inflows and outflows by speeding up the collection of checks received and slowing down the payment of checks issued. Excess cash is generally held as marketable securities. Here, safety is the watchword, and rarely will a financial manager sacrifice safety for higher yields.

OUTLINE

I. **Cash balances vary widely both among industries and among firms, depending upon specific conditions and on the owners' and financial manager aversion to risk.**

   A. Firms hold cash for two primary reasons:
   1. *Transactions balances* are held to provide the cash needed to conduct normal business operations.
   2. *Compensating balances* are often required by bank for providing loans and services.

   B. Two secondary reasons are also cited:
   1. *Precautionary balances* are held in reserve for random fluctuations in cash inflows and outflows.
   2. *Speculative balances* are held to enable the firm to take advantage of bargain purchases.

   C. Most firms do not segregate funds for each of these motives, but they do consider them in setting their overall cash positions.

II. **Cash is a nonearning asset. Excessive cash balances reduce the rate of return on equity and hence the value of a firm's stock.**

   A. A *cash budget* projects cash inflows and outflows over some specified period of time, based on sales and the level of fixed assets and inventories that will be required to meet the forecasted sales level. Cash budgeting was discussed in Chapter 9.

   B. *Improved forecasts* of cash inflows and outflows will permit a smaller cash balance.

III. **A carefully constructed cash budget, along with a well thought-out target cash balance, is a necessary starting point for good cash management. However, other factors also contribute to sound cash management.**

A. *Synchronizing cash inflows and outflows* permits a reduction in the firm's target cash balance.

B. Both *speeding collections* and *slowing payments* permit a firm to operate with smaller cash balances.
   1. *Float* is the difference between the balance shown in a firm's checkbook and the balance on the bank's books. It is an indication that the firm is more efficient in making collections than are the recipients of its checks.
   2. The use of a *lock-box plan* can substantially reduce the time required to process checks and thus to receive payments.
   3. *Slowing payments* improves efficiency by increasing float.
   4. The use of *drafts* rather than checks also increases float.

C. Firms often maintain bank balances in excess of transactions needs as a means of compensating the bank for various services. These balances are called *compensating balances*. The banks in turn earn income on these funds by lending them to their borrowing customers.
   1. Compensating balances also are required by some bank loan agreements.
   2. Compensating balances may be established as an absolute minimum or as a minimum average balance over some time period, generally a month.

D. Many banks in countries other than the United States use *overdraft systems* in which depositors write checks in excess of their actual balances. These banks then automatically extend loans to cover the shortages. Overdraft systems are becoming increasingly popular in the United States.

IV. **A firm can accelerate the cash-gathering process by streamlining collections, utilizing a cash-concentration system, and forecasting cash inflows and outflows.**

A. A *lockbox system* can reduce mail-time float and processing float.
   1. In a lockbox system, customers mail checks to a post office box in a specified city. A local bank then collects the checks, deposits them, starts the clearing process and notifies the selling firm that payment has been received.
   2. Processing time is further reduced because it takes less time for banks to collect local checks.

B. A *cash-gathering system* consists of a network of banks used to channel funds to where they can be utilized most effectively.
   1. Local *depository banks* operate lockboxes.
   2. Funds are channeled to *regional concentration banks* where they are available for disbursement.
   3. The *primary bank* is the overall control bank for the firm's cash-gathering network. The main advantages of centralizing the firm's pool of cash include:
      a. Better control is achieved.
      b. Unused cash is minimized. Excess cash in one local bank can be transferred to the central bank and then sent to other banks where it is needed or else be invested in marketable securities.

V. A transfer mechanism is a means of moving funds among accounts at different banks.

    A. *Depository transfer checks (DTCs)* are checks used for deposit only to a firm's account at a particular bank. *Electronic depository transfer checks (EDTCs)* eliminate mail-time float.

    B. *Wire transfers* make funds transferred from one bank to another immediately available.

    C. The cost of a transfer mechanism is related to its speed.
        1. Wire transfers are instantaneous, but cost $6 to $8 each.
        2. Mail DTCs cost $0.40 to $0.50, but may take 2 to 7 days.
        3. By relating the cost of a faster mechanism to the value of the extra interest which could be earned by the funds after transfer, the breakeven transfer size can be found:

$$S^* = C/I \, T,$$

    where

        S^* = the breakeven size of transfer above which the faster, higher cost mechanism should be used.

        C = the incremental cost of the faster mechanism.

        I = the applicable daily interest rate.

        T = the difference in transfer time in days.

        4. This formula has been criticized on several counts:
            a. Funds in the depository bank are assumed to have no value when in fact they earn service credits which may reduce bank service charges.
            b. Timing the use of transfer alternatives may eliminate the advantage of a faster mechanism.

VI. Firms should incur the costs of cash management activities only so long as they provide adequate returns.

    A. Larger firms, with more invested in cash assets, can better afford cash management personnel and services.

    B. Higher interest rates make cash management services more valuable. If a firm can operate with a reduced cash position, it can increase earning assets or reduce expensive borrowing.

    C. Smaller firms often use cash management services offered by large banks.

VII. Marketable securities typically provide lower yields than a firm's operating assets, yet they are often held in sizable amounts.

A. Marketable securities are held as a *substitute for cash balances*. The securities are sold when cash is needed for transactions.

B. A second use of marketable securities is as a *temporary investment*.
   1. Seasonal or cyclical operations may generate surplus cash at some times and deficits at other times. Marketable securities may be used to smooth out these cash fluctuation/
   2. Marketable se urities may be used to accumulate funds for a known financial requirement s ch as a bond redemption or a major tax payment.
   3. Proceeds fr m a major stock or bond issue may be temporarily invested in marketable ecurities until they are needed for permanent investment in operating assets.

C. A firm's m rketable securities policy is an integral part of its overall working capital policy.
   1. A fir with a *conservative working capital financing policy*, which has long-term capi al exceeding permanent assets, will hold marketable securities when inv ntories and receivables are low. This is the least risky policy, but has the lo est expected return.
   2. firm with an *aggressive policy* will never carry marketable securities and will orrow heavily to meet peak needs. This is the most risky policy, but provides the highest expected return.
   3 A firm with a *moderate policy*, where maturities are matched, will meet peak seasonal increases in inventories and receivables with short-term loans, but it will also carry marketable securities during the peak season.

D. A wide variety of securities, differing in terms of default risk, interest rate risk, liquidity risk, and expected rate of return, are available.
   1. *Default risk* is the risk that an issuer will not be able to make promised interest payments or to repay principal amounts on schedule.
   2. *Interest rate risk* involves the changes in security prices that occur with changes in interest rates.
   3. *Purchasing power risk* is the risk that inflation will reduce the purchasing power of a given sum of money.
   4. *Liquidity risk* refers to whether an asset can be sold at or near its current market price.
   5. Most firms emphasize safety in their marketable securities portfolios even though such an investment policy requires a sacrifice in terms of the rates of return earned on the portfolios.

E. Many types of securities are available for investment of surplus cash. Among those most suitable for holding as near-cash reserves are U.S. Treasury bills, commercial paper, negotiable certificates of deposit, money market funds, and Eurodollar time deposits.

VI. One of the key elements in a firm's cash budget is the target cash balance. The target cash balance is normally set as the larger of the firm's transactions balances plus precautionary balances or its required compensating balances.

    A. The Baumol model applies inventory methodology (EOQ model) to cash balances.
        1. The optimal cash holdings to be transferred from marketable securities or borrowed, C*, can be found by the equation:

$$C* = \sqrt{\frac{2(F)(T)}{k}}.$$

        Here F = fixed costs of borrowing or of converting marketable securities into cash, T = total amount of net new cash needed for transactions over the entire period, usually a year, and k = the opportunity cost of holding cash.
        2. Assuming no precautionary balances, the optimal average cash balance is C*/2.
        3. The Baumol model is simplistic in many respects, but it can provide a useful starting point for establishing a target cash balance.

DEFINITIONAL QUESTIONS

1. The funds needed to carry on the everyday business activities of the firm are referred to as _____ balances.

2. _____ balances are maintained in order to allow for random, unforeseen fluctuations in cash _____ and _____.

3. Cash balances held to enable the firm to take advantage of bargain purchases are know as _____ balances.

4. _____ balances are maintained to pay banks for services they perform.

5. The most important tool in cash management is the _____ _____.

6. Efficient cash management is often concerned with speeding up the _____ of checks received and slowing down the _____ of checks issued.

7. One method for improving the collection process is the use of a _____ system.

8. Many firms delay the actual payment of bills by the use of _____ rather than checks.

9. The difference between a firm's balance on its own books and its balance as carried on the bank's books is known as _____.

10. In a cash-gathering system, local depository banks channel funds to a regional _____ bank.

11. Three mechanisms by which firms transfer funds between accounts at different banks are _____ _____ _____, _____ depository transfer checks, and _____ _____.

12. As a general rule, a firm should invest in cash management operations so long as the marginal _____ on the cash saved exceed the marginal _____ of freeing this cash.

13. Compensating balances may be determined as an absolute _____ amount or as a minimum _____ amount over some period of time.

14. A procedure whereby a bank automatically extends a loan to cover checks in excess of the actual balance in an account is known as an _____ system.

15. Business firms subject to _____ patterns of cash flows may invest _____ funds in short-term securities and then liquidate them when cash _____ occur.

16. _____ risk refers to an issuer's inability to make interest payments and to repay the _____ at maturity.

17. The prices of _____ bonds are much more sensitive to changes in interest rates than are the prices of _____ bonds.

CONCEPTUAL QUESTIONS

18. Money market funds are suitable vehicles for investment of surplus cash, especially for small firms.

    a. True   b. False

19. Which of the following actions would *not* be consistent with good cash management?

    a. Increased synchronization of cash flows
    b. Use of drafts in disbursing funds
    c. Use of lock-boxes in funds collection
    d. Maintaining an average cash balance equal to that required as a compensating balance or that which minimizes total cost.
    e. Minimize the use of float.

20. Which of the following investments is not likely to be a proper investment for temporarily idle cash?

    a. Commercial paper
    b. Treasury bills
    c. Recently issued long-term AAA corporate bonds
    d. Treasury bonds due within one year
    e. AAA corporate bonds due within one year

21. The term "interest rate risk" refers to the probability that a firm will be unable to continue making interest payments on its debt.

    a. True   b. False

PROBLEMS

22. The Mill Company has a daily average collection of checks of $250,000. It takes the company 4 days to convert the checks to cash. Assume a lockbox system could be employed which would reduce the cash conversion period to 3 days. The lockbox system would have a net cost of $25,000 per year, but any additional funds made available could be invested to net 8 percent per year. Should Mill adopt the lockbox system?

    a. Yes; the system would free $250,000 in funds.
    b. Yes; the benefits of the lock-box system exceed the costs.
    c. No; the benefit is only $10,000.
    d. No; the firm would lose $5,000 per year if the system were used.
    e. The benefits and costs are equal, hence the firm is indifferent toward the system.

23. The Ryder Company has been practicing cash management for some time by using the Baumol model to determine cash balances. Recently, when the interest rate on marketable securities was 10 percent, the model called for an average cash balance of $1,000. A rapid increase in interest rates has driven this rate up to 15 percent. The firm incurs a cost of $20 per transaction. Ryder does not carry any precautionary balances. What is the appropriate average cash balance now?

    a. $596.97
    b. $604.73
    c. $816.50
    d. $1,632.99
    e. $1,333.33

24. The Northrup Corporation needs to transfer $30,000 in excess cash from its field office in Miami to its regional concentration bank in Dallas. A mail depository transfer check will cost $0.50 and take two days to arrive in Dallas, while a wire transfer will cost $8.00 and will be immediately available. Northrup earns 12 percent annual interest on funds in its concentration bank. Which transfer method should be used?

    a. DTC; it will save Northrup $7.50 over using the wire transfer.
    b. DTC; the breakeven transfer volume is $11,250, indicating that the DTC should be used.
    c. The breakeven transfer size is $30,000, hence the firm is indifferent between the two methods.
    d. wire; the breakeven transfer volume is $11,250, indicating that the wire transfer should be used.
    e. wire; the breakeven volume is $25,000, indicating that the wire transfer should be used.

ANSWERS
AND SOLUTIONS

1. transactions

2. Precautionary; inflows; outflows

3. speculative

4. compensating

5. cash budget

6. collection; payment

7. lock-box

8. drafts

9. float

10. concentration

11. depository transfer checks; electronic; wire transfers

12. returns; costs

13. minimum; average

14. overdraft

15. seasonal; surplus; shortages

16. Default; principal

17. long-term; short-term

18. a. They offer safety and liquidity, the two most important factors in choosing marketable securities.

19. e. Management should try to maximize float.
20. c. Long-term bonds have too much interest rate risk for the firm's liquid asset portfolio.

21. b. Interest rate risk stems from the loss of value of a security if interest rates rise. *Default risk* refers to the probability of missing interest payments.

22. d. Currently, Mill has 4($250,000) = $1,000,000 in unavailable collections. If lockboxes were used, this could be reduced to $750,000. Thus, $250,000 would be available to invest at 8 percent, resulting in an annual return of 0.08($250,000) = $20,000. If the system costs $25,000, Mill would lose $5,000 per year by adopting the system.

23. c. The model is

$$C^* = \sqrt{\frac{2(F)(T)}{k}}$$

Initially, the average cash balance, $C^*/2$, is $1,000, thus $C^* = \$2,000$. Therefore,

$$\$2,000 = \sqrt{\frac{2(\$20)(T)}{0.10}}$$

$$\$4,000,000 = \frac{2(\$20)(T)}{0.10}$$

$$\$4,000,000 = \$400T$$
$$\$10,000 = T.$$

Therefore the new average cash balance is

$$C^* = \sqrt{\frac{2(\$20)(\$10,000)}{0.15}}$$

$$C^* = \$1,632.99$$

$$C^*/2 = \$816.50.$$

24. d. The breakeven transfer size is found as

$$S^* = \frac{\Delta C}{I\Delta T}.$$

For the Northrup Company

$$S^* = \frac{\$8.00 - \$0.50}{(0.12/360)(2)} = = \$11,250.$$

The breakeven transfer volume, above which the wire transfer is preferred, is $11,250. Since Northrup needs to transfer $30,000, it should use a wire transfer.

Note that if you round 0.12/360 to 0.0003, you will get $12,500 as the breakeven transfer volume. $11,250 is the exact solution.

CHAPTER 12
CREDIT MANAGEMENT

OVERVIEW

The average firm has about 20 percent of its assets in receivables and another 20 percent in inventories. Effective management of these two accounts is therefore vital to profitability. In general, firms would rather sell for cash than on credit, but granting credit normally stimulates sales. The investment in receivables is dependent on the firm's credit policy, which reflects four variables: 1) the credit period if no discount is taken, 2) the credit standards, 3) collection policy, and 4) cash discounts offered. Easier credit stimulates sales, but it also has some costs, and the optimal credit policy involves a tradeoff between these benefits and costs.

OUTLINE

I. **The typical manufacturing firm has about 20 percent of its total assets invested in accounts receivable, and effective management of these assets is important to the profitability of the firm.**

    A. Accounts receivable are created when a firm sells goods or performs services on credit rather than on a cash basis.

    B. The total amount of accounts receivable outstanding is determined by 1) the volume of credit sales and 2) the average length of time between sales and collections.

    C. The investment in receivables, like any asset, must be financed in some manner. Financing has a cost, so any relaxation of credit policy which increases receivables also increases the firm's cost of funds.

II. **Receivables must be actively managed to insure that they are paid off on time. Two tools are commonly used to monitor a firm's receivables.**

    A. The first is the *average collection period (ACP)*.
        1. The ACP measures the average length of time it takes a firm's customers to pay off their credit purchases.
        2. The ACP is calculated by dividing the receivables balance by average daily credit sales.
        3. The ACP can be compared with the industry average and with the firm's own credit terms, and its trend over time can be plotted, to get an indication of how well customers are adhering to the prescribed credit terms and how its collections compare with the industry average.

    B. A second tool used to monitor the receivables position is the *aging schedule*.
        1. The aging schedule breaks down a firm's receivables by the ages of the accounts.
        2. The aging schedule points out the percentage of receivables owed by late paying customers.

III. **The major controllable variables that affect sales are sales price, product quality, advertising, and the firm's credit policy. The credit policy consists of 1) the credit period, 2) credit standards, 3) collection policy, and 4) discounts offered.**

A. The *credit period* is the length of time for which credit is granted to customers who do not take discounts. Increasing the credit period often stimulates sales, but there is a cost involved in carrying the receivables for a longer period.

B. *Credit standards* relate to decisions about who will be granted credit. If the firm extended credit sales to only the strongest of customers, it would never have bad debt losses. However, it would probably be losing some sales.

 1. A key element in setting credit standards is the evaluation of credit risk. To evaluate credit risk, credit managers consider the five Cs of credit.
   a. *Character.* This refers to the likelihood that customers will try to honor their obligations.
   b. *Capacity.* This is a subjective appraisal of the customer's ability to pay.
   c. *Capital.* This is measured by the amount of equity the customer has, or, more generally, by the customer's overall financial strength as measured by a ratio analysis.
   d. *Collateral.* This is represented by assets the customer may offer as security to obtain credit.
   e. *Conditions.* This refers to the impact of general or specific economic trends on the customer's ability to pay off receivables.
 2. Two major sources of external credit information are available: (1) credit associations and (2) credit-reporting agencies such as Dun & Bradstreet (D&B).
 3. Modern credit managers classify customers into five or six categories according to degree of risk. Then, the credit manager concentrates time and attention on the weakest customers. This is referred to as *management by exception.*
 4. *Credit scoring systems* use *multiple discriminant analysis (MDA)* to assess credit risk in a quantitative manner. MDA gives the probability that a given customer will default.

C. *Collection policy* refers to the procedures the firm follows to collect past-due accounts. The collection process can be expensive in terms of both direct costs and lost goodwill, but some firmness is needed to prevent an undue lengthening of the collection period and to minimize outright losses.

D. The last variable in the credit policy decision is *cash discounts offered.* Cash discounts (1) attract customers and (2) encourage early payment, but they also reduce the dollar amount collected on each discount sale.

E. It is possible sometimes to sell on credit and assess a carrying charge on the receivables that are outstanding, making credit sales more profitable than cash sales.

IV. **When offering credit, the selling firm can use any of a variety of credit instruments. Different types of instruments work best at different times, depending on the nature of the product and on the buyer's ability to pay.**

A. An *open account* is used for most credit. With an open account, the only formal evidence of credit is an *invoice* which accompanies the shipment and which the buyer signs to indicate that goods have been received.

B. A *promissory note* may be used as evidence of the credit obligation. Notes are used for certain "big ticket" items where a longer credit period is granted, where interest is to be charged, and/or where the seller lacks confidence in the buyer's ability to pay and therefore wants a legally stronger credit instrument.

C. A *draft* is a cross between a check and promissory note; it looks like a check, but it is often dated for future payment. The draft is signed by the buyer upon receipt of the goods. A specific type of draft is chosen based on the seller's objectives. Common types of drafts are as follows:
   1. Commercial draft; payable immediately; looks just like a check.
   2. Sight draft; similar to a commercial draft.
   3. Time draft or trade acceptance; dated for future payment.
   4. Banker's acceptance; dated for future payment by the bank, which makes it much less risky.

D. A *conditional sales contract* allows the seller retains legal ownership of the goods until the buyer has completed payment.

V. **Easing the credit policy normally stimulates sales. As sales rise, costs also rise (1) because more goods are produced; (2) because additional receivables are outstanding and must be financed, and (3) because bad debt expenses rise.**

A. The question when considering a credit policy change is whether sales revenues will rise more than costs.

B. The way to answer this question is to compare projected income statements which reflect the incremental changes in expected sales revenues and costs that would result from proposed changes in the credit policy.

C. In a credit policy analysis, determine the firm's cost of carrying receivables before and after the change in credit policy.
   1. The cost of carrying receivables is the product of
      a. the average collection period;
      b. sales per day;
      c. the variable cost ratio; and
      d. the cost of capital invested in receivables.
   2. Only variable costs are considered because only this portion needs to be financed.

D. The change in the level of bad debt losses and the dollar value of the discounts taken must also be determined.

E. If expected sales revenues minus expected expenses is greater after the proposed change in credit policy than before, then profits will increase and the change in credit policy should be undertaken.

F. There is quite a bit of uncertainty in a credit policy analysis: (1) It is hard to tell how a change in credit policy will affect demand. (2) The effects on bad debt losses is uncertain. (3) The variable cost ratio may change as a result of economies or diseconomies of scale. (4) Competitors may match the change. The final decision must be based on judgment.

DEFINITIONAL QUESTIONS

1. _____ _____ are created when goods are sold or services are performed on credit.

2. A firm's outstanding accounts receivable will be determined by the _____ of credit sales and the length of time between _____ and _____.

3. Sales volume and the collection period will be affected by a firm's _____ _____.

4. Extremely strict credit standards will result in lost _____.

5. Effective credit standards require a balance between the _____ costs of credit and the marginal _____ on increased sales.

6. The five Cs of credit refer to _____, _____, _____, _____, and _____.

7. Credit terms generally specify the _____ for which credit is granted and any _____ _____ that are offered for early payment.

8. The optimal credit terms involve a tradeoff between increased _____ and the cost of carrying additional _____ _____.

9. _____ policy refers to the manner in which a firm tries to obtain payment from past-due accounts.

10. Two popular methods for monitoring receivables are _____ _____ _____ and the _____ _____.

11. Credit sales may be especially profitable if _____ is charged on accounts receivable.

12. _____ _____ are local groups which meet to exchange credit information.

13. Most credit is offered on _____ _____, which means that the only formal evidence of credit is the invoice.

14. If a seller wants a stronger legal claim against a creditor, or wants to charge interest until the account is settled, then the seller will require the buyer to sign a _____ _____.

CONCEPTUAL QUESTIONS

15. A firm changes its credit policy from 2/10, net 30, to 3/10, net 30. The change is to meet competition, so no increase in sales is expected. The firm's average investment in accounts receivable will probably increase as a result of the change.

   a. True   b. False

16. An aging schedule is constructed by a firm to keep track of when its accounts payable are due.

    a. True   b. False

17. The goal of credit policy is to

    a. Minimize bad debt losses.
    b. Minimize the ACP.
    c. Maximize sales.
    d. Minimize collection expenses.
    e. Extend credit to the point where marginal profits equal marginal costs.

18. If a credit policy change increases the firm's accounts receivable, the entire amount of the increase must be financed by some external source of funds.

    a. True   b. False

PROBLEMS

(The following data apply to the next three problems.)

Simmons Brick Company sells on terms of 3/10, net 30. Gross sales for the year are $1,200,000 and the collections department estimates that 30 percent of the customers pay on the tenth day and take discounts; 40 percent pay on the thirtieth day; and the remaining 30 percent pay, on average, 40 days after the purchase. Assume 360 days per year.

19. What is the average collection period?

    a. 10 days
    b. 13 days
    c. 20 days
    d. 27 days
    e. 40 days

20. What is the current receivables balance?

    a. $60,000
    b. $70,000
    c. $75,000
    d. $80,000
    e. $90,000

21. What would be the new receivables balance if Simmons toughened up on its collection policy, with the result that all nondiscount customers paid on the thirtieth day?

a. $60,000
b. $70,000
c. $75,000
d. $80,000
e. $90,000

(The following data apply to the next three problems.)

Furston, Inc., a retail firm, currently has sales of $1 million. Its credit period and average collection period are both 30 days, and 1 percent of its sales end up as bad debts. Furston's credit manager estimates that if the firm extends its credit period to 45 days, sales will increase by $100,000, but its bad debt losses on the incremental sales would be 3 percent. Variable costs are 40 percent, and the cost of carrying receivables, k, is 15 percent. Assume a tax rate of 40 percent and 360 days per year.

22. What would be the incremental investment in receivables if the change were made?

a. $3,250
b. $12,352
c. $21,667
d. $33,891
e. $41,667

23. What would be the incremental cost of carrying receivables?

a. $0
b. $3,250
c. $5,000
d. $8,250
e. $10,000

24.
What would be the incremental change in profits?

a. $15,875
b. $26,875
c. $29,250
d. $32,250
e. $41,857

(The following data apply to the next two problems.)

Hodes Furniture currently has annual sales of $2,000,000. Its average collection period is 40 days, and bad debts are 5 percent of sales. The credit and collection manager is considering instituting a stricter collection policy, whereby bad debts would be reduced to 2 percent of total sales, and the average collection period would fall to 30 days. However, sales would also fall by an estimated $250,000 annually. Variable costs are 60 percent of sales and the cost of carrying receivables is 12 percent. Assume a tax rate of 40 percent and 360 days per year.

25. What would be the incremental investment in receivables if the change were made?

    a. -$16,667
    b. -$27,167
    c. -$48,611
    d. -$45,833
    e. -$72,431

26. What would be the incremental change in profits?

    a. -$16,667
    b. -$17,700
    c. -$20,250
    d. -$25,750
    e. -$31,825

ANSWERS AND SOLUTIONS

1. Accounts receivable

2. volume; sales; collections

3. credit policy

4. sales

5. marginal; profits

6. character; capacity; capital; collateral; conditions

7. period; cash discounts

8. sales; accounts receivable

9. Collection

10. average collection period; aging schedules

11. interest

12. Credit associations

13. open account

14. promissory note

15. b. No new customers are being generated. The current customers pay either on Day 10 or Day 30. The increase in trade discount will induce some customers who are now paying on Day 30 to pay on Day 10. Thus, the average collection period will be shortened, and this will cause a decline in accounts receivable.

16. b. The aging schedule breaks down accounts receivable according to how long they have been outstanding.

17. e. The goal of credit policy is to maximize overall profits. This is achieved when the marginal profits equal the marginal costs.

18. b. Receivables are based on the sales price, which generally includes a profit, but only the actual cash outlays associated with receivables must be financed. The remainder, or profit, appears on the balance sheet as an increase in retained earnings.

19. d. 0.3(10 days) + 0.4(30 days) + 0.3(40 days) = 27 days.

20. e. Receivables = (ACP)(Sales/360) = 27($1,200,000/360) = $90,000.

21. d. New average collection period = 0.3(10) + 0.7(30) = 24 days.

Sales per day = $1,200,000/360 = $3,333.33.

Receivables = $3,333.33(24 days) = $80,000.00.

Thus, the average receivables would drop from $90,000 to $80,000. Furthermore, sales may decline as a result of the tighter credit and reduce receivables even more. Also, some additional customers may now take discounts, which would further reduce receivables.

22. c. The incremental receivable investment would be calculated as follows:

Old credit policy: (ACP)(Sales per day)(Variable cost ratio)

$$(30)\,(\frac{\$1,000,000}{360})\,(0.4) = \$33,333.$$

New credit policy: (ACP)(Sales per day)(Variable cost ratio)

$$(45)\,(\frac{\$1,100,000}{360})\,(0.4) = \$55,000.$$

The incremental investment in receivables is:

$$\$55,000 - \$33,333 = \$21,667.$$

23. b. The incremental cost of carrying receivables would be calculated as follows:

Old credit policy: (ACP)(Sales per day)(Variable cost ratio)(Cost of funds)

$$(30)(\frac{\$1,000,000}{360})(0.4)(0.15) = \$5,000.$$

New credit policy: (ACP)(Sales per day)(Variable cost ratio)(Cost of funds)

$$(45)(\frac{\$1,100,000}{360})(0.4)(0.15) = \$8,250.$$

Thus, the incremental cost is $8,250 - $5,000 = $3,250.

24. d.

	Income Statement under Current Policy	Effect of Change	Income Statement under New Policy
Gross sales	$1,000,000	$100,000	$1,100,000
Less discounts			
Net sales			
Production costs	400,000	40,000	440,000
Gross profit before credit costs	$ 600,000	$ 60,000	$ 660,000
Credit related costs:			
Cost of carrying receivables	5,000	3,250	8,250
Collection expenses			
Bad debt losses	10,000	3,000	13,000
Gross profit	$ 585,000	$ 53,750	$ 638,750
Taxes (40%)	234,000	21,500	255,500
Net income	$ 351,000	$ 32,250	$ 383,250

25. d. The incremental change in receivables investment would be calculated as follows:

Old credit policy: (ACP)(Sales per day)(Variable cost ratio)

$$(40)(\frac{\$2,000,000}{360})(0.6) = \$133,333.$$

New credit policy: (ACP)(Sales per day)(Variable cost ratio)

$$(30)(\frac{\$1,750,000}{360})(0.6) = \$87,500.$$

The incremental change in receivables is $87,500 - $133,333 = -$45,833.

26. b.

	Income Statement under Current Policy	Effect of Change	Income Statement under New Policy
Sales	$2,000,000	($250,000)	$1,750,000
Less discounts			
Net sales			
Production costs	1,200,000	150,000	1,050,000
Gross profit before credit costs	$ 800,000	($100,000)	$ 700,000
Credit related costs:			
Cost of carrying receivables	16,000	5,500	10,500
Collection expenses			
Bad debt losses	100,000	65,000	35,000
Gross profit	$ 684,000	($ 29,500)	$ 654,500
Tax (40%)	273,600	11,800	261,800
Net income	$ 410,400	($ 17,700)	$ 392,700

CHAPTER 13
INVENTORY MANAGEMENT

OVERVIEW

Inventory management focuses on three basic questions: (1) How many units should be ordered (or produced) at a given time? (2) At what point should inventory be ordered (or produced)? (3) What inventory items warrant special attention? Since inventories must be acquired prior to sales, accurate sales forecasts are essential if these questions are to be answered correctly. It should be noted that inventory models center around the balancing of a set of costs that decline with larger holdings, and another set of costs that increase with larger holdings. The Economic Ordering Quantity (EOQ) model is a formal model which balances these two sets of costs and minimizes the total costs of ordering and carrying inventories.

OUTLINE

I. **Inventories are essential to the operation of most businesses.**

   A. The typical manufacturing firm has about 20 percent of its assets in inventories.

   B. Inventories are commonly classified into three categories.
      1. Raw materials
      2. Work-in-process
      3. Finished goods

   C. Inventories are greatly influenced by the level of sales, and since inventories must be acquired before sales can take place, an accurate sales forecast is critical to effective inventory management.

II. **The goal of inventory management is to provide the level of inventories necessary for efficient operations at the minimum cost. The first step in developing an inventory model is to identify the costs associated with ordering and carrying inventories:**

   A. *Carrying costs* generally rise in direct proportion to the average amount of inventory held.
      1. Carrying costs include the following:
         a. Cost of the capital tied up in inventories
         b. Storage costs
         c. Insurance costs
         d. Property taxes
         e. Depreciation and obsolescence
      2. Let TCC = total carrying costs, C = annual carrying costs as a percentage of inventory value, P = purchase price per unit of inventory, and A = average number of units held in inventory. Then,

$$\text{Total carrying costs} = TCC = (C)(P)(A).$$

   Note that as the average inventory held, A, increases, so does total carrying cost.

B. *Ordering costs* are fixed costs per order, but total ordering costs decline as the number of orders decrease.
   1. Ordering costs include the costs of placing and receiving orders.
   2. Let TOC = total ordering costs, F = fixed costs associated with placing and receiving an order, and N = the number of orders placed per year. Then,

$$\text{Total ordering costs} = \text{TOC} = (F)(N).$$

Note that TOC increases as the number of orders, N, increases. Note also that to lower N, the firm must order more each time it places an order, and that will mean larger average inventories. Thus, carrying costs are minimized by ordering frequently and holding low average inventories, but that will raise ordering costs. Thus, minimizing total costs involves balancing these two sets of costs.

C. The costs of running short of inventory, or *stock-out costs*, will be dealt with later, when safety stocks are discussed.

D. Total inventory costs, TIC, equal the sum of carrying costs and ordering costs:

$$\text{TIC} = \text{TCC} + \text{TOC} = (C)(P)(A) + (F)(N).$$

   1. Now recognize that if Q units are ordered each time an order is placed, and assuming (1) that inventories are used evenly over the year and (2) that inventory levels are run down to zero immediately prior to receipt of each order, then the average inventory level will be one-half the number ordered: $A = Q/2$.
   2. Further, if Q units are ordered each time, and S units are required over the year, then the firm must place N orders per year, where $N = S/Q$.
   3. Using these relationships for A and N, the total inventory cost equation can be rewritten as

$$\text{TIC} = \text{Carrying Costs} + \text{Ordering Costs}$$

$$\text{TIC} = (C)(P)\left(\frac{Q}{2}\right) + \frac{(F)(S)}{Q}.$$

III. Inventories are obviously necessary, but it is equally obvious that inventory levels that are too high or too low are costly to the firm.

A. The *Economic Ordering Quantity (EOQ)* model minimizes total inventory costs.

B. The model, which is derived by minimizing the total inventory cost function, is

$$\text{EOQ} = \sqrt{\frac{2(F)(S)}{(C)(P)}}.$$

Here:

   1. EOQ is the optimal quantity to order each time an order is placed.
   2. F = fixed costs of placing and receiving an order.
   3. S = annual sales in units.
   4. C = carrying cost expressed as a percentage of inventory value.
   5. P = purchase price the firm must pay per unit of inventory.

C. The assumptions of the model are as follows:
1. There is no uncertainty regarding the sales forecast.
2. Inventory usage is evenly distributed over time.
3. Orders are always received on schedule.

D. If orders could be received instantaneously, the order point would be zero. However, if time must lapse between placing an order and receiving it, then the order point must be found as follows:
1. Find the daily rate of usage.
2. The lead time is the number of days required to place an order and receive delivery.
3. The order point = daily usage x lead time.

E. Demand, rate of usage, and order lead time cannot always be known with certainty. Therefore, firms add a *safety stock* to their inventories to permit them to continue operations if (1) shipping delays are encountered or (2) the usage rate increases after an order has been placed. The safety stock is designed to avoid running out of inventory and suffering stock-out costs.
1. At the optimal level of safety stock, the probable cost of running out of inventory is just offset by the cost of carrying the additional inventory.
2. The costs of a stock-out include the following:
   a. Customer ill-will
   b. Production delays and added production costs
   c. Profits on lost sales
3. The probability of a stock-out is influenced by fluctuations in the usage rate and the delivery time.
4. Inclusion of a safety stock does not affect the EOQ, although it does affect the average inventory held.
   a. The average inventory with the safety stock is A = EOQ/2 + Safety stock.
   b. The order point is increased by the amount of the safety stock.
   c. Total inventory costs are increased by the carrying costs of the safety stock.

V. The EOQ model, plus the safety stock analysis, helps firms establish proper inventory levels, but inventory management also includes the inventory ordering and control system. One element of this system is the order point, or the inventory level at which a company should place an order. There are several methods available to determine when the order point is reached.

A. One simple control procedure is the *red-line* method. A red line is drawn inside the bin where the inventory is stocked. When the red line shows, an order is placed.

B. The *two-bin* method has inventory items stocked in two bins. When the working bin is empty, an order is placed and inventory is drawn from the second bin.

C. Large companies employ much more sophisticated *computerized inventory control systems.*

V. **Inventory management should focus on those items which are most critical to the firm. The ABC classification method groups inventory into three classes.**

    A. Category A items, which are most critical, are reviewed often, say monthly, and inventory levels and order quantities are adjusted as needed.

    B. Category B items, which are of average importance to the firm, are reviewed and adjusted less frequently.

    C. Category C items, the least critical, are reviewed and adjusted the least often, say annually.

VI. **During inflation, or if sales are seasonal or cyclical, the EOQ must be updated frequently.**

    A. Values used in the EOQ model may not remain constant for an appreciable length of time.

    B. The firm needs a more flexible inventory management system so it can take advantage of bargains and provide for future contingencies.

    C. The basic logic for inventory models is still valid, but finding the optimal quantity becomes more difficult.

VII. **Two other inventory-related issues should be mentioned:**

    A. The *just-in-time method* coordinates a manufacturer's production with suppliers' so that raw materials arrive from suppliers just as they are needed in the production process.

    B. *Out-sourcing* is the practice of purchasing components rather than making them in-house. Out-sourcing is often combined with just-in-time systems to reduce inventory levels.

DEFINITIONAL QUESTIONS

1. Inventories are usually classified as _____ _____, _____-_____-_____and _____ _____.

2. The _____ classification method is used to focus managerial resources on those inventory items deemed most critical.

3. Storage costs, obsolescence, and other costs that _____ with larger inventories are known as _____ costs.

4. Ordering and receiving costs are _____ related to average inventory size.

5. The _____ _____ quantity minimizes the total costs of ordering and holding inventories.

6. When the level of inventories reaches the _____ _____, the EOQ amount should be ordered.

7. A _____ _____ must be maintained in order to allow for shipping delays and changes in the rate of _____.

8. Running out of an item of inventory is called a _____-_____.

CONCEPTUAL QUESTIONS

9. The costs of a stock-out do *not* include

   a. Disruption of production schedules.
   b. Loss of customer goodwill.
   c. Depreciation and obsolescence.
   d. Loss of sales.
   e. Answers c and d above.

10. The economic ordering quantity (EOQ) is the order quantity that provides the minimum total cost; that is, both the ordering and carrying cost components are minimized.

    a. True   b. False

11. The addition of a safety stock to the EOQ model

    a. Increases the EOQ proportionately.
    b. Raises the order point.
    c. Lowers the order point.
    d. Does not change the total inventory costs.
    e. Results in greater variability in the time required to receive deliveries.

PROBLEMS

(The following data apply to the next four problems.)

The South Florida Lawn Supply Company is reviewing its inventory policy regarding lawn seed. The following relationships and conditions are known by management to exist:

(1) Orders must be placed in multiples of 100 bags.
(2) Requirements for the year are 16,200 bags.
(3) The purchase price per bag is $5.00.
(4) The carrying cost is 20 percent of inventory value.
(5) The fixed costs per order are $25.
(6) The desired safety stock is 300 bags; this amount is on hand initially.
(7) Five days are required for delivery.
(8) Assume 360 days per year.

12. What is the economic ordering quantity?

    a. 600 bags
    b. 700 bags
    c. 800 bags
    d. 900 bags
    e. 1,000 bags

13. How many orders should South Florida Lawn Supply place each year?

    a. 22
    b. 20
    c. 18
    d. 16
    e. 14

14. What is the reorder point?

    a. 750 bags
    b. 525 bags
    c. 345 bags
    d. 300 bags
    e. 225 bags

15. What is the average inventory level?

    a. 750 bags
    b. 525 bags
    c. 345 bags
    d. 300 bags
    e. 225 bags

(The following data apply to the next 6 problems.)

The Magnuson Company is trying to determine its optimal inventory policy. The following relationships and conditions exist for the firm:

(1) Annual sales are 120,000 units.
(2) The purchase price per unit is $500.
(3) The carrying cost is 20 percent of inventory value.
(4) The fixed costs per order are $600.
(5) The optimal safety stock is 500 units, which are already on hand.
(6) Assume 360 days per year.

16. What is the economic ordering quantity?

    a. 600 units
    b. 800 units
    c. 1,000 units
    d. 1,200 units
    e. 1,400 units

17. What is the maximum inventory the company will hold?

   a. 1,300 units
   b. 1,400 units
   c. 1,500 units
   d. 1,600 units
   e. 1,700 units

18. What is the average inventory the company will hold?

   a. 600 units
   b. 850 units
   c. 1,100 units
   d. 1,200 units
   e. 1,700 units

19. How often will the company order?

   a. Every 2.0 days
   b. Every 3.60 days
   c. Every 5.25 days
   d. Every 2 weeks
   e. Continually

20. What are the firm's annual total inventory costs disregarding the safety stock?

   a. $50,000
   b. $120,000
   c. $150,000
   d. $170,000
   e. $200,000

21. What are the annual total inventory costs including the safety stock?

   a. $50,000
   b. $120,000
   c. $150,000
   d. $170,000
   e. $200,000

ANSWERS AND SOLUTIONS

1. raw materials; work-in-process; finished goods

2. ABC

3. increase; carrying

4. inversely

5. economic ordering

6. order point

7. safety stock; usage

8. stock-out

9. c. Depreciation and obsolescence are inventory carrying costs.

10. b. The total cost, or the *sum* of the ordering and carrying costs, is minimized, but neither of these component costs is minimized. For example, to minimize carrying costs, no inventory would be kept on hand at all, but then ordering costs would be very large.

11. b. The addition of a safety stock increases the reorder point by the amount of the safety stock.

12.
$$EOQ = \sqrt{\frac{2(F)(S)}{(C)(P)}} = \sqrt{\frac{2(\$25)(16,200)}{0.20(\$5)}} = \sqrt{\frac{\$810,000}{\$1.00}} = 900 \text{ bags.}$$

13.
$$\frac{16,200 \text{ bags per year}}{900 \text{ bags per order}} = 18 \text{ orders per year.}$$

14. b. Daily rate of use = 16,200/360 = 45 bags.

Reorder point = 300 + 5(45) = 525 bags.

Thus, South Florida Lawn Supply Company will have 1,200 bags on hand immediately after a shipment is received, will use 45 bags per day, will reorder when the stock is down to 525 bags (which is 5 days' requirements, plus the safety stock), and will be down to 300 bags just before a shipment arrives.

15. a. Average inventory level = EOQ/2 + Safety stock = 900/2 + 300 = 750 bags.

Note that the inventory fluctuates between 1,200 and 300 bags.

16.
$$EOQ = \sqrt{\frac{2(F)(S)}{(C)(P)}} = \sqrt{\frac{2(\$600)(120,000)}{0.20(\$500)}} = \sqrt{\frac{\$144,000,000}{\$100}}$$
$$= 1,200 \text{ units.}$$

17. e. Maximum inventory = EOQ + Safety stock = 1,200 + 500 = 1,700 units.

18. c. Average inventory = EOQ/2 + Safety stock = 600 + 500 = 1,100 units.

19. b.
$$\frac{120,000 \text{ units per year}}{1,200 \text{ units per order}} = 100 \text{ orders per year.}$$

$$\frac{360 \text{ days per year}}{100 \text{ orders per year}} = 3.60 \text{ days.}$$

The firm must place one order every 3.60 days.

20.

$$TIC = (C)(P)(Q/2) + \frac{(F)(S)}{Q}$$

$$= 0.2(\$500)(1,200/2) + \frac{\$600(120,000)}{1,200}$$

$$= \$60,000 + \$60,000 = \$120,000.$$

Note that total carrying costs equal total ordering costs at the EOQ.

21. d. Now, the average inventory is EOQ/2 + Safety stock = 1,100 units rather than EOQ/2 = 600 units.

$$TIC = 0.2(\$500)(1,100) + \frac{\$600(120,000)}{1,200}$$

$$= \$110,000 + \$60,000 = \$170,000.$$

Note that a safety stock increases the cost of carrying inventories.

CHAPTER 14
SHORT-TERM FINANCING

OVERVIEW

Short-term credit is defined as debt originally scheduled for repayment within one year. There are four major types of short-term credit: (1) accruals, (2) accounts payable, or trade credit, (3) bank loans, and (4) commercial paper. Companies use accruals on a regular basis, but this usage is not discretionary. Trade credit, bank loans, and commercial paper are controllable, at least within limits. In many situations, lenders require security when furnishing short-term credit, and this security is often in the form of accounts receivable and inventories.

I. **Accrued wages and taxes increase and decrease spontaneously as a firm's operations expand and contract.**

   A. This type of debt is "free" in the sense that no interest is paid on funds raised through accruals.

   B. The amount of accruals is determined by economic forces, industry custom, and tax payment dates established by law. Thus, firms have little control over the supply of capital from this source.

II. **Accounts payable, or trade credit, is the largest single category of short-term debt.**

   A. Trade credit is a spontaneous source of funds in that it arises from ordinary business transactions. Most firms make purchases on credit, recording the debt as an account payable.

   B. An increase in sales will be accompanied by an increase in inventory purchases, which will automatically generate additional financing.

   C. Trade credit can be divided into two components.
     1. *Free trade credit* is that credit received during the discount period.
     2. Costly trade credit is obtained by forgoing discounts. This costly component should be used only when it is less expensive than funds obtained from other sources.

   D. The costly component of trade credit is based on discounts lost by not paying invoices within the discount period.
     1. For example, if credit terms are 2/10, net 30, the cost of 20 additional days credit is 2 percent of the dollar value of the purchases made.

2. The following equation may be used to calculate the approximate cost of costly trade credit; that is the annual percentage cost of not taking discounts:

$$\% \text{ cost} = \frac{\text{Discount }\%}{100 - \text{Discount }\%} \times \frac{360}{\text{Days credit is} - \text{Discount}}_{\text{outstanding} \quad \text{period}}$$

E. Competitive conditions may permit firms to lower the cost of trade credit by taking discounts beyond the discount period or by paying late. Such practices, called "stretching," reduce the cost of trade credit, but they also result in poor relationships with suppliers.

III. **Bank loans, which appear on a firm's balance sheet as notes payable, represent another important source of short-term financing.**

A. Bank loans are not generated spontaneously but must be negotiated and renewed on a regular basis.

B. About two-thirds of all bank loans mature in a year or less, although banks do make longer-term loans.

C. The main features of bank loans include the following:
  1. When a firm obtains a bank loan, it executes a *promissory note* specifying the following items:
     a. The amount borrowed;
     b. The percentage interest rate;
     c. The repayment schedule;
     d. Any collateral offered as security; and
     e. Any other terms of the loan, such as guarantees by third parties, limitations on additional debt, and the like.
  2. Banks normally require regular borrowers to maintain *compensating balances* equal to 10 to 20 percent of the face value of loans. Such required balances generally increase the effective interest rate on the loan.
  3. A *line of credit* is an informal understanding between the bank and the borrower concerning the maximum loan balance the bank will allow.
  4. A *revolving credit agreement* is a formal line of credit often used by large firms. Normally, the borrower will pay the bank a *commitment fee* to compensate the bank for guaranteeing that the funds will be available. This fee is paid in addition to the regular interest charge on funds actually borrowed.

D. The interest cost of loans will vary for different types of borrowers and for all borrowers over time. Rates charged will vary depending on economic conditions, the risk of the borrower, and the size of the loan. Interest charges on bank loans can be calculated in several ways:
  1. *Regular, or simple, interest.* The interest payment is determined by multiplying the loan amount, or face value, by the stated interest rate. Principal and interest are then paid at the end of the loan period.

$$\text{Effective rate}_{\text{Simple}} = \frac{\text{Interest}}{\text{Amount received}}.$$

2. On a simple interest loan of less than one year the effective rate will be higher due to the compounding effect.

$$\text{Effective rate}_\text{Simple} = (1 + \frac{k_\text{Nom}}{m})^m - 1.0.$$

Here k_Nom is the nominal, or stated, interest rate expressed as a decimal and m is the number of compounding periods per year (four for a quarterly loan or twelve for a monthly loan).

3. *Discount interest.* Under this method, the bank deducts interest in advance. The effective rate of interest is higher than the nominal, or stated, rate.

$$\text{Effective rate}_\text{Discount} = \frac{\text{Interest}}{\text{Face value} - \text{Interest}}.$$

Alternatively,

$$\text{Effective rate}_\text{Discount} = \frac{\text{Nominal rate (\%)}}{1.0 - \frac{\text{Nominal rate}}{\text{(decimal fraction)}}}.$$

4. Effective rates on discount loans for less than one year have higher effective discount rates and are found using this formula:

$$\text{Effective rate}_\text{Discount} = (1.0 + \frac{\text{Interest}}{\text{Face value} - \text{Interest}})^m - 1.0.$$

Here interest and face value are in dollars. A $1,000 loan at 12 percent for one month, discount interest, would have an effective rate of 12.82 percent.

$$\text{Effective rate} = (1.0 + (\frac{\$10}{\$1,000 - \$10}))^{12} - 1.0 = 12.82\%.$$

5. *Installment loans: add-on interest.* Interest charges are calculated and then added on to the funds received to determine the face value of the note, which is paid off in equal installments. The borrower has use of the full amount of the funds received only until the first installment is paid. The effective rate is approximately double the stated rate, because the average amount of the loan outstanding is only about half the face amount borrowed.

$$\begin{array}{c}\text{Approximate}\\ \text{effective rate} \\ \text{Add-on} \end{array} = \frac{\text{Interest paid}}{\text{Loan amount}/2}.$$

14-3

6. Compensating balances tend to raise the effective interest rate on bank loans.
    a. In general, this formula is used to find the effective interest rate when compensating balances apply and interest is paid at the end of the period:

$$\text{Effective rate} \atop \text{Simple/CB} = \frac{\text{Nominal rate (\%)}}{1.0 - \left(\begin{array}{c}\text{Compensating balance} \\ \text{(decimal fraction)}\end{array}\right)}.$$

    b. The analysis can be extended to the case where compensating balances are required and the loan is based on discount interest:

$$\text{Effective rate}_{\text{Discount}} =$$

$$\frac{\text{Nominal rate (\%)}}{1.0 - \left(\begin{array}{ccc}\text{Compensating} & & \text{Nominal} \\ \text{balance} & - & \text{rate} \\ \text{(dec. fraction)} & & \text{(dec. fraction)}\end{array}\right)}.$$

    c. It should be noted that when compensating balances or discount interest or both apply, the borrower must borrow a face amount significantly greater than the funds actually received. For a discount loan with a compensating balance, the face amount is calculated as follows:

$$\text{Face value} = \frac{\text{Funds required}}{1.0 - \left(\begin{array}{ccc}\text{Compensating} & & \text{Nominal} \\ \text{balance} & - & \text{interest rate} \\ \text{(dec. fraction)} & & \text{(dec. fraction)}\end{array}\right)}.$$

E. Choosing a bank involves an analysis of the following variables:
   1. *Policies toward risk.* Some banks are quite conservative, while others are more willing to make risky loans.
   2. *Counsel and advice of bank personnel.* A bank's ability to provide counsel and advice is particularly important to firms in their formative years.
   3. *Loyalty of the bank.* This variable deals with a bank's willingness to support customers during difficult economic times.
   4. *Degree of loan specialization.* A bank may specialize in making loans to a particular type of business. Firms should seek out a bank which is familiar with their particular type of business.
   5. *Size of the bank.* This is an important consideration for large companies when establishing a borrowing relationship because most banks cannot lend to a single customer more than 10 percent of the total amount of the bank's capital.
   6. *Other services.* The availability of services such as lockbox systems should also be taken into account when selecting a bank.

IV. **Commercial paper, another source of short-term credit, is an unsecured promissory note. It is generally sold to other business firms, to insurance companies, to banks, and to money market mutual funds. Only large, financially strong firms are able to tap the commercial paper market.**

A. *Maturities* of commercial paper range from a few days to nine months, but the great majority mature in two to six months.

B. *Interest rates* on prime commercial paper generally range from one to two percentage points below the stated prime rate; this is also about 1/4 of a percentage point above the T-bill rate. However, rates fluctuate daily with supply and demand conditions in the marketplace, and since no compensating balance is required, the effective cost is even lower in comparison to bank loans.

C. Using commercial paper permits a corporation to tap a wide range of credit sources.

D. A disadvantage of the commercial paper market vis-a'-vis bank loans is that the impersonal nature of the market makes it difficult for firms to use commercial paper at times when they are in temporary financial distress.

V. For a strong firm, borrowing on an unsecured basis is generally cheaper and simpler than on a secured loan basis because of the administrative costs associated with the use of security. However, lenders will refuse credit without some form of collateral if a borrower's credit standing is questionable.

A. Most secured short-term business loans involve the pledge of short-term assets such as accounts receivable or inventories.

B. The legal procedures for establishing loan security have been standardized and simplified in the *Uniform Commercial Code.*

VI. Accounts receivable financing involves either the pledging of receivables or the selling (factoring) of receivables.

A. In *pledging* accounts receivable as security for financing, no notification is made to the buyer of the goods, and the lender has recourse to the seller of the goods in case of default. The receivable is not sold to the lender; it is merely used as a security for a loan.

B. In *factoring*, the buyer of the goods makes payment directly to the factor, who has no recourse to the seller of the goods in case of default. The receivable is sold outright to the factoring firm.

C. The cost of receivables financing can be quite high.
  1. Interest rates on borrowed funds under receivables financing are usually above the prevailing prime rate.
    a. The credit rating of the borrower is usually below that of firms qualifying for prime rate loans.
    b. The processing of the invoices (receivables) involves additional expenses.
  2. Factoring charges consist of two elements.
    a. A fee for credit checking of 1 to 3 percent.
    b. An interest charge (somewhat above the prevailing prime rate) on the fund.
    c. Also, if the risk is high, the factor may purchase the invoices at a discount from face value.

D. There are several advantages of receivables financing.
  1. It is flexible--credit expands with sales.

     2. The security provided may allow the firm to receive financing that would otherwise be unobtainable.

     3. Factoring may provide the services of a credit department.

E. The disadvantages of accounts receivable financing are:
1. When invoices are numerous, administrative costs may be high.
2. The firm is using a highly liquid asset as security, which may disturb other creditors and limit the availability of trade credit.

F. In the future, accounts receivable financing will increase in relative importance as automation reduces the cost and increases the convenience of employing receivables financing. Credit card use is a prime example of a type of automated accounts receivable financing.

VII. A large volume of credit is secured by business inventories.

A. The *blanket inventory lien* gives the lending institution a lien against all inventories of the borrowing firm. However, the firm is free to sell the inventories, which reduces the value of the collateral.

B. A *trust receipt* is an instrument acknowledging that the borrower holds goods in trust for the lender. The borrower may keep the goods in his possession, but he must remit the proceeds of the sale of the specific goods to the lender at the end of each day.

C. A third means of inventory financing is *warehouse financing*. In warehouse financing, a third party acts as a supervisory agent for the lender.

QUESTIONS

1. _____ wages and taxes are a common source of short-term credit. However, most firms have little control over the _____ of these accounts.

2. Accounts payable, or _____ _____, is the largest single source of short-term credit for most businesses.

3. Trade credit is a _____ source of funds in the sense that it automatically increases when sales increase.

4. Trade credit can be divided into two components: _____ trade credit and _____ trade credit.

5. _____ trade credit is that credit received during the _____ period.

6. _____ trade credit should only be used when the cost of the trade credit is less than the cost of funds from _____ sources.

7. The instrument signed when bank credit is obtained is called a _____ _____.

8. Most banks require borrowers to keep _____ _____ on deposit with the bank equal to 10 or 20 percent of the face value of the loan.

9. Maturities on commercial paper generally range from _____ to _____ months, with interest rates set one to two percentage points below the _____ rate. This is also about 1/4 of a percentage point above the _____ rate.

10. A _____ loan is one where collateral such as _____ or _____ have been pledged in support of the loan.

11. A _____ _____ _____ is an understanding between a bank and a borrower as to the maximum loan that will be permitted.

12. The fee paid to a bank to institute a revolving credit agreement is known as a _____ fee.

13. Commercial paper can only be issued by _____, _____ _____ firms.

14. If interest charges are deducted in advance, this is known as _____ interest, and the effective rate is higher than the _____ interest rate.

15. With an _____ loan, the average amount of the usable funds during the loan period is equal to approximately _____ of the face amount of the loan.

CONCEPTUAL QUESTIONS

16. Accruals are "free" in the sense that no interest must be paid on these funds.

    a. True   b. False

17. The effect of compensating balances is to decrease the effective interest rate of a loan.

    a. True   b. False

18. Which of the following statements concerning commercial paper is correct?

    a. Commercial paper is secured debt of large, financially strong firms.
    b. Commercial paper is sold primarily to individual investors.
    c. Maturities of commercial paper generally exceed nine months.
    d. Commercial paper interest rates are typically 1.25 to 1.50 percentage points above the stated prime rate.
    e. None of the above statements is correct.

PROBLEMS

19. A firm buys on terms of 2/10, net 30, but generally does not pay until 40 days after the invoice date. Its purchases total $1,080,000 per year. How much "non-free" trade credit does the firm use on average each year?

    a. $120,000
    b. $90,000
    c. $60,000
    d. $30,000
    e. $20,000

20. Refer to Problem 20. What is the approximate cost of the "non-free" trade credit?

    a. 16.2%
    b. 19.4%
    c. 21.9%
    d. 24.5%
    e. 27.4%

21. Lawton Pipelines, Inc., has developed plans for a new pump that will allow more economical operation of the company's oil pipelines. Management estimates that $2,400,000 will be required to put this new pump into operation. Funds can be obtained from a bank at 10 percent *discount* interest, or the company can finance the expansion by delaying payment to its suppliers. Presently, Lawton purchases under terms of 2/10, net 40, but management believes payment could be delayed 30 additional days without penalty; that is, payment could be made in 70 days. Which means of financing should Lawton use? (Use the approximate cost of trade credit.)

    a. Trade credit, since the cost is about 12.24 percent.
    b. Trade credit, since the cost is about 3.13 percentage points less than the bank loan.
    c. Bank loan, since the cost is about 1.13 percentage points less than trade credit.
    d. Bank loan, since the cost is about 3.13 percentage points less than trade credit.
    e. The firm could use either since the costs are the same.

(The following data apply to the next four problems.)

You plan to borrow $10,000 from your bank, which offers to lend you the money at a 10 percent nominal, or stated, rate on a 1-year loan.

22. What is the effective interest rate if the loan is a discount loan?

    a. 11.1%
    b. 13.3%
    c. 15.0%
    d. 17.5%
    e. 20.0%

23. What is the approximate effective interest rate if the loan is an add-on interest loan with 12 monthly payments?

    a. 11.1%
    b. 13.3%
    c. 15.0%
    d. 17.5%
    e. 20.0%

24. What is the effective interest rate if the loan is a discount loan with a 15 percent compensating balance?

    a. 11.1%
    b. 13.3%
    c. 15.0%
    d. 17.5%
    e. 20.0%

25. Under the terms of Problem 24, how much would you have to borrow to have the use of $10,000?

    a. $10,000
    b. $11,111
    c. $12,000
    d. $13,333
    e. $15,000

ANSWERS

1. Accrued; size

2. trade credit

3. spontaneous

4. free; costly

5. Free; discount

6. Costly; other

7. promissory note

8. compensating balances

9. two; six; prime; T-bill

10. secured; receivables; inventories

11. line of credit

12. commitment

13. large; financially strong

14. discount; simple (or nominal or stated)

15. installment; one-half

16. a. Neither workers nor the IRS require interest payments on wages and taxes that are not paid as soon as they are earned.

17. b. Compensating balances *increase* the effective rate.

18. e. Commercial paper is the unsecured debt of strong firms. It generally has a maturity of less than 6 months and is sold primarily to other corporations and financial institutions. Rates on commercial paper are typically below the prime rate.

19. b. $1,080,000/360 = $3,000 in purchases per day. Typically, there will be $3,000(40) = $120,000 of accounts payable on the books at any given time. Of this, $3,000(10) is "free" credit, while $3,000(30) = $90,000 is "non-free" credit.

20. d.

$$\text{Approx. cost} = \frac{\text{Discount \%}}{100 - \text{Discount \%}} \times \frac{360}{\text{Days credit is outstanding} - \text{Discount period}}$$

$$= \frac{2\%}{100\% - 2\%} \times \frac{360}{40 - 10} = \frac{2}{98} \times \frac{360}{30} = 24.5\%.$$

21. c.

$$\text{Effective rate on the discount loan} = \frac{\text{Interest}}{\text{Face value} - \text{Interest}}$$

$$= \frac{(\$2,400,000)(0.10)}{\$2,400,000 - (\$2,400,000)(0.10)}$$

$$= \frac{\$240,000}{\$2,160,000} = 0.1111 = 11.11\%.$$

Credit terms are 2/10, net 40, but delaying payments 30 additional days is the equivalent of 2/10, net 70. Assuming no penalty, the approximate cost is as follows:

$$\begin{array}{c}\text{Approximate}\\\text{cost}\end{array} = \frac{\text{Discount \%}}{100 - \text{Discount \%}} \times \frac{360}{\begin{array}{c}\text{Days credit is}\\\text{outstanding}\end{array} - \begin{array}{c}\text{Discount}\\\text{period}\end{array}}.$$

$$= \frac{2\%}{100\% - 2\%} \times \frac{360}{70 - 10}$$

$$= \frac{2}{98} \times \frac{360}{60} = 0.0204(6) = 12.24\%.$$

Therefore, the loan cost is 1.13 percentage points less than trade credit.

22. a.
$$\begin{array}{c}\text{Effective}\\\text{rate}\end{array} = \frac{\$10,000(0.10)}{\$10,000 - \$10,000(0.10)} = \frac{\$1,000}{\$9,000} = 11.1\%.$$

23. e. Approximate effective rate = $1,000/$5,000 = 20.0%.

24. b.
$$\text{Effective rate} = \frac{10\%}{1 - 0.15 - 0.10} = 13.3\%.$$

25. d.
$$\frac{\$10,000}{1 - 0.15 - 0.10} = \$13,333,$$

since 0.15($13,333) = $2,000 is required for the compensating balance, and 0.10($13,333) = $1,333 is required for the immediate interest payment.

CHAPTER 15
CAPITAL BUDGETING TECHNIQUES

OVERVIEW

Capital budgeting is similar in principle to security valuation in that future cash flows are estimated, risks are appraised and reflected in a cost of capital discount rate, and all cash flows are evaluated on a present value basis. Three methods are frequently used to determine which projects should be included in a firm's capital budget: (1) payback, (2) net present value (NPV), and (3) internal rate of return (IRR). The payback method has deficiencies, and thus should not be used as the sole criterion for making capital budgeting decisions. The NPV and IRR methods both lead to the same accept/reject decisions on independent projects. However, the methods may conflict when ranking mutually exclusive projects which differ in scale or timing. When conflicts occur, the NPV method should be used to make the final decision.

OUTLINE

I. **Capital budgeting is the process of identifying and then analyzing fixed asset investment proposals.**

 A. The discounting process is essential in capital budgeting, as fixed assets are expected to provide cash flows for some years into the future.

 B. Analyzing capital expenditure proposals has a cost, so firms classify projects into different categories to help differentiate the level of analysis required.
 1. Replacement--maintenance of business
 2. Replacement--cost reduction
 3. Expansion of existing products or markets
 4. Expansion into new products or markets
 5. Safety and environmental projects
 6. Other, a catchall for miscellaneous projects

 Normally, a more detailed analysis is required for expansion and new product decisions than for simple replacement and maintenance decisions. Also, projects requiring larger investments will be analyzed more carefully than smaller projects.

 C. The capital budgeting process involves similar concepts and procedures to those used in security valuation.
 1. Cash flows are estimated, including the value of the asset at some specified terminal date.
 2. The riskiness of the projected cash flows is determined.

3. Given the general level of money costs and the riskiness of the projected cash flows, a discount rate is determined and used to calculate the present value of the project.

4. The present value of the benefits is then compared to the required outlay, or cost of the project. If the benefits exceed the cost--that is, if the net present value (NPV) is positive--then the project should be accepted since it will increase the value of the firm.

II. **Estimating the cash flows associated with a project is the most important, but also the most difficult, step in the capital budgeting process. Cash flow estimation will be discussed in detail in the next chapter, but once cash flow estimates have been made for various projects, different methods can be used to evaluate the proposals to decide which ones should be accepted for inclusion in the capital budget. The three most frequently used methods are (1) payback (or payback period), (2) net present value (NPV), and (3) internal rate of return (IRR).**

A. *The payback period* is defined as the number of years it takes a firm to recover its original investment in a project. The payback period is determined by summing each year's inflows until their cumulative total equals the initial outlay. Although payback is sometimes useful as a measure of project liquidity or as a risk indicator, it has two major weaknesses which may cause it to lead to incorrect decisions:
   1. It ignores cash flows beyond the payback period. This penalizes long-term projects, which may be vital to the firm's long-term success.
   2. It ignores the time value of money, because it assigns equal weight to cash flows received in each year during the payback period.

B. Methods that take into account the time value of money are called *discounted cash flow techniques*. One such method is the *net present value (NPV) method*.
   1. To calculate the NPV, find the present value of each cash flow, including the initial (negative) outflow, and sum these PVs to find the NPV.
   2. If the NPV is positive, the project should be accepted; if negative, it should be rejected. By taking on a project with a positive NPV, the value of the firm is increased, and the position of the stockholders is improved.
   3. If two projects are mutually exclusive (that is, if only one can be accepted), the one with the higher NPV should be chosen, assuming the NPV is positive. If both projects have negative NPVs, neither should be chosen.

C. The *internal rate of return (IRR)* is defined as the discount rate which equates the present value of the expected future cash inflows to the present value of the outflows.
   1. The equation for calculating the IRR is as follows, where CF_t is the cash flow for the year t:

$$\sum_{t=0}^{n} \frac{CF_t}{(1 + r)^t} = 0.$$

This is an equation with one unknown, r, and we can solve for the value of r that will make the equation equal to zero. The solution value of r is defined as the internal rate of return: r = IRR.

2. The IRR formula is simply the NPV formula solved for the particular discount rate that causes the NPV to equal zero.
3. The IRR can be found by trial and error, by using a graphical analysis of the net present value profile, or by using a financial calculator or computer.

D. A *net present value profile* is a plot of a project's net present value at various discount rates. It can be used to determine a single project's IRR, and also to choose between two mutually exclusive projects.
   1. The point at which the NPV profile crosses the horizontal axis is the project's IRR.
   2. The NPV and IRR criteria always lead to the same accept/reject decision for independent projects.
   3. If two mutually exclusive projects have NPV profiles which intersect, there may be a conflict in project choice between the NPV and IRR methods.
   4. Conflicts can occur under two circumstances.
      a. The projects differ in scale; for example, one project costs $100,000 while the other project costs $1 million.
      b. The projects differ in cash flow timing; that is, one project has larger cash flows in its early years, while the other has larger cash flows in its later years. Note that cash flow timing does not necessarily refer to project life, but rather to the relative sizes of the flows.
   5. The underlying cause of conflicts in project rankings lies in differing reinvestment rate assumptions.
      a. The NPV method implicitly assumes that project cash flows are reinvested at the project's cost of capital.
      b. The IRR method implicitly assumes that project cash flows are reinvested at the project's IRR.
      c. The opportunity cost of project cash flows is the project's cost of capital. If these cash flows were not available to the firm, and if the firm needed capital to invest in new projects, then the funds would be obtained from the capital markets, and the cost would be the firm's overall cost of capital. Thus, the assumption of reinvestment at the cost of capital is the correct assumption, which makes the NPV decision rule superior to the IRR decision rule.

E. The best method to use is the one that consistently leads to correct capital budgeting decisions. Only the NPV method does this. The NPV method:
   1. Considers all cash flows throughout the life of the project.
   2. Considers the time value of money.
   3. Selects that project from a set of mutually exclusive projects which maximizes the firm's stock value.

III. **The post-audit, or post-completion audit, is an important element of the capital budgeting process.**

A. The post-audit involves a comparison of actual results with those predicted, and it explains any differences.

B. The purpose of the post-audit is to improve forecasting techniques and operations by providing an incentive to help make performance match expectations.

IV. This chapter has outlined the basic procedures for analyzing capital projects; however, there are additional issues which can complicate the process. They are discussed in Chapter 16.

DEFINITIONAL QUESTIONS

1. A firm's _____ _____ outlines its planned expenditures on fixed assets.

2. The most difficult step in the analysis of capital expenditure proposals involves estimating future _____ _____.

3. The number of years necessary to return the original investment in a project is known as the _____ _____.

4. One important weakness of payback analysis is the fact that _____ _____ beyond the payback period are _____.

5. The net present value (NPV) method of evaluating investment proposals takes into account the _____ value of _____.

6. A capital investment proposal should be accepted if its NPV is _____.

7. If two projects are _____ _____, the one with the _____ positive NPV should be selected.

8. In the IRR approach, a discount rate is sought which makes the value of the NPV equal to _____.

9. A net present value profile shows the relationship between a project's _____ and the _____ _____ used to calculate the NPV.

10. If an independent project's _____ is greater than the project's cost of capital, it should be accepted.

11. If two mutually exclusive projects are being evaluated, and one project has a higher NPV while the other project has a higher IRR, the project with the higher _____ should be preferred.

12. The NPV method implicitly assumes reinvestment at the project's _____ _____ _____, while the IRR method implicitly assumes reinvestment at the _____ _____ _____.

13. The process of comparing a project's actual results with its projected results is known as a _____-_____.

14. The primary objective of the post-audit is to improve _____.

15. The internal rate of return (IRR) is the _____ rate that equates the present value of the _____ _____ with the present value of the _____ _____.

CONCEPTUAL QUESTIONS

16. The NPV of a project with cash flows that come in relatively slowly is *more sensitive* to changes in the discount rate than is the NPV of a project with cash flows that come in more rapidly.

    a. True   b. False

17. The NPV method is preferred over the IRR method because the NPV method's reinvestment rate assumption is the correct assumption.

    a. True   b. False

18. When you find the yield to maturity on a bond, you are finding the bond's net present value (NPV).

    a. True   b. False

19. Other things held constant, a decrease in the cost of capital (discount rate) will cause an *increase* in a project's IRR.

    a. True   b. False

20. The IRR method can be used in place of the NPV method for all independent projects, because the two methods then result in identical decisions.

    a. True   b. False

PROBLEMS

21. Your firm is considering a fast-food concession at the 1990 World's Fair. The cash flow pattern is somewhat unusual since you must build the stands, operate them for 2 years, and then tear the stands down and restore the sites to their original condition. You estimate the net cash flows to be as follows:

Time	Expected Net Cash Flow
0	($800,000)
1	700,000
2	700,000
3	(400,000)

What is the approximate IRR of this venture?

a. 5%
b. 15%
c. 25%
d. 35%
e. 45%

(The following data apply to the next three problems.)

Toya Motors needs a new machine for production of its 1988-1989 models. The financial vice president has appointed you to do the capital budgeting analysis. You have identified two different machines that are capable of performing the job. You have completed the cash flow analysis, and the expected net cash flows are as follows:

	Expected Net Cash Flow	
Year	Machine B----Machine O	
0	($5,000)	($5,000)
1	2,085	0
2	2,085	0
3	2,085	0
4	2,085	9,677

22. What is the payback period for Machine B?

a. 1.0 years
b. 2.0 years
c. 2.4 years
d. 2.6 years
e. 3.0 years

23. The cost of capital is uncertain at this time, so you construct NPV profiles to assist in the final decision. The profiles for Machines B and O cross at what cost of capital?

a. 6%
b. 10%
c. 18%
d. 24%
e. They do not cross.

24. If the cost of capital for the project is 14 percent at the time the decision is made, which machine would you choose?

a. Machine B; it has the higher positive NPV.
b. Machine 0; it has the higher positive NPV.
c. Neither; both have negative NPVs.
d. Either; both have the same NPV.
e. Machine B; it has the higher IRR.

(The following data apply to the next four problems.)

The director of capital budgeting for Giant, Inc., has identified two mutually exclusive projects, L and S, with the following expected net cash flows:

| | Expected Net Cash Flow | |
Year	Project L	Project S
0	($100)	($100)
1	10	70
2	60	50
3	80	20

Both projects have a cost of capital of 10 percent.

25. What is the payback period for Project S?

 a. 1.6 years
 b. 1.8 years
 c. 2.1 years
 d. 2.5 years
 e. 2.8 years

26. What is Project L's NPV?

 a. $50.00
 b. $34.25
 c. $22.64
 d. $18.79
 e. $10.06

27. What is Project L's IRR?

 a. 18.1%
 b. 19.7%
 c. 21.4%
 d. 23.6%
 e. 24.2%

28. Plot the NPV profiles for the two projects. Where is the crossover point?

 a. 6.9%
 b. 7.8%
 c. 8.7%
 d. 9.6%
 e. 9.9%

ANSWERS AND SOLUTIONS

1. capital budget

2. cash flows

3. payback period

4. cash flows; ignored

5. time; money

6. positive

7. mutually exclusive; higher

8. zero

9. NPV; discount rate

10. IRR

11. NPV

12. cost of capital; internal rate of return

13. post-audit

14. forecasts

15. discount; cash inflows; cash outflows (or initial cost)

16. a. The more the cash flows are spread over time, the greater is the effect of a change in discount rate. This is because the compounding process has a greater effect on distant than close-in cash flows.

17. a. Project cash flows are substitutes for outside capital. Thus, the opportunity cost of cash flows is the firm's cost of capital, adjusted for risk. The NPV method uses this cost as the reinvestment rate, while the IRR method assumes reinvestment at the IRR.

18. b. The yield to maturity on a bond is the bond's IRR.

19. b. The computation of IRR is independent of the project's cost of capital.

20. a. Both the NPV and IRR methods lead to the same accept/reject decisions for independent projects. Thus, the IRR method can be used as a proxy for the NPV method when choosing independent projects.

21. c. Unless you have a calculator that performs IRR calculations, the IRR must be obtained by trial and error or graphically. (The calculator solution is 25.48 percent.)

22. c. After Year 1, there is $5,000 - $2,085 = $2,915 remaining to pay back. After Year 2, only $2,915 - $2,085 = $830 is remaining. In Year 3, another $2,085 is collected. Assuming that the Year 3 cash flow occurs evenly over time, then payback occurs $830/$2,085 = 0.4 of the way through Year 3. Thus, the payback period is 2.4 years.

23. b. To solve graphically, construct the NPV profiles:

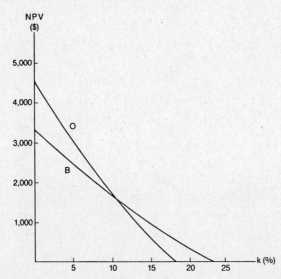

The Y intercept is the NPV when k = 0%. For B, 4($2,085) - $5,000 = $3,340. For O, $9,677 - $5,000 = $4,677. The X intercept is the discount rate when NPV = $0, or the IRR. For B, $5,000 = $2,085(PVIFA$_{IRR,4}$); IRR - 24%. For O, $5,000 = $9,677(PVIF$_{IRR,4}$); IRR - 18%. The graph is an approximation since we are only using two points to plot lines that are curvilinear. However, it shows that there is a crossover point, and that it occurs somewhere in the vicinity of k = 10%.

24. a. Refer to the NPV profiles. When k = 14%, we are to the right of the crossover point and Machine B has the higher NPV. You can verify this fact by calculating the NPVs. NPV$_B$ = $1,075 and NPV$_O$ = $730. Note that Machine B also has the higher IRR. However, the NPV method should be used when evaluating mutually exclusive projects. Note that had the project cost of capital been 8 percent, then Machine O would be chosen on the basis of the higher NPV.

25. a. After the first year, there is only $30 remaining to be repaid, and $50 is received in Year 2. Assuming an even cash flow throughout the year, the payback period is 1 + $30/$50 = 1.6 years.

26. d. NPV$_L$ = -$100 + $10/1.10 + $60/(1.10)^2 + $80/(1.10)^3 = -$100 + $9.09 + $49.59 + $60.11 = $18.79.

(Calculator solution is $18.78.)

27. a. We used a calculator to find IRR$_L$ = 18.1%.

15-9

28. c. The NPV profiles plot as follows:

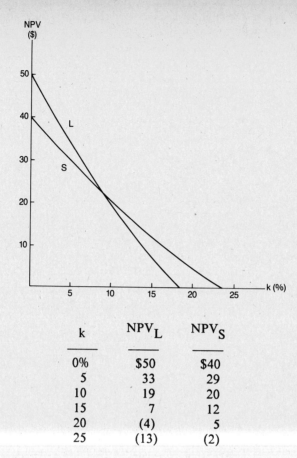

k	NPV_L	NPV_S
0%	$50	$40
5	33	29
10	19	20
15	7	12
20	(4)	5
25	(13)	(2)

By looking at the graph, the approximate crossover rate is 8.7%.

CHAPTER 16
PROJECT CASH FLOWS AND RISK

OVERVIEW

One of the most critical steps in capital budgeting analysis is *cash flow estimation*. The key to correct cash flow estimation is to consider only *incremental cash flows*. However, the process is complicated by such factors as sunk costs, opportunity costs, net working capital changes, salvage values, and tax effects. Cash flow estimation for replacement projects is similar to that for new or expansion projects, except that there are more flows to consider when analyzing replacement projects.

The analysis of project risk focuses on two issues: (1) the project's effect on the probability of bankruptcy or at least low earnings (corporate risk) and (2) the effect of a project on the firm's beta coefficient (market risk). Corporate risk affects the financial strength of the firm, and this, in turn, influences its ability to use debt, to maintain smooth operations over time, and to avoid crises that might consume the energy of the firm's managers and disrupt its employees, customers, suppliers, and community. Beta risk directly affects the value of the firm's stock. In practice, both measuring risk and incorporating risk into capital budgeting decisions involves judgment.

OUTLINE

I. **The most important, and also the most difficult, step in project analysis is estimating the cash flows. The key concept in the process is to consider only the relevant cash flows, which are defined as those cash flows which are affected by the decision. Capital budgeting decisions must be based on cash flows rather than accounting income, and only incremental cash flows should be considered.**

   A. *Cash flow* must be distinguished from *accounting income*.
      1. Operating cash flow is, as a general approximation, a project's net income plus depreciation.
      2. A project's operating cash flow in any year can be calculated as $(S - OC)(1 - T) + TD$, where S = sales revenues, OC = operating costs (less depreciation), T = marginal tax rate, and D = depreciation expense, with all items applying to the project in question.

   B. There are three aspects of cash flow estimation which often present special problems in determining incremental cash flows:
      1. A *sunk cost* is an outlay that has already occurred or has been committed. Sunk costs are not incremental--they do not depend on the decision at hand--and hence they should not be included in the analysis.

2. All relevant *opportunity costs* must be included in the analysis. For example, IBM owns land in Alachua County, Florida. If IBM were analyzing a project which used that land, it would have to include the current net market value of the land as an opportunity cost, because if the project were not undertaken, IBM could sell the land. Note that the relevant opportunity cost is the current net market value, not the price paid to acquire the asset.

3. The analysis must include the *effects* of a proposed project on the firm's *existing projects*. If the introduction of a new liquid detergent would reduce sales of a firm's existing line, then the reduction must be included in the analysis as a cost of the project. This is called, in economics, an *externality*.

C. Normally, additional inventories are required to support a new project, and expanded sales also produce additional accounts receivable, both of which must be financed. On the other hand, accounts payable and accruals may also increase, and this reduces the need to finance inventories and receivables.

1. The difference between the projected increase in current assets and the projected increase in current liabilities is the projected *change in net working capital*.

2. If the change is positive (as it normally is), additional financing above that required for fixed assets is needed.

3. Conversely, if the change is negative, the project is generating a cash inflow from working capital changes.

D. Assuming that all investment cash outflows occur at t = 0, an expansion project's cash flows are estimated as follows:

1. Consider the cash flows which occur at the time the investment is made; that is, at t = 0.

   a. Record the purchase price of the asset, plus any transportation and installation costs.

   b. Show any changes in net working capital.

   c. The net of these items is the project's *net investment outlay*.

2. Consider the future cash flows from operations.

   a. First, look at the effects of the new equipment on revenues and costs. An incremental increase in revenues would produce a cash inflow, while an incremental increase in cash operating costs would produce a cash outflow. After combining the revenue and cost effects into a single incremental cash inflow for each year, multiply by (1 - T) to obtain the after-tax cash inflow.

   b. Then, the depreciation expense in each year is multiplied by the tax rate to find the tax savings due to depreciation.

   c. The sum of the after-tax revenue and cost components, and the depreciation tax savings in each year is the cash flow from operations.

   d. Note that the annual operating cash flows could also be developed using a project income statement. Here cash flow equals project net income plus project depreciation.

3. Consider the additional cash flows which are projected to occur at the end of the project's life.

   a. The *salvage value* represents a cash inflow in the final year. However, any tax effects must also be included.

b. Any net working capital change that occurred at t=0 is offset now. For example, if the project had an increase in net working capital and hence an outflow at t=0, an equal inflow would occur at the end of the project.
4. Finally, place all the cash flows for each year on a time line to determine the net cash flows on a year-by-year basis. Discount them at the cost of capital to find the NPV. Set the NPV = 0 to find the IRR.

E. The analysis becomes somewhat more involved if cash outflows (investment costs) occur over more than one year, as we must find the PV of the investment outlays. However, the principles remain the same.

II. **Replacement decision analysis is somewhat different from that for expansion projects. The following changes must be made to the procedures outlined above in Paragraph I.**

A. Determine the net initial cash outlay at t=0.
1. Payment for the new equipment is an outflow.
2. The cash received from the sale of the old equipment is an inflow.
3. However, the sale of the old machine will usually have tax effects. If the old equipment is sold below book value, there will be a tax savings; if the equipment is sold at a profit, taxes must be paid. The tax effect is equal to the loss or gain times the firm's marginal tax rate.

B. The cash flow from operations must also be calculated differently.
1. First, look at the effects of the new equipment on revenues and costs. An incremental increase in revenues would produce a cash inflow, while an incremental increase in costs would produce a cash outflow, just as before. But, the incremental flows must take account of the flows that would have been generated by the old asset. After combining the revenue and cost effects into a single incremental cash inflow, multiply by $(1 - T)$ to obtain the after-tax cash inflow or outflow.
2. The depreciation expense on the old equipment must be subtracted from the depreciation expense on the new equipment to get the net change in depreciation. This amount is then multiplied by the tax rate to find the tax savings from the change in depreciation.
3. Any salvage value on the old machine, adjusted for tax effects, must be included as a cash outflow at the end of the project's life. Accepting the new project causes the firm to forgo the old machine's salvage value, so this value must be included as an opportunity cost.

C. The text analysis assumes that the replacement project has the same expected life as the remaining years of usage on the old machine. If this is not true, an adjustment must be made to account for differing project lives.

III. **Risk analysis is particularly important in the capital budgeting process because of the large amounts of capital involved and the long-term nature of the investments being considered. The higher the risk associated with a proposed investment, the greater is the rate of return the project must earn to compensate for that risk.**

IV. Two separate and distinct kinds of risk have been identified in capital budgeting; corporate risk and beta risk. The corporate risk of a capital budgeting project reflects the probability that the project will incur losses which will destabilize the firm's earnings or even cause the firm to go bankrupt.

   A. A project with a high degree of corporate risk will not necessarily raise the firm's beta.

   B. For example, by investing in a large number of projects, the corporation can diversify away some of the risks inherent in individual projects.

   C. Corporate risk is important for three reasons.

      1. Undiversified stockholders will be more concerned about corporate risk than beta risk. This is particularly true for the owners of small businesses.
      2. Empirical studies show that even well-diversified investors consider both beta and corporate risk to be important when setting required returns.
      3. A firm that is relatively unstable will find it difficult to attract and retain good employees, and both customers and suppliers will be reluctant to depend on the firm. These facts lower the sales and profits of a firm with excessive corporate risk.

V. Both quantitative and qualitative techniques can be used to analyze corporate risk.

   A. The starting point for analyzing corporate risk is a determination of the uncertainty associated with a project's cash flows.
      1. Note that estimated cash flows are really expected values of a probability distribution of possible results from a project. Thus, a project's NPV is also an expected value from a probability distribution.
      2. The shape of the probability distribution provides an indication of the degree of uncertainty.
         a. A "flat" distribution would indicate a high degree of uncertainty about the actual cash flows.
         b. A "tight" (or peaked) distribution would indicate that the actual results will probably be close to the expected value.

   B. *Sensitivity analysis* is one technique used in risk analysis.
      1. This involves changing one key variable at a time and observing how sensitive the project's NPV is to the change.
      2. Sensitivity analysis spotlights the factors that have the greatest effect on NPV. Then, extra effort can be spent to carefully forecast these critical items.
      3. If small changes in relatively uncertain variables will cause a large change in NPV, the project has a high degree of corporate risk.

   C. *Scenario analysis* involves setting optimistic, pessimistic, and base case, or expected, values for the key variables affecting the proposed investment. Cash flows and NPVs can then be estimated under these three sets of conditions.

D. *Computer simulation,* or *Monte Carlo simulation,* is a very powerful tool that requires sophisticated financial planning software.

   1. A simulation model requires that a probability distribution be constructed for each of the important variables affecting the project's cash flows, and hence NPV.

   2. These distributions may be based on past data, if any exists, or on the judgment of experienced operating personnel.

   3. The computer then randomly selects values of each of these variables and combines them into a cash flow estimate for the project. This process is repeated many times to develop a probability distribution for NPV.

   4. The expected value of the NPV distribution as well as its standard deviation can then be used to help assess the project's riskiness.

VI. Portfolio considerations play an important role in the overall capital budgeting process.

   A. The returns on an individual project may be very uncertain, but if the project is small in relation to the total firm, and if its returns are not highly correlated with the firm's other assets, then the project may not be very risky in either the corporate or beta sense.

   B. Through planned diversification, corporations can stabilize earnings and reduce corporate risk. However, investors can diversify their stock portfolios more easily than firms can diversify their assets, so corporate diversification just to reduce risk is not likely to raise stock prices.

VII. Beta, or market, risk, measures risk from the standpoint of an equity investor holding a diversified stock portfolio.

   A. Beta analysis can be used to determine the appropriate project cost of capital.

   1. The required rate of return on equity, k_s, is equal to the risk-free rate of return, k_{RF}, plus a risk premium equal to the firm's beta coefficient, b, times the market risk premium, $k_M - k_{RF}$:

$$k_s = k_{RF} + b(k_M - k_{RF}).$$

   2. For example, if a firm has a beta of 0.9, k_M = 12%, and k_{RF} = 7%, then its required rate of return would be k_s = 7% + 0.9(5%) = 11.5%. Stockholders should be willing to let the firm invest their money if the firm can earn 11.5 percent or more on its equity capital.

   B. The acceptance of a particular capital budgeting project may cause a firm's overall beta to rise or fall, causing a change in the required rate of return.

   1. The impact of any one project on a firm's beta will depend upon the size of the project relative to the existing "portfolio" of projects.

   2. According to the Gordon model, $P_0 = D_1/(k_s - g)$, and holding other factors constant, an increase in a firm's beta coefficient will result in a higher required return, k_s, and, thus, a decrease in price. Therefore, to maintain a given price, there must be an *increase* in the expected rate of growth, in the current dividend, or both. These factors, in turn, will result in an increase in the expected return on the stock. Therefore, an increase in the firm's beta coefficient will cause the stock price to decline unless the increased beta is offset by a higher expected rate of return.

3. Given the proportions of the new investment and the existing projects, it is possible to calculate the required return on a new investment needed to offset the project's effect on the firm's beta.

C. If the beta coefficient for each project can be determined, then individual projects' costs of equity capital can be found as follows:

$$k_{s(Project)} = k_{RF} + b_{Project}(k_M - k_{RF}).$$

High beta (or high-risk) projects will have a relatively high cost of equity capital, while low beta projects will have a correspondingly low cost of capital.

D. However, it is very difficult to estimate the beta for a particular project, and for some projects, such as a new computer billing system, the beta may not be meaningful.
   1. One approach to estimating project betas is the *"pure play" method*. Here the firm must find another company which is exclusively engaged in the same business line as the project.
   2. Another way of estimating project betas is the *accounting beta method*. Here a project's (or perhaps a division's) return on assets (ROA) is regressed against the average ROA of a large sample of firms, say the S&P 500. The resulting accounting beta is then used as a proxy for the market beta.

VIII. **Using risk-adjusted discount rates is probably the best way of accounting for risk in the capital budgeting process.**

A. The overall cost of capital for a firm may be estimated with a fair degree of accuracy.

B. Increasing the discount rate for high-risk projects and lowering it for low-risk projects is a somewhat arbitrary process, and one which requires considerable judgment, but it may help improve the capital budgeting process.

C. Diversified companies with divisions of varying risk may use a two-step process to determine a project's risk-adjusted discount rate.
   1. First, divisional costs of capital are established for each of the major operating divisions.
   2. Then, within the division, projects classified as high-risk would have an increased discount rate while low-risk projects would have a lowered discount rate.

IX. **Capital budgeting is normally an application of a classical economic principle: A firm should expand to the point where its marginal profits equal its marginal costs. In other words, keep accepting projects as long as the benefits exceed the costs. However, some firms set an absolute limit on the size of their capital budgets. This is called capital rationing.**

DEFINITIONAL QUESTIONS

1. An increase in net working capital would show up as a cash _____ at t=0, and then again as a cash _____ at the _____ of the project's life.

2. A _____ _____ is a cash outlay which has already occurred or has been committed.

3. In general, a project's operating cash flow in any year is equal to the project's _____ _____ plus its _____ expense.

4. In replacement analysis, two cash flows that occur at t = 0 that are not present in expansion projects are the price received from the sale of the _____ equipment and the _____ effects of the sale.

5. In replacement analysis, the depreciation tax savings or loss is based on the _____ in depreciation expense between the old and new asset.

6. An _____ cash flow represents the change in the firm's total cash flow that occurs as a direct result of project acceptance.

7. The _____ the risk associated with an investment, the greater the _____ _____ _____ needed to compensate investors.

8. Two types of separate risk have been identified in capital budgeting decisions: _____ risk and _____ risk.

9. The required rate of return on a company's stock is equal to the _____ rate plus a _____ for risk.

10. The risk premium on a stock is equal to the stock's _____ times the market risk premium.

11. An increase in the overall beta coefficient will cause the firm's stock price to _____ unless this increase is offset by a _____ expected rate of return.

12. Measuring corporate risk involves determining the uncertainty of a project's _____ _____.

13. Cash flow estimates are really _____ _____ taken from _____ distributions.

14. A commonly used method of risk analysis is based on constructing optimistic, pessimistic, and expected value estimates for the key variables. This method is called _____ _____.

15. In project analysis, changing one key variable at a time and determining the effect on NPV is known as _____ _____.

16. One purpose of sensitivity analysis is to determine which of the _____ have the _____ influence on the project's NPV.

17. A project with a high degree of corporate risk will not necessarily affect the firm's _____ to any great extent.

18. Beneficial_____ occurs when returns on various projects' cash flows are not highly _____ with each other.

19. Diversification is aimed at stabilizing _____, reducing _____, and raising the firm's _____ _____.

20. Riskier projects should be evaluated with a higher _____ _____ _____ than average-risk projects.

CONCEPTUAL QUESTIONS

21. In general, the value of land currently owned by a firm is irrelevant to a capital budgeting decision because the cost of that property is a sunk cost.

    a. True   b. False

22. McDonald's is planning to open a new store across from the student union. Annual revenues are expected to be $5 million. However, opening the new location will cause annual revenues to drop by $3 million at McDonald's existing stadium location. The relevant sales revenues for the capital budgeting analysis are $2 million per year.

    a. True   b. False

23. In a replacement decision, the salvage value of the old asset need not be considered since the current market value of the asset is included in the analysis.

    a. True   b. False

24. Even if the beta of a project being considered has a value of zero, acceptance of the project will affect the market risk of the firm.

    a. True   b. False

25. When projects of different risk are to be considered in capital budgeting, any project will be acceptable to the firm if the project's IRR is greater than the firm's weighted average cost of capital.

    a. True   b. False

26. In capital budgeting decisions, corporate risk will be of least interest to

    a. Employees.
    b. Stockholders with few shares.
    c. Institutional investors.
    d. Creditors.
    e. The local community.

27. When using the pure play approach, the analyzing firm uses the proxy firm's beta as an estimate of the project's beta, providing the proxy firm has the same leverage and tax rate as the subject firm.

    a. True   b. False

28. If a cash *outflow* is judged to be riskier than average, then the firm's marginal cost of capital must be adjusted *downward* to reflect this differential.

    a. True   b. False

PROBLEMS

29. The capital budgeting director of National Products, Inc., is evaluating a new project that would decrease operating costs by $30,000 per year without affecting revenues. The project's cost is $50,000. The project will be depreciated using the ACRS method over its 3-year life. It will have a *zero salvage value* after 3 years. The marginal tax rate of National Products is 34 percent, and the project's cost of capital is 12 percent. What is the project's NPV?

    a. $7,068
    b. $8,324
    c. $9,875
    d. $10,214
    e. $11,182

30. Your firm has a marginal tax rate of 40 percent and a cost of capital of 14 percent. You are performing a capital budgeting analysis on a new project that will cost $500,000. The project is expected to have a useful life of 10 years, although its ACRS class life is only 5 years. The project is expected to increase the firm's net income by $61,257 per year and to have a salvage value of $35,000 at the end of 10 years. What is the project's NPV?

    a. $95,356
    b. $108,359
    c. $135,256
    d. $162,185
    e. $181,321

31. The Board of Directors of National Brewing, Inc., is considering the acquisition of a new still. The still is priced at $600,000 but would require $60,000 in transportation costs and $40,000 for installation. The still has a useful life of 10 years but will be depreciated over its 5-year ACRS life. It is expected to have a salvage value of $10,000 at the end of 10 years. The still would increase revenues by $120,000 per year and increase yearly operating costs by $20,000 per year. Additionally, the still would require a $30,000 increase in net working capital. The firm's marginal tax rate is 40 percent, and the project's cost of capital is 10 percent. What is the NPV of the still?

   a. $18,430
   b. -$12,352
   c. -$65,204
   d. -$129,300
   e. -$203,450

(The following data apply to the next three problems.)

As the capital budgeting director of Union Mills, Inc., you are analyzing the replacement of an automated loom system. The old system was purchased 5 years ago for $200,000; it falls into the ACRS 5-year class; and it has 5 years of remaining life and a $50,000 salvage value five years from now. The current market value of the old system is $100,000. The new system has a price of $300,000, plus an additional $50,000 in installation costs. The new system falls into the ACRS 5-year class, has a 5-year economic life, and a $100,000 salvage value. The new system will require a $40,000 increase in the spare parts inventory. The primary advantage of the new system is that it will decrease operating costs by $40,000 per year. Union Mills has a 12 percent cost of capital and a marginal tax rate of 34 percent.

32. What is the net cash investment at Year 0?

   a. $350,000
   b. $324,000
   c. $295,000
   d. $40,000
   e. $23,200

33. What is the annual net operating cash inflow in Year 1?

   a. $50,200
   b. $43,950
   c. $39,825
   d. $33,350
   e. $31,475

34. What is the net cash flow in the final year (Year 5)?

    a. $31,360
    b. $43,060
    c. $116,060
    d. $121,930
    e. $171,000

35. Initially, United Products has a beta of 1.30. The risk-free rate is 12 percent, and the required rate of return on the market is 18 percent. The firm now sells 10 percent of its assets, having a beta of 1.30, and uses the proceeds to purchase a new product line with a beta of 1.00. What is the new overall required rate of return for United Products?

    a. 15.11%
    b. 16.24%
    c. 17.48%
    d. 18.00%
    e. 19.62%

36. Consolidated, Inc., uses a weighted average cost of capital of 12 percent to evaluate average-risk projects and adds/subtracts two percentage points to evaluate projects of greater/ lesser risk. Currently, two mutually exclusive projects are under consideration. Both have a net cost of $200,000 and last 4 years. Project A, which is riskier than average, will produce yearly after-tax net cash flows of $71,000. Project B, which has less-than-average risk, will produce an after-tax net cash flow of $146,000 in Years 3 and 4 only. What should Consolidated do?

    a. Accept Project B with an NPV of $9,412.
    b. Accept both projects since both NPVs are greater than   zero.
    c. Accept Project A with an NPV of $6,874.
    d. Accept neither project since both NPVs are less than zero.
    e. Accept Project A with an NPV of $15,652.

37. Union Industries, an all equity-financed firm, is considering the purchase of a plant that produces plastic products. The plant is expected to generate a rate of return of 17 percent, and the plant's estimated beta is 2.00. The risk-free rate is 12 percent, and the market risk premium is 6 percent. Union should make the investment.

    a. True   b. False

38. Diversified Products (DP) is considering the formation of a new division which will double the assets of the firm. DP is an all-equity firm which has a current required rate of return of 20 percent. The risk-free rate is 10 percent, and the market risk premium is 5 percent. If DP wants to reduce its required rate of return to 18 percent, what is the maximum beta the new division could have?

    a. 1.00
    b. 1.10
    c. 1.20
    d. 1.25
    e. 1.30

39. Midwest Motors is choosing between two automobile washing/waxing machines on the basis of cost. The expected net costs of the two machines are as follows:

Year	Machine A	Machine B
0	($20,000)	($10,000)
1	(5,000)	(8,000)
2	(5,000)	(8,000)
3	(5,000)	(8,000)
4	(5,000)	(8,000)

The firm's cost of capital is 10 percent. Machine B is judged to be a riskier-than-average project, while Machine A is considered less risky than average. The firm's policy is to add or subtract 2 percentage points to adjust for risk. The firm should choose Machine B.

a. True   b. False

ANSWERS AND SOLUTIONS

1. outflow; inflow; end

2. sunk cost

3. net income; depreciation

4. old; tax

5. difference

6. incremental

7. greater; rate of return

8. corporate; beta (market)

9. risk-free; premium

10. beta

11. fall; higher

12. cash flows

13. expected values; probability

14. scenario analysis

15. sensitivity analysis

16. variables; greatest

17. beta

18. diversification; correlated

19. earnings; risk; stock price

20. cost of capital (or discount rate)

21. b. The net market value of land currently owned is an opportunity cost of the project. If the project is not undertaken, the land could be sold to realize its current market value less any taxes and expenses. Thus, project acceptance means forgoing this cash inflow.

22. a. Incremental revenues, which are relevant in a capital budgeting decision, must consider the effects on other parts of the firm.

23. b. In an incremental analysis, the cash flows assuming replacement are compared with the cash flows assuming the old asset is retained. If the old asset is retained, it will produce a salvage value cash flow which must be included, with tax effects, in the replacement analysis.

24. a. The addition of an asset with a beta of zero would normally lower the beta of the firm, thus lowering the firm's market risk. (The starting beta of most firms is greater than zero.)

25. b. The only time this statement holds is when all projects being evaluated have the same risk as the firm's current average project. Otherwise, the cost of capital must be adjusted for project risk.

26. c. Institutional investors are well diversified and, therefore, more concerned with beta risk.

27. a. However, the proxy firm's beta must be adjusted for leverage and tax effects if they are different.

28. a. The present value of a cash *outflow* (cash cost) must be *increased* to penalize it for above-average risk, and the present value will be increased only if the discount rate is *decreased*.

29. e. The only cash outflow is the $50,000 cost of the project. Cash inflows consist of the reduction in operating costs, equal to $30,000(0.66) = $19,800 on an after-tax basis, and depreciation. The value of the depreciation cash flows generated by the project is the amount of tax savings. After-tax depreciation cash flows are found by multiplying the depreciable basis, $50,000, by the recovery percentages in each year, and then multiplying this product by the tax rate. The allowances in each year are 34, 33, and 33 percent, respectively, and the depreciation tax savings in each year are as follows:

$$Dep_1 = \$50,000(0.34)(0.34) = \$5,780.$$

$$Dep_2 = \$50,000(0.33)(0.34) = \$5,610.$$

$$Dep_3 = \$50,000(0.33)(0.34) = \$5,610.$$

The project's cash flows are placed on a time line as follows:

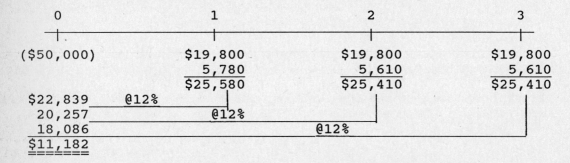

```
        0                   1                   2                   3
        +                   +                   +                   +
  ($50,000)            $19,800             $19,800             $19,800
                         5,780               5,610               5,610
                       $25,580             $25,410             $25,410
  $22,839     @12%
   20,257              @12%
   18,086                               @12%
  $11,182
```

30. e. In this case, the *net income* of the project is $61,257. Net cash flow = Net income + Depreciation = $61,257 + Depreciation. The depreciation allowed in each year is calculated as follows:

$$Depr._1 = \$500,000(0.20) = \$100,000.$$

$$Depr._2 = \$500,000(0.32) = \$160,000.$$

$$Depr._{3-5} = \$500,000(0.20) = \$100,000.$$

$$Depr._{4-5} = \$500,000(0.14) = \$70,000.$$

$$Depr._{6-10} = \$0.$$

In the final year (Year 10), the firm receives $35,000 from the sale of the machine. However, the book value of the machine is $0. Thus, the firm would have to pay 0.4($35,000) = $14,000 in taxes, and the net salvage value is $35,000 - $14,000 = $21,000. The time line is as follows:

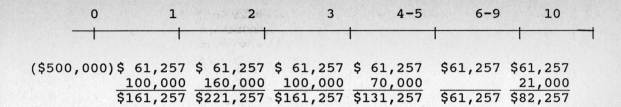

0	1	2	3	4-5	6-9	10
($500,000)	$ 61,257	$ 61,257	$ 61,257	$ 61,257	$61,257	$61,257
	100,000	160,000	100,000	70,000		21,000
	$161,257	$221,257	$161,257	$131,257	$61,257	$82,257

The project's NPV can be found by discounting each of the cash flows at the firm's 14 percent cost of capital. The project's NPV, found by using a financial calculator with an NPV function, is $181,321.

31. d. The initial net investment is $730,000:

Price	($600,000)
Transportation	(60,000)
Installation	(40,000)
Change in net working capital	(30,000)
Initial net investment	($730,000)

The annual net cash flows are equal to the net after-tax increase in revenues, 0.6($120,000 - $20,000) = $60,000, plus the depreciation tax savings. In Year 10, the firm will recover its investment in net working capital of $30,000 and gain the net salvage value of $6,000. The annual depreciation tax savings is calculated as the depreciable basis times the applicable depreciation allowance times the tax rate. The depreciable basis is equal to the cost of the still plus transportation and installation, or $700,000.

$$\text{Dep}_1 = \$700,000(0.20)(0.4) = \$56,000.$$

$$\text{Dep}_2 = \$700,000(0.32)(0.4) = \$89,600.$$

$$\text{Dep}_3 = \$700,000(0.20)(0.4) = \$56,000.$$

$$\text{Dep 4-5} = \$700,000(0.14)(0.4) = \$39,200.$$

$$\text{Dep}_{6-10} = \$0.$$

The net salvage value is $10,000(0.6) = $6,000. Therefore, the time line is as follows:

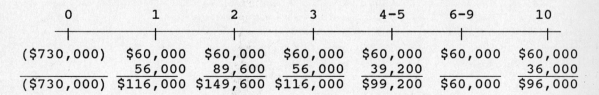

0	1	2	3	4-5	6-9	10
($730,000)	$60,000	$60,000	$60,000	$60,000	$60,000	$60,000
	56,000	89,600	56,000	39,200		36,000
($730,000)	$116,000	$149,600	$116,000	$99,200	$60,000	$96,000

The project's NPV using a 10 percent cost of capital is -$129,300.

32. b.

Price of new machine	($300,000)
Installation	(50,000)
Sale of old machine	+100,000
Tax on sale	*(34,000)
Increase in net working capital	(40,000)
	($324,000)

*The old machine has been depreciated down to zero, since it falls into the ACRS 5-year class and it has been in operation for 5 years. Now, the old machine has a market value of $100,000. The full $100,000 (purchase price minus book value) is treated as ordinary income and is taxed at 34 percent. Thus, Union Mills must pay a tax of 0.34($100,000) = $34,000 on the sale of the old asset.

33. a. The after-tax revenue/cost component is 0.66($40,000) = $26,400. As for the tax savings due to depreciation, the depreciable basis for the new machine is $350,000. Further, the ACRS depreciation allowance for Year 1 of a 5-year class asset is 20 percent. Thus, the depreciation expense on the new machine is 0.20($350,000) = $70,000. The old machine has been fully depreciated, so its depreciation expense in Year 1 is $0, and the change in depreciation due to the replacement decision is an increase of $70,000. The tax savings is 0.34($70,000) = $23,800. Therefore, the Year 1 net cash flow from operations is $26,400 + $23,800 = $50,200.

34. c. In the final year, Year 5, the net cash flow is composed of 0.66($40,000) = $26,400 in after-tax cost decrease and 0.34(0.14)($350,000) = $16,660 in depreciation tax savings, for a total of $43,060, plus the applicable nonoperating cash flows. Thus, we have the following:

From operations	$ 43,060
Salvage value of new machine	100,000
Tax on new machine salvage value	-34,000
Salvage value of old machine	-50,000
Tax on old machine salvage value	17,000
Change in working capital	40,000
Net cash flow	$116,060

Note that the salvage value of the old machine is a cash outflow. This is an opportunity cost, since buying the new machine deprives Union Mills of the salvage value of the old machine. Additionally, salvage tax effects must be considered. Also note that the change in working capital considered at t = 0, an outflow, is exactly offset by an inflow at the end of the project. This is because it is assumed that the project will terminate and the increase in working capital is no longer required.

35. e. New b = 0.9(1.30) + 0.1(1.00) = 1.27.

New k = 12% + 1.27(18% - 12%) = 19.62%.

36. a. Look at the time lines:

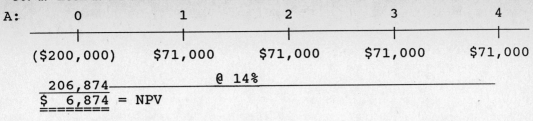

A:

0	1	2	3	4
($200,000)	$71,000	$71,000	$71,000	$71,000

@ 14%

206,874

$ 6,874 = NPV

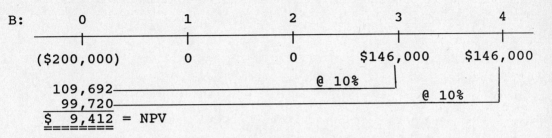

B:

0	1	2	3	4
($200,000)	0	0	$146,000	$146,000

@ 10%

@ 10%

109,692

99,720

$ 9,412 = NPV

Note that both discount rates are adjusted for risk. Since the projects are mutually exclusive, the project with the higher NPV is chosen.

37. b. The project's required rate of return on equity and overall cost of capital is 24 percent:

$$k_{s(Project)} = 12\% + 2(6\%) = 24\%.$$

Since the expected return is only 17 percent, the plant should not be purchased.

38. c. First, find the current beta of the firm:

$$k = 10\% + b(5\%) = 20\%$$

$$b = 2.00.$$

Now find the beta required to lower the required rate of return to 18 percent:

$$k = 10\% + b(5\%) = 18\%$$

$$b = 1.60.$$

Finally, if the firm doubles with the formation of the new division, 50 percent of the expanded firm's assets will be old assets, while 50 percent will be assets from the new division. Thus, $0.5(2.00) + 0.5(b_{Div.}) = 1.60$; $b_{Div.} = 1.20$.

39. b. These are cash outflows, so the risk adjustment process is reversed. Thus, the project cost of capital for Machine A is 12 percent, while the project cost of capital for B is 8 percent.

$$PV_{Project\ A} = (\$35,187)$$

$$PV_{Project\ B} = (\$36,497)$$

We see that with the correct risk adjustment, the PV of costs for Machine A is less than the PV of costs for Machine B, and hence Machine A should be selected.

CHAPTER 17
THE COST OF CAPITAL

OVERVIEW

The firm's marginal cost of capital (MCC) schedule is developed in the following manner: First, the cost of capital must be estimated for each component of the firm's capital structure. These components are normally debt, preferred equity, and common equity. The next task is to combine the component costs to form a weighted average cost of capital. The weights are based on the firm's target capital structure. Capital typically has an increasing cost if the firm expands beyond certain limits. The point at which the cost of capital increases is called a break point, and the MCC schedule is often drawn as a step-function which increases due to increases in one or more of the capital components.

The investment opportunity schedule (IOS) is a plot of the firm's potential projects arrayed in descending order of IRR. The intersection of the MCC and the IOS defines the firm's optimal capital budget as well as the relevant marginal cost of capital used to evaluate all new projects with the same risk as the firm's other assets.

OUTLINE

I. **Determination of the cost of capital is an important aspect of financial management. The two primary uses of the cost of capital are (1) in capital budgeting and (2) in helping to establish the optimal capital structure.**

   A. The appropriate cost of capital for most decisions is a *weighted average cost*.

   B. *Capital components* are items on the right-hand side of the balance sheet such as debt, preferred stock, common stock, and retained earnings.

   C. Each element of capital has a *component cost* which can be identified as follows:
   1. k_d = interest rate on new debt, before tax.
   2. $k_d(1 - T)$ = after-tax cost of debt, where T is the marginal tax rate.
   3. k_p = component cost of preferred stock.
   4. k_s = component cost of retained earnings; it is equal to the required rate of return on common stock.
   5. k_e = cost of external capital obtained by issuing additional common stock; it must be distinguished from equity raised through retained earnings due to flotation costs when stock is issued.
   6. k_a = the weighted average, or composite, cost of capital.

II. **The cost of each capital component can be determined as follows:**

   A. The after-tax cost of debt, $k_d(1 - T)$, is defined as the interest rate that must be paid on new debt capital, reduced by (1 - T) because interest payments are tax deductible.
   1. For example, if Firm A has a tax rate of 40 percent and can borrow at a rate of 14 percent, then its after-tax cost of debt is k_d = 14%(1 - 0.40) = 14%(0.60) = 8.4%.

2. The tax deductibility of interest payments has the effect of causing the federal government to pay part of the interest charges.
3. k_d is applicable to new debt only, not to any previously outstanding debt.

B. The component cost of preferred stock, k_p, is the preferred dividend, D_p, divided by the issuance price net of flotation costs, P_n, or $k_p = D_p/P_n$. Note that no tax adjustment is made since preferred stock dividends are paid from after-tax earnings.

C. The cost of equity obtained by retaining earnings, k_s, is the rate of return stockholders require on the firm's common stock. There are three approaches used to determine k_s.
1. One approach is to use the *Capital Asset Pricing Model (CAPM)* as follows:
   a. Determine the riskless rate, k_{RF}, usually based on U.S. Treasury securities.
   b. Use the stock's beta coefficient as an index of risk.
   c. Estimate the required rate of return on the market, or on an "average" stock, k_M.
   d. Determine the required rate of return on the firm's stock using the SML.
   e. If $k_{RF} = 10\%$, $k_M = 15\%$, and the beta of Firm A is 1.3, then $k_s = 10\% + 1.3(5\%) = 16.5\%$.
2. A simple but useful approach to determine k_s is the *bond-yield-plus-risk-premium approach* in which a risk premium is added to the firm's own cost of long-term debt.
   a. Using this approach, k_s is found as follows:

   $$k_s = \text{Bond rate} + \text{Risk premium.}$$

   b. A risk premium of from 2 to 4 percentage points is commonly used with this approach.
   c. If Firm A uses a risk premium of 3 percentage points, and its bond rate is 14 percent, then

   $$k_s = 14\% + 3\% = 17\%.$$

3. The required rate of return, k_s, may also be estimated by the *discounted cash flow (DCF) approach*. This approach combines the expected dividend yield, D_1/P_0, with the expected future growth rate, g, of earnings and dividends, or

   $$k_s = D_1/P_0 + g.$$

   a. The DCF approach assumes that stocks are normally in equilibrium and that growth is expected to be at a constant rate. If growth is not constant, then a nonconstant growth model must be used.
   b. The expected growth rate may be based on projections of past growth rates, if they have been relatively stable, or on expected future growth rates as estimated in some other manner.
   c. If Firm A last paid $4.00 in annual dividends which are expected to grow at a constant 10 percent per year, and Firm A's stock is selling for $63.00 per share, then

   $$k_s = \frac{\$4(1.10)}{\$63} + 10\% = 16.98\%.$$

4. If Firm A cannot earn about 17 percent on reinvested equity capital, then it should pay its earnings to stockholders and let them invest directly in other assets that do provide this return. Thus, k_s is an *opportunity cost*.
5. It is recommended that all three approaches be used in estimating the required rate of return on common stock. When the methods produce widely different results, judgment must be used in selecting the best estimate.

D. The cost of new common stock, or external equity capital, k_e, is higher than the cost of retained earnings, k_s, because of *flotation costs* of new common stock.
1. To allow for flotation costs, F, we must adjust the DCF formula for the required rate of return as follows:

$$k_e = \frac{D_1}{P_0(1 - F)} + g.$$

2. If Firm A incurred flotation costs of 12 percent in issuing new common shares, the required rate of return would be as follows:

$$k_e = \frac{\$4.00(1.10)}{\$63.00(1 - 0.12)} + 10\% = 7.94\% + 10\% = 17.94\%.$$

3. If Firm A can earn 17.94 percent on investments financed by new common stock, then earnings, dividends, and the growth rate will be maintained, and the price per share will not fall. If it earns more than 17.94 percent, the price will rise; while if it earns less, the price will fall.

III. **The proportions of debt and equity in a firm's target capital structure are used to calculate the weighted average cost of capital.**

A. The calculation of the weighted average cost of capital is shown below for a firm which finances 30 percent with debt, 10 percent with preferred stock, and 60 percent with common equity and which has the following after-tax component costs:

Component	Weight	x After-tax Cost	= Weighted Cost
		%	%
Debt	0.3	7.6	2.28
Preferred	0.1	12.6	1.26
Common	0.6	16.5	9.90
			k_a = 13.44%

B. In more general terms, and in equation format,

$$k_a = w_d(k_d)(1 - T) + w_p(k_p) + w_s(k_s \text{ or } k_e).$$

C. The capital structure that minimizes a firm's weighted average cost of capital also maximizes its stock price.

17-3

IV. The marginal cost of capital is defined as the cost of raising another dollar of new capital. In general, the marginal cost of any factor of production, including capital, will eventually rise as more and more of the factor is used.

A. Firms raise capital in accordance with their target capital structures.

B. As companies raise larger and larger sums during a given time period, the component costs begin to rise. This causes an increase in the weighted average cost of each additional dollar of new capital.

C. Suppose that a firm needs $500,000 in new capital. Its capital structure is 60 percent common equity, 30 percent debt and 10 percent preferred stock, and its marginal tax rate is 40 percent. The before-tax cost of debt is 14 percent and the cost of preferred stock is 12.6 percent. The firm will need to raise 0.6($500,000) = $300,000 in common equity. It expects retained earnings for the year to be $100,000; therefore, it needs to sell $300,000 - $100,000 = $200,000 of new common stock. The cost of retained earnings is 16.0 percent, but the cost of new equity is 16.8 percent. The average cost of capital, using retained earnings, is:

$$k_a = w_d k_d (1 - T) + w_p k_p + w_s k_e$$

$$= (0.3)(14\%)(0.60) + (0.1)(12.6\%) + (0.6)(16.0\%)$$

$$= 13.38\%,$$

while the average cost of capital, using new equity, is:

$$k_a = w_d k_d (1 - T) + w_p k_p + w_s k_s$$

$$= (0.3)(14\%)(0.60) + (0.1)(12.6\%) + (0.6)(16.8\%)$$

$$= 13.86\%.$$

D. The point at which the marginal cost of capital increases is called a *break point*. The retained earnings break point is calculated as Retained earnings/Equity fraction. For the firm discussed in Part C, this break point is $100,000/0.6 = $166,667. That is, when $166,667 of new capital is raised, the firm will have used 0.6($166,667) = $100,000 of retained earnings. After that, more costly new common equity must be used.

V. The marginal cost of capital (MCC) schedule shows the relationship between the cost of each dollar raised, k_a, and the total amount of capital raised during the year. The MCC schedule for the firm discussed in Part IV above is shown on the next page:

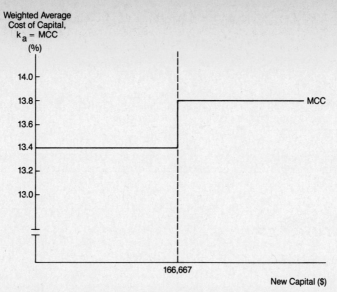

Weighted Average
Cost of Capital,
k_a = MCC
(%)

14.0

13.8 — MCC

13.6

13.4

13.2

13.0

166,667

New Capital ($)

A. The optimal capital structure is the one that produces the lowest MCC schedule.

B. In general, a break will occur in the MCC schedule any time the cost of one of the components rises.

    1. The break point is determined by the following equation:

$$\text{Break point} = \frac{\text{Total amount of lower-cost capital of a given type}}{\text{Fraction of this type of capital in the optimal structure}}.$$

    2. If there are no break points, there will be one MCC. If there are n break points, there will be n + 1 different MCCs.

C. For ease in calculating the MCC schedule, first identify the points where breaks occur, then determine the cost of capital for each component in the intervals between breaks, and, finally, calculate the weighted averages of these costs for each interval.

VI. The optimal capital budget and a firm's marginal cost of capital are interrelated.

A. The *investment opportunity schedule (IOS)* is a plot of the firm's potential projects in descending order of IRR.

B. The marginal cost of capital (MCC) schedule is a plot of the firm's weighted average cost of capital.

C. The intersection of the IOS and MCC schedules determines the cost of capital that is used in the capital budgeting process. This discount rate is influenced both by the shape of the MCC curve and by the set of available projects.

D. The discount rate determined by the intersection of the MCC curve and IOS should be used to find the NPV of new projects that are as risky as the firm's existing assets, but it should be adjusted upward or downward to find NPVs for projects with higher or lower risk.

DEFINITIONAL QUESTIONS

1. The firm should calculate its cost of capital as a _____ _____ of the after-tax costs of the various types of funds it uses.

2. Capital components are items on the right-hand side of the balance sheet such as (1) _____, (2) _____ _____, (3) _____ _____, and (4) _____ _____.

3. The cost of equity capital is defined as the _____ _____ _____ stockholders require on the firm's common stock.

4. There are _____ approaches that can be used to determine the cost of retained earnings.

5. Assigning a cost to retained earnings is based on the _____ _____ principle.

6. The cost of external equity capital is higher than the cost of retained earnings due to _____ _____.

7. Using the Capital Asset Pricing Model (CAPM), the required rate of return on common stock is found as a function of the _____ _____, the firm's _____ _____, and the required rate of return on an average _____.

8. The cost of common equity may also be found by adding a _____ _____ to the interest rate on the firm's own _____-_____ _____.

9. The required rate of return may also be estimated as the _____ _____ on the common stock plus the expected _____ _____ in dividends.

10. The proportions of _____, _____ _____, and _____ _____ in the target capital structure should be used to calculate the _____ _____ cost of capital.

11. The _____ cost of capital is the cost of raising another dollar of capital.

12. The MCC schedule can be used to help determine the _____ _____ to be used in the capital budgeting process.

13. The _____ _____ _____ graphs a firm's capital projects in descending order of each project's _____ _____ _____ _____.

CONCEPTUAL QUESTIONS

14. If a firm obtains all of its common equity from retained earnings, its MCC schedule would always be flat; that is, there would be no break points.

   a. True   b. False

15. If there are n break points in the MCC schedule, there will be n + 1 different MCCs.

    a. True   b. False

16. Funds acquired by the firm through preferred stock have a cost to the firm equal to the preferred dividend divided by the price investors paid for one share.

    a. True   b. False

17. Which of the following statements *could* be true concerning the costs of debt and equity?

    a. The cost of debt for Firm A is greater than the cost of equity for Firm A.
    b. The cost of debt for Firm A is greater than the cost of equity for Firm B.
    c. The cost of retained earnings for Firm A is less than the cost of external equity for Firm A.
    d. The cost of retained earnings for Firm A is less than the cost of debt for Firm A.
    e. Statements b and c could both be true.

PROBLEMS

18. Roland Corporation's next expected dividend (D_1) is $2.50. The firm has maintained a constant payout ratio of 50 percent during the past 7 years. Seven years ago its EPS was $1.50. The firm's beta coefficient is 1.2. The required return on an average stock in the market is 13 percent, and the risk-free rate is 7 percent. Roland's A-rated bonds are yielding 10 percent, and its current stock price is $30. Which of the following values is the most reasonable estimate of Roland's cost of retained earnings, k_s?

    a. 10%
    b. 12%
    c. 14%
    d. 20%
    e. 26%

19. The director of capital budgeting for See-Saw, Inc., manufacturers of playground equipment, is considering a plan to expand production facilities in order to meet an increase in demand. He estimates that this expansion will produce an IRR of 11 percent. The firm's target capital structure calls for a debt/equity ratio of 0.8.

    See-Saw currently has a bond issue outstanding which will mature in 25 years and has a 7 percent annual coupon rate. The bonds are currently selling for $804. The firm has maintained a constant growth rate of 6 percent. See-Saw's next expected dividend is $2 and its current stock price is $40. Its tax rate is 40 percent. Should it undertake the expansion? (Assume that there is no preferred stock outstanding and that any new debt will have a 25 year maturity.)

    a. No; the expected return is 2.5 percentage points lower than the cost of capital.
    b. No; the expected return is 1.0 percentage points lower than the cost of capital.
    c. Yes; the expected return is 0.5 percentage points higher than the cost of capital.
    d. Yes; the expected return is 1.0 percentage points higher than the cost of capital.
    e. Yes; the expected return is 2.5 percentage points higher than the cost of capital.

20. Midterm Corporation's present capital structure, which is also its target capital structure, calls for 50 percent debt and 50 percent common equity. The firm has only one potential project, an expansion program with a 10.2 percent IRR and a cost of $20 million but which is completely divisible; that is, Midterm can invest any amount up to $20 million. Midterm expects to retain $3 million of earnings next year. It can raise up to $5 million in new debt at a before-tax cost of 8 percent, and all debt after the first $5 million will have a cost of 10 percent. The cost of retained earnings is 12 percent; Midterm can sell any amount of new common stock desired at a constant cost of new equity of 15 percent. The firm's marginal tax rate is 40 percent. What is Midterm's optimal capital budget?

a. $0 million
b. $5 million
c. $6 million
d. $10 million
e. $20 million

21. The management of Florida Phosphate Industries is planning next year's capital budget. FPI projects net income of $10,500, and its payout ratio is 40 percent. The company's earnings and dividends are growing at a constant rate of 5 percent; the last dividend, D_0, was $0.90; and the current equilibrium stock price is $8.59. FPI can raise up to $10,000 of debt at a 12 percent before-tax cost, the next $10,000 will cost 14 percent, and all debt after $20,000 will cost 16 percent. If FPI issues new common stock, a 10 percent flotation cost will be incurred on the first $16,000 issued, while flotation costs will be 20 percent on all new stock issued after the first $16,000. FPI is at its optimal capital structure, which is 40 percent debt and 60 percent equity, and the firm's marginal tax rate is 40 percent. FPI has the following independent, indivisible, and equally risky investment opportunities:

Project	Cost	IRR
	$	%
A	15,000	17
B	20,000	14
C	15,000	16
D	12,000	15

What is FPI's optimal capital budget?

a. $62,000
b. $42,000
c. $30,000
d. $15,000
e. $0

22. Refer to Problem 21. Management neglected to incorporate project risk differentials into the analysis. FPI's policy is to add 2 percentage points to the IRR of those projects significantly less risky than average and to subtract 2 percentage points from the IRR of those which are substantially more risky than average. Management judges Project A to be of high risk, Projects C and D to be of average risk, and Project B to be of low risk. No projects are divisible. What is the optimal capital budget after adjustment for project risk? Assume that if the Company has a choice between two projects of equal risk (after adjustment), and one project uses all the available funds at a certain cost whereas the other project does not, the Company will choose the project that uses all the available funds.

    a. $62,000
    b. $50,000
    c. $42,000
    d. $30,000
    e. $15,000

23. Gator Products Company (GPC) is at its optimal capital structure of 70 percent common equity and 30 percent debt. GPC's MCC and IOS schedules for next year intersect at a 14 percent marginal cost of capital. At the intersection, the IOS schedule is vertical and the MCC schedule is horizontal. GPC has a marginal tax rate of 40 percent. Next year's dividend is expected to be $2.00 per share, and GPC has a constant growth in earnings and dividends of 6 percent. The after-tax cost of equity used in the MCC at the intersection is based on new equity with a flotation cost of 10 percent, while the before-tax cost of debt is 12 percent. What is GPC's current equilibrium stock price?

    a. $12.73
    b. $17.23
    c. $20.37
    d. $23.70
    e. $37.20

ANSWERS AND SOLUTIONS

1. weighted average

2. debt; preferred stock; common stock; retained earnings

3. rate of return

4. three

5. opportunity cost

6. flotation costs

7. risk-free rate (k_{RF}); beta coefficient (b); stock (k_M)

8. risk premium; long-term debt

9. dividend yield; growth rate

10. debt; preferred stock; common equity; weighted average

11. marginal

12. discount rate

13. Investment Opportunity Schedule (IOS); internal rate of return (IRR)

14. b. The component cost of debt and/or preferred equity might increase, thus causing break points in the MCC schedule.

15. a.

16. b. Flotation costs must be subtracted from the investor's cost to get the net issuance price, which is then used to calculate the cost of preferred stock.

17. e. If Firm A has more business risk than Firm B, Firm A's cost of debt could be greater than Firm B's cost of equity. Also, the cost of retained earnings is less than the cost of external equity because of flotation costs.

18. c. Use all three methods to estimate k_s.

(1) *CAPM:* $k_s = k_{RF} + b(k_M - k_{RF}) = 7\% + 1.2(13\% - 7\%) = 14.2\%$.

(2) *Risk Premium:* k_s = Bond yield + Risk premium = 10% + approximately 4% = 14%.

(3) *DCF:*

$$k_s = D_1/P_0 + g = \$2.50/\$30 + g, \text{ where g can be estimated as follows:}$$

$$\$0.75 = \$2.50(PVIF_{k,7})$$

$$PVIF_{k,7} = \$0.75/\$2.50 = 0.3000.$$

Thus k, which is the compound growth rate, g, is about 19%, or, using a calculator, 18.8%. Therefore, $k_s = 0.083 + 0.188 = 27.1\%$.

Roland Corporation has apparently been experiencing supernormal growth during the past 7 years, and it is not reasonable to assume that this growth will continue. The first two methods yield a k_s of about 14 percent, which appears reasonable.

19. e. Cost of equity $= k_s = \$2/\$40 + 0.06 = 0.11 = 11\%$.

Cost of debt $= k_d = $ Yield to maturity on outstanding bonds based on current market price.

$$V = C(PVIFA_{k_d,25}) + M(PVIF_{k_d,25}),$$

$$\$804 = \$70(PVIFA_{k_d,25}) + \$1,000(PVIF_{k_d,25}).$$

Solving by trial and error gives $k_d = 9\%$. In determining the capital structure weights, note that debt/equity $= 0.8$ or, for example, $4/5$. Therefore, debt/assets is

$$\frac{D}{A} = \frac{Debt}{Debt + Equity} = \frac{4}{4 + 5} = \frac{4}{9}$$

and equity/assets $= 5/9$. Hence, the weighted average cost of capital is

$$k_a = k_d(1 - T)(D/A) + k_s(1 - D/A)$$

$$= 0.09(1 - 0.4)(4/9) + 0.11(5/9)$$

$$= 0.024 + 0.061 = 0.085 = 8.5\%.$$

The cost of capital is 8.5 percent, while the expansion project's IRR is 11.0 percent. Since the expected return is 2.5 percentage points higher than the cost, the expansion should be undertaken.

20. d. First, look only at debt:

Now, look only at equity:

Now combine debt and equity and look at total capital:

The break points are calculated as follows:

$$E_1 = \$3,000,000/0.5 = \$6,000,000.$$

$$D_1 = \$5,000,000/0.5 = \$10,000,000.$$

Now, determine the weighted average cost of capital for intervals A, B, and C:

$$k_a = w_d(k_d)(1 - T) + w_s(k_s \text{ or } k_e).$$

$$A = 0.5(8\%)(0.6) + 0.5(12\%) = 8.4\%.$$

$$B = 0.5(8\%)(0.6) + 0.5(15\%) = 9.9\%.$$

$$C = 0.5(10\%)(0.6) + 0.5(15\%) = 10.5\%.$$

Finally, graph the IOS and MCC schedules.

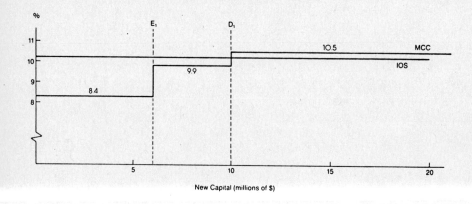

Thus, the optimal capital budget is $10 million.

21. b. First look only at debt:

<pre>
        12%   D₁   14%   D₂   16%
                                                          ($ of debt)
    ┬─────────────┬───────────────────┬──────────────────
    $0 $10,000 $20,000
</pre>

Now, look only at equity:

<pre>
        16%   E₁   17.22%   E₂   18.75%
                                                          ($ of equity)
    ┬─────────────┬───────────────────┬──────────────────
    $0 $6,300 $22,300
</pre>

Retained earnings are forecast to be $10,500(0.6) = $6,300. The cost of retained earnings is as follows:

17-12

$$k_s = \frac{D_0(1 + g)}{P_0} + g = \frac{\$0.90(1.05)}{\$8.59} + 0.05 = 0.16 = 16.0\%.$$

The cost of new equity is as follows:

$$k_{e1} = \frac{D_0(1 + g)}{P_0(1 - F)} + g = \frac{\$0.90(1.05)}{\$8.59(1 - 0.10)} + 0.05 = 0.1722 = 17.22\%.$$

$$k_{e2} = \frac{\$0.90(1.05)}{\$8.59(1 - 0.20)} + 0.05 = 0.1875 = 18.75\%.$$

Now, combine debt and equity and look at total capital:

```
      A    E₁   B    D₁   C    E₂   D    D₂   E                ($ of capital)
 ┼─────────┼─────────┼─────────┼─────────┼──────────
$0      $10,500  $25,000  $37,167  $50,000
```

The break points are calculated as follows:

E_1 = \$6,300/0.60 = \$10,500.
D_1 = \$10,000/0.40 = \$25,000.
E_2 = \$22,300/0.60 = \$37,167.
D_2 = \$20,000/0.40 = \$50,000.

Now, determine the weighted average cost of capital for intervals A through E:

$$k_a = w_d(k_d)(1 - T) + w_s(k_s \text{ or } k_e)$$

A = 0.4(12%)(0.6) + 0.6(16.00%) = 12.48%.
B = 0.4(12%)(0.6) + 0.6(17.22%) = 13.21%.
C = 0.4(14%)(0.6) + 0.6(17.22%) = 13.69%.
D = 0.4(14%)(0.6) + 0.6(18.75%) = 14.61%.
E = 0.4(16%)(0.6) + 0.6(18.75%) = 15.09%.

Finally, graph the MCC and IOS schedules:

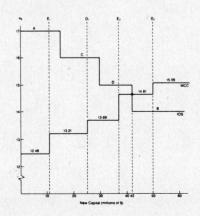

Therefore, the optimal capital budget is \$42,000. Projects A, C, and D are accepted.

22. b. First, determine the risk-adjusted IRRs:

Project	Cost $	IRR %	Risk	Risk-adjusted IRR %
A	15,000	17	High	15
B	20,000	14	Low	16
C	15,000	16	Avg.	16
D	12,000	15	Avg.	15

Now, regraph the IOS and MCC schedules:

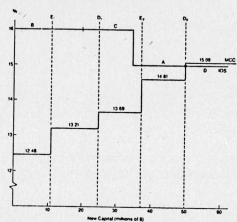

Note that Projects B and C are graphed first, and then the IOS can be ordered with A first or with D first. With A first, total cost of Projects B, C, and A is $50,000, which coincides with a break point. Clearly, Project D is not acceptable. Therefore, the optimal capital budget is $50,000.

23. c. At the intersection of the IOS and MCC schedules, $k_a = 14\%$. Therefore,

$$w_d(k_d)(1 - T) + w_s(k_e) = k_a = 14\%$$

$$0.3(12\%)(0.6) + 0.7(k_e) = 14\%$$

$$k_e = 16.91\%.$$

Now, at equilibrium:

$$\hat{k}_e = k_e = \frac{D_1}{P_0(1 - F)} + g$$

$$0.1691 = \frac{\$2.00}{P_0(1 - 0.10)} + 0.06$$

$$0.1091 = \frac{\$2.222}{P_0}$$

$$P_0 = \$20.37.$$

CHAPTER 18
CAPITAL STRUCTURE AND FINANCIAL LEVERAGE

OVERVIEW

Capital structure theory suggests that some optimal capital structure exists which simultaneously maximizes a firm's stock price and minimizes its cost of capital. The use of debt tends to increase earnings per share, which will lead to a higher stock price, but at the same time, the use of debt also increases the risk borne by stockholders, which lowers the stock price. The optimal capital structure strikes a balance between these risk and return effects. While it is difficult to determine the optimal capital structure with precision, it is possible to identify the factors that influence it. The target may change over time as conditions vary, but, at any given moment, a well-managed firm's management has a specific structure in mind, and financing decisions are made so as to be consistent with this target structure.

OUTLINE

I. **Capital structure refers to decisions involving a choice between risk and expected return.**

   A. Additional debt increases the riskiness of the firm, but added leverage can also result in higher returns.

   B. The optimal capital structure balances risk and return to maximize the stock price. The structure that maximizes stock price also minimizes the firm's cost of capital.

   C. A firm has a certain amount of risk in its operations, even if no debt is used. This is *business risk*. The greater the amount of a firm's business risk, the less debt should be included in its capital structure.

   D. A major reason for using debt is the fact that interest is tax deductible. Therefore, the higher a firm's tax rate, the more debt it should include in its capital structure.

   E. Also influencing a firm's capital structure is the potential future need for funds--the larger the potential future funds requirements, the greater the need for *reserve borrowing capacity*, and hence the lower the optimal debt ratio.

II. **Business risk is the uncertainty inherent in estimates of future operating income. It represents the riskiness of the firm's operations when no debt is used.**

   A. Operating income is also referred to as earnings before interest and taxes (EBIT).

   B. Business risk depends on the following factors:
      1. Demand variability (variability of sales in units)
      2. Sales price variability
      3. Input price variability
      4. Ability to adjust output prices for changes in input prices
      5. Operating leverage (the extent to which costs are fixed)

C. *Operating leverage* is the degree to which a firm uses fixed costs in its production processes.
   1. Firms that have a high percentage of fixed costs are said to have a high *degree of operating leverage.*
   2. High operating leverage implies that a relatively small change in sales will result in a large change in operating income.
   3. The higher a firm's degree of operating leverage, the higher its breakeven point tends to be.
   4. In general, the higher a firm's operating leverage, the higher its business risk.
   5. Production technology limits control over the amount of fixed costs and operating leverage.
   6. However, firms do have some control over the type of production processes they employ. Therefore, a firm's capital budgeting decisions will have an impact on its operating leverage and business risk.

III. **Financial leverage refers to the firm's use of fixed-charge securities such as debt and preferred stock, rather than common stock, in its capital structure. By using financial leverage, the firm concentrates its business risk on the common stockholders.**

   A. The degree to which a firm employs fixed charge capital--debt and preferred stock-- will affect its expected earnings per share and the riskiness of these earnings.

   B. EBIT *does* depend on operating leverage, but it does *not* depend on financial leverage, at least for "reasonable" amounts of leverage.

   C. Financial leverage will cause earnings per share to rise if the return on assets is greater than the cost of debt. However, the degree of risk associated with the firm will also increase as leverage increases.

   D. As financial leverage increases, the cost of debt will also rise due to the increased risk of not being able to meet the fixed charges.

   E. Financial leverage increases the potential return to common stockholders, but it also increases the potential variability in earnings per share.

   F. A firm should choose that capital structure which maximizes the price of its stock. This capital structure is called the optimal, or *target, capital structure.*

IV. **Changes in the use of financial leverage will affect EPS and stock price.**

   A. At first, EPS will rise as the use of debt increases. Interest charges rise, but the number of outstanding shares will fall as equity is replaced by debt. The formula for EPS is:

$$\text{EPS} = \frac{(\text{Sales} - F - \text{VC} - \text{Interest})(1 - \text{Tax rate})}{\text{Shares outstanding}}.$$

   B. At some point EPS will peak. Beyond this point interest rates will rise so fast that EPS is depressed in spite of the fact that the number of shares outstanding is falling.

C. Risk, as measured by the standard deviation of EPS, rises continuously as the use of debt increases.

D. The expected stock price will at first increase with financial leverage, will then reach a peak, and finally it will decline.
   1. The optimal capital structure is found when the expected stock price is maximized.
   2. Management should set its target capital structure at this ratio of debt/assets.

E. The financial structure that maximizes EPS usually has more debt than the one which results in the highest stock price.

V. **Operating leverage and financial leverage are interrelated: A reduction in operating leverage would normally lead to an increase in the optimal amount of financial leverage, while an increase in operating leverage would lead to a decrease in the optimal amount of debt.**

   A. The *degree of operating leverage (DOL)* is defined as the percentage change in operating income (EBIT) associated with a given percentage change in sales volume.
      1. The formula used to analyze a single product is:

      $$DOL = \frac{Q(P - V)}{Q(P - V) - F}.$$

      Q = units of output
      P = sales price per unit
      V = variable cost per unit
      F = fixed operating costs

      2. The formula to analyze an entire firm is:

      $$DOL = \frac{S - VC}{S - VC - F}.$$

      S = sales in dollars
      VC = total variable costs
      F = fixed costs

   To find the effects on EBIT of a particular percentage change in sales, multiply the percentage change in sales times the DOL.

   B. Financial leverage affects earnings after interest and taxes. The *degree of financial leverage (DFL)* is the percentage change in earnings available to common stockholders (EPS) associated with a particular percentage change in EBIT.
      1. The formula for DFL is:

      $$DFL = \frac{EBIT}{EBIT - I}.$$

      2. To find the effects on income available to common stockholders, multiply the percentage change in EBIT by DFL. The greater the degree of financial leverage, the greater the impact of a given change in EBIT on EPS.

C. *Degree of total leverage (DTL)* combines DOL and DFL to show how a given change in sales will affect EPS.

1. One formula for DTL is:

$$DTL = \frac{S - VC}{S - VC - F - I}.$$

2. The degree of total leverage can also be found as:

$$DTL = (DOL)(DFL).$$

DTL shows the interrelationship between operating and financial leverage.

VI. **There are problems with using the type of leverage analyses described in the text.**

A. It is extremely difficult to determine the relationships among financial leverage, P/E ratios, and equity capitalization rates (k_s). Therefore, it is frequently difficult to use stock price analysis to determine a target capital structure.

B. Established management teams are often conservative; they may be more interested in survival than in maximizing expected stock prices.

C. Firms that provide vital services (utilities) must put long-run viability above short-run stock price maximization or cost of capital minimization.

D. Because of these factors, management may place considerable emphasis on the times-interest-earned ratio and the fixed charge coverage ratio when establishing the firm's financial structure. The higher these ratios, the less likely it is that a firm will be unable to meet all of its fixed charge obligations and thus face bankruptcy. The TIE ratio is calculated as:

$$TIE = \frac{EBIT}{Interest\ charges}.$$

VII. **Capital structure theory attempts to estimate the target capital structure for a firm.**

A. Capital structure theory as set forth by *Modigliani and Miller* states that, due to the tax deductibility of interest on debt, a firm's value rises continuously as it uses more debt. This theory holds only under a very restrictive set of assumptions.

B. These assumptions, however, do not hold true in the real world. For example, debt costs rise as the debt ratio rises, EBIT declines at extreme leverage, expected tax rates fall and reduce the value of the tax shelter, and the probability of bankruptcy increases as the debt level rises. Therefore, at some point, bankruptcy-related costs exceed the benefit of additional debt. This point denotes the target capital structure.

VIII. **A firm's capital structure can change because of merger activity.**

A. The acquiring firm may issue debt to purchase the target firm's stock.

B. This action will change the combined firm's capital structure.

C. This use of debt increases the value sufficiently to cover the premium offered for the stock and to provide a profit for the acquiring firm.

IX. **The following factors will all have some influence on the firm's choice of a target capital structure.**

   A. *Sales stability.* If sales are stable, a firm will be more likely to take on increased debt and higher fixed charges.

   B. *Types of assets (asset structure).* Firms whose assets can readily be pledged as collateral for loans will tend to operate with a higher degree of financial leverage.

   C. *Operating leverage.* Lower operating leverage generally permits a firm to employ more debt.

   D. *Growth rate.* Firms that are growing rapidly generally need large amounts of external capital. The flotation costs associated with debt are generally less than those for common stock, so rapidly growing firms tend to use more debt.

   E. *Profitability.* A high degree of profitability would indicate an ability to carry a high level of debt. However, many profitable firms are able to meet most of their financing needs with retained earnings, and do so.

   F. *Taxes.* Interest charges are tax deductible, while dividend payments are not. This factor favors the use of debt over equity for firms in high tax brackets.

   G. *Control.* Management may not wish to increase the shares of stock outstanding for fear of losing voting control of the company.

   H. *Management attitudes.* Managements vary in their attitudes toward risk. More conservative managers will use stock rather than debt for financing, while less conservative managers will use more debt.

   I. *Lender and rating agency attitudes.* This factor will penalize firms that go beyond the average for their industry in the use of financial leverage.

   J. *Market conditions.* At any point in time, securities markets may favor either debt or equity.

   K. *Firm's internal conditions.* Expected future earnings patterns and internal factors will influence management's choice of debt versus equity.

   L. *Financial flexibility.* Most treasurers have as a goal to always be in a position to raise the capital needed to support operations, even under bad conditions. Therefore, they want to always maintain some *reserve borrowing capacity*.

X. **There are wide variations in the use of financial leverage both among industries and among individual firms within each industry.**

DEFINITIONAL QUESTIONS

1. Determination of an _____ capital structure requires consideration of both _____ and _____.

2. A firm's _____ capital structure is generally set equal to the estimated optimal structure.

3. Business risk refers to the uncertainty about expected _____ _____, or _____.

4. The factors that influence a firm's business risk include the variability of (1) _____ in units, (2) _____ _____, and (3) _____ _____.

5. Business risk represents the riskiness of the firm's operations if it uses no _____; financial risk represents the additional risk borne by common stockholders as a result of using _____.

6. Common stockholders are compensated for bearing financial risk by a higher _____ _____.

7. Expected EPS generally _____ as the debt/assets ratio increases.

8. As financial leverage increases, the stock price will first begin to rise, but it will then decline as financial leverage becomes excessive because potential _____ _____ becomes increasingly important.

9. Firms that have a high ratio of fixed to variable costs are said to operate with a high degree of _____ _____.

10. Operating leverage refers to the use of _____ _____.

11. Financial leverage refers to the use of _____ financing.

12. Difficulties in determining the relationship between _____/_____ ratios, _____ capitalization rates, and the degree of _____ _____ have made some managers reluctant to rely heavily on stock price analysis to help determine the optimal capital structure.

13. Conservative financial managers may try to maintain a target _____ _____ that does not maximize the firm's _____ _____.

14. Some managers may be more concerned with _____ than with maximizing stock prices.

15. The _____ ratio and the _____ _____ _____ ratio give some indication of a firm's risk of default on its fixed charges.

16. The _____ _____ _____ _____ is defined as the percentage change in EBIT associated with a given change in sales volume.

17. The _____ _____ _____ _____ is defined as the percentage change in EPS associated with a given change in EBIT.

18. The _____ _____ _____ _____ is defined as the percentage change in EPS associated with a given change in sales volume.

19. Debt has a _____ advantage over equity in that _____ is a deductible expense while _____ are not.

20. Management may prefer additional _____ as opposed to common stock in order to help maintain _____ of the company.

CONCEPTUAL QUESTIONS

21. Firm A has a higher degree of business risk than Firm B. Firm A can offset this by increasing its operating leverage.

    a. True   b. False

22. Two firms operate in different industries, but they have the same expected EPS and the same standard deviation of expected EPS. Thus, the two firms must have the same financial risk.

    a. True   b. False

23. As a general rule, the capital structure that maximizes stock price also:

    a. Maximizes the weighted average cost of capital.
    b. Maximizes EPS.
    c. Maximizes bankruptcy costs.
    d. Minimizes the weighted average cost of capital.
    e. Minimizes the required rate of return on equity.

24. A decrease in the debt ratio will normally have no effect on:

    a. Financial risk.
    b. Total risk.
    c. Business risk.
    d. Systematic risk.
    e. Firm-unique risk.

25. Two firms could have identical financial and operating leverage yet have different degrees of business risk.

    a. True   b. False

PROBLEMS

26. Brown Products is a new firm just starting operations. The firm will produce backpacks which will sell for $22.00 apiece. Fixed costs are $500,000 per year, and variable costs are $2.00 per unit of production. The company expects to sell 50,000 backpacks per year, and its effective tax rate is 40 percent. Brown needs $2 million to build facilities, obtain working capital, and start operations. If Brown borrows part of the money, the interest charges will depend on the amount borrowed as follows:

Amount Borrowed	Percentage of Debt in Capital Structure	Interest Rate on Total Amount Borrowed
200,000	10	9.00
400,000	20	9.50
600,000	30	10.00
800,000	40	15.00
1,000,000	50	19.00
1,200,000	60	26.00

Assume that stock can be sold at a price of $20 per share on the initial offering, regardless of how much debt the company uses. Then after the company begins operating, its price will be determined as a multiple of its earnings per share. The multiple (or the P/E ratio) will depend upon the capital structure as follows:

Debt/Assets	P/E	Debt/Assets	P/E
0.0	12.5	40.0	8.0
10.0	12.0	50.0	6.0
20.0	11.5	60.0	5.0
30.0	10.0		

What is Brown's optimal capital structure, which maximizes stock price, as measured by the debt/assets ratio?

a. 10%
b. 20%
c. 30%
d. 40%
e. 50%

27. Refer to Problem 26. What is Brown's degree of operating leverage at the expected level of sales?

a. 1.00
b. 1.08
c. 2.00
d. 2.16
e. 3.00

28. Refer to Problem 26. What is Brown's degree of financial leverage at the expected level of sales?

   a. 1.00
   b. 1.08
   c. 2.00
   d. 2.16
   e. 3.00

29. Refer to Problem 26. What is Brown's degree of total leverage at the expected level of sales and optimal capital structure?

   a. 1.00
   b. 1.08
   c. 2.00
   d. 2.16
   e. 3.00

30. Bicycles, Inc., currently sells 75,000 units annually. At this sales level, its net operating income (EBIT) is $4 million and the degree of total leverage is 2.0. The firm's debt consists of $20 million in bonds with a 10 percent coupon. Bicycles is considering a new assembly line which would entail an increase in fixed cost, resulting in a degree of operating leverage of 1.8. However, the firm desires to maintain the degree of total leverage at 2.0. Assuming that EBIT remains at $4 million, what dollar amount of bonds must be retired to accomplish adding the assembly line yet retain the old degree of total leverage.

   a. $10 million
   b. $12 million
   c. $14 million
   d. $16 million
   e. $18 million

ANSWERS AND SOLUTIONS

1. optimal; risk; return

2. target

3. operating income; EBIT

4. sales; sales prices; operating costs

5. debt; debt

6. expected return

7. increases

8. bankruptcy costs

9. operating leverage

10. fixed costs

11. debt (or fixed-charge)

12. P/E; equity; financial leverage

13. capital structure; stock price

14. survival

15. debt; times-interest-earned (or fixed charge coverage)

16. degree of operating leverage (DOL)

17. degree of financial leverage (DFL)

18. degree of total leverage (DTL)

19. tax; interest; dividends

20. debt; control

21. b. Increasing operating leverage will increase Firm A's business risk; therefore, Firm A should use *less* operating leverage.

22. b. The two firms would have the same *total* risk. However, they could have different combinations of business and financial risk.

23. d.

24. c. Business risk measures the riskiness of the firm's operation assuming no debt is used.

25. a. Business risk consists of several elements in addition to operating leverage, for example, sales variability, and it does not depend on financial risk at all.

26. b. The first step is to calculate EBIT:

```
Sales in dollars [50,000($22)]              $1,100,000
     Less:  Fixed costs                         500,000
            Variable costs [50,000($2)]         100,000
     EBIT                                    $  500,000
                                             ===========
```

The second step is to calculate the EPS at each debt/assets ratio using the formula:

$$EPS = \frac{(EBIT - I)(1 - T)}{Shares\ outstanding}.$$

Recognize (1) that I = interest charges = (dollars of debt)(interest rate at each D/A ratio), and (2) that shares outstanding = (assets - debt)/initial price per share = ($2,000,000 - debt)/$20.00.

D/A %	EPS $	D/A %	EPS $
0	3.00	40	3.80
10	3.21	50	3.72
20	3.47	60	2.82
30	3.77		

Finally, the third step is to calculate the stock price at each debt/assets ratio using the following formula: price = (P/E)(EPS).

D/A %	Price $	D/A %	Price $
0	37.50	40	30.40
10	38.52	50	22.32
20	39.91	60	14.10
30	37.70		

Thus, a debt/assets ratio of 20 percent maximizes stock price. This is the optimal capital structure.

27. c.

$$\text{DOL} = \frac{PQ - VQ}{PQ - VQ - F} = \frac{\$22(50,000) - \$2(50,000)}{\$22(50,000) - \$2(50,000) - \$500,000}$$

$$= 2.00.$$

28. b.

$$\text{DFL} = \frac{EBIT}{EBIT - I} = \frac{PQ - VQ - F}{PQ - VQ - F - I}$$

$$= \frac{\$1,100,000 - \$100,000 - \$500,000}{\$1,100,000 - \$100,000 - \$500,000 - \$38,000}$$

$$= \frac{\$500,000}{\$462,000} = 1.08.$$

29. d.

$$DTL = \frac{PQ - VQ}{PQ - VQ - F - I}$$

$$= \frac{\$1,100,000 - \$100,000}{\$1,100,000 - \$100,000 - \$500,000 - \$38,000}$$

$$= \frac{\$1,000,000}{\$462,000} = 2.16,$$

or

$$DTL = (DOL)(DFL) = (2.00)(1.08) = 2.16.$$

30. d.

$$DOL = \frac{PQ - VQ}{PQ - VQ - F} = 1.8.$$

But,

$$PQ - VQ - F = EBIT = \$4 \text{ million.}$$

Therefore,

$$\frac{PQ - VQ}{\$4 \text{ million}} = 1.8$$

$$PQ - VQ = \$7.2 \text{ million.}$$

Now,

$$DTL = \frac{PQ - VQ}{PQ - VQ - F - I} = 2.0$$

$$\frac{\$7.2 \text{ million}}{\$4.0 \text{ million} - I} = 2.0$$

$$I = \$0.40 \text{ million.}$$

Therefore, the new interest payment must be $0.40 million. The current interest payment is 0.10($20 million) = $2.0 million. Thus, the interest payment must be reduced by $1.60 million by retiring bonds. This would require that $1.60/0.10 = $16 million of bonds be retired.

CHAPTER 19
DIVIDEND POLICY

OVERVIEW

Dividend policy involves the decision to pay out earnings as dividends or to retain and reinvest them in the firm. Any change in dividend policy has both favorable and unfavorable effects on the firm's stock price: higher dividends mean higher immediate cash flows to investors, which is good, but lower future growth, which is bad. The optimal dividend policy balances these opposing forces and maximizes stock price. Two theories regarding the relationship between dividend payout and stock price have been proposed: (1) *dividend irrelevance*, which states that dividend policy has no effect on the firm's stock price, and (2) the *"bird-in-the-hand"* theory, which states that investors prefer dividends because they are less risky than potential capital gains. In addition, the water is muddied because of the existence of *signaling* and *clientele* effects. It is simply not possible to state that any one dividend policy is correct, and hence it is impossible to develop a precise model for use in establishing dividend policy. Thus, financial managers must consider a number of factors when setting their firms' dividend policies.

OUTLINE

I. **Dividend policy involves the decision to pay out earnings versus retaining them for reinvestment in the firm.**

    A. The constant growth stock model, $P_0 = D_1/(k_s - g)$ shows that paying out more dividends will increase stock price. However, if this results in insufficient equity funds to meet investment needs, then the firm must sell new common stock and incur flotation costs, which will cause the price of the stock to decrease.

    B. The optimal dividend policy strikes a balance between investors' desire for current cash flows (dividends) and future expected growth so as to maximize the value of the firm's stock.

    C. *Modigliani and Miller (MM)* argue that a firm's value is determined solely by its basic earnings power and its risk class. Thus, the value of the firm depends on asset investment policy only, and not on how the firm's net income is split between dividends and retained earnings.
        1. MM prove their proposition, but only under a set of restrictive assumptions, including (1) zero personal taxes, (2) independence between dividend policy and equity costs, and (3) zero flotation costs.
        2. Obviously, firms and investors do pay taxes and do incur flotation costs, and investors may apply a different capitalization rate (k_s) to firms that pay out more rather than less of their earnings. Thus, the MM conclusions on dividend irrelevance may not be valid under real-world conditions.

D. The most critical assumption of MM's dividend irrelevance theory is that dividend policy does not affect the required rate of return on equity, k_s.

    1. Myron Gordon and John Lintner argue that k_s increases as the dividend payout is reduced because investors are more sure of receiving dividend payments than income from capital gains that presumably result from retained earnings.

    2. MM call the Gordon-Lintner argument the "bird-in-the-hand" theory because Gordon and Lintner believe that investors view dividends in the hand as being less risky than capital gains in the bush. In MM's view, however, most investors are going to reinvest their dividends in the same or similar firms, and the riskiness of the firm's cash flows to investors in the long run is solely a function of the firm's asset cash flows.

E. Note that each of these theories leads to a different prescription for financial managers.

    1. According to MM, there is no optimal dividend payout policy--one is as good as another.

    2. Gordon and Lintner argue that the cost of equity increases as the payout ratio is reduced, and hence, that firms should retain a high fraction of their earnings only if internal investment opportunities promise high rates of return.

F. Unfortunately, empirical testing has not produced definitive results regarding which theory is correct.

II. There are two other issues which have a bearing on optimal dividend policy.

A. It has been observed that a dividend increase announcement is often accompanied by an increase in the price of the stock.

    1. This might be interpreted by some to mean that investors prefer dividends over capital gains, thus supporting the Gordon-Lintner hypothesis.

    2. However, MM argue that a dividend increase is a *signal* to investors that the firm's management forecasts good future earnings. Thus, MM argue that investors' reactions to dividend announcements do not necessarily show that investors prefer dividends to retained earnings. Rather, the fact that the stock price changes merely indicates that there is an important *information content* in dividend announcements. This is referred to as the *information content, or signaling, hypothesis.*

B. MM also suggest that a *clientele effect* might exist.

    1. Some stockholders--for example, retirees--prefer current income; therefore, they would want the firm to pay out a high percentage of its earnings as dividends.

    2. Other stockholders have no need for current income--for example, doctors in their peak earning years-- and they would simply reinvest any dividends received, after first paying income taxes on the dividend income. Therefore, they would want the firm to retain most of its earnings.

    3. Thus, a firm establishes a dividend policy and then attracts a specific clientele that is drawn to this dividend policy.

    4. Empirical evidence supports the contention that a *clientele effect* does exist.

        a. MM argue that one clientele is as good as another, so the existence of a clientele effect does not imply that one payout policy is better than another.

        b. However, MM offer no proof that the aggregate makeup of investors permits firms to disregard clientele effects.

III. The theories offer conflicting advice, yet managers must take action. Here are the actual dividend policies that firms follow in practice:

A. *Residual dividend policy.* This policy is based on the premise that investors prefer to have a firm retain and reinvest earnings rather than pay them out in dividends if the rate of return the firm can earn on reinvested earnings exceeds the rate of return investors can obtain for themselves on other investments of comparable risk. Further, it is less expensive for the firm to use retained earnings than it is to issue new common stock. A firm using the residual policy would follow these four steps:

1. Determine the optimal capital budget.
2. Determine the amount of equity required to finance the optimal capital budget, recognizing that the funds used will consist of both equity and debt to preserve the optimal capital structure.
3. To the extent possible, use retained earnings to supply the equity required.
4. Pay dividends only if more earnings are available than are needed to support the optimal capital budget.

B. *Constant, or steadily increasing, dividends per share.* A company which uses this procedure implies to shareholders that the regular dividend will at least be maintained and, accordingly, that earnings will be sufficient to cover it. Some other features of this policy are as follows:

1. Dividends are increased only when earnings have increased and seem stable enough to maintain the new dividend level.
2. Dividend payments will be maintained, at least temporarily, even if earnings fall below the level of the dividend payment. Firms try very hard never to reduce the regular dividend.
3. Most corporations follow this type of policy.
   a. Stable dividends or a stable dividend growth rate will tend to stabilize a firm's stock price movements.
   b. Investors who rely on dividends for income normally prefer a stable dividend policy.
   c. A stable growth rate policy confirms investors' estimates of the growth factor, and hence reduces risk perceptions.
4. Because of these factors, many people think that a stable dividend policy (including a steady growth rate) will maximize the price of a firm's stock.

C. *Constant payout ratio.* Only a few firms pay out a constant percentage of their yearly earnings. This would normally result in an unpredictable dividend stream and would not please most investors.

D. *Low regular dividend plus extras.* This policy is often followed by firms with relatively volatile earnings from year to year. The low regular dividend can usually be maintained even when earnings decline, and "extra" dividends can be paid when excess funds are available.

IV. Firms usually pay dividends on a quarterly basis in accordance with the following payment procedures:

A. *Declaration date.* This is the day on which the board of directors declares the dividend. At this time they set the amount of the dividend to be paid, the holder-of-record date, and the payment date.

B. *Holder-of-record date.* This is the date the stock transfer books of the corporation are closed. Holders of record who purchased shares before the ex-dividend date will receive the announced dividend.

C. *Ex-dividend date.* This date is four days prior to the holder-of-record date. Shares purchased after the ex-dividend date are not entitled to the dividend. This practice is a convention of the brokerage business which allows sufficient time for stock transfers to be made on the books of the corporation.

D. *Payment date.* This is the day when dividend checks are actually mailed to the holders of record.

V. Many firms have instituted dividend reinvestment plans whereby stockholders simply reinvest their dividends in additional shares of the corporation. Income taxes on the amount of the dividends must be paid even though stock rather than cash is received.

VI. Regardless of the debate on the relevancy of dividend policy, it is possible to identify several factors which influence dividend policy. These factors are grouped into four broad categories.

A. *Constraints on dividend payments:*
1. Bond indenture provisions
2. Impairment of capital rule
3. Availability of cash
4. Tax on improperly accumulated earnings

B. *Investment opportunities:*
1. Location of the IOS schedule
2. Ability to accelerate or postpone projects

C. *Availability and costs of alternative sources of capital:*
1. Flotation costs of selling new stock
2. Capital structure flexibility--how steep is the average cost of capital schedule, and how much would it cost to substitute debt for equity?
3. Management control

D. *Effects of dividend policy on k_s:*
1. Stockholder preference for current versus future income
2. Risk of dividends versus capital gains
3. Information content of dividends

VII. Stock dividends and stock splits are often used to lower a firm's stock price, and, at the same time, to conserve its cash resources.

A. The effect of a stock split is an increase in the number of shares outstanding and a reduction in the par, or stated, value of the shares. For example, if a firm had 1,000 shares of stock outstanding with a par value of $100 per share, a 2-for-1 split would reduce the par value to $50 and increase the number of shares to 2,000.
1. The total net worth of the firm remains unchanged.
2. The stock split does not involve any cash payment, only additional certificates representing new shares.

B. A stock dividend requires an accounting entry transfer from retained earnings to the common stock and paid-in capital accounts and an accompanying pro-rata distribution of new shares to the existing stockholders.
   1. Dollars transferred from retained earnings = (Number of shares outstanding)(Percentage of the stock dividend)(Market price of the stock).
   2. Again, no cash is involved with this "dividend." Net worth remains unchanged, and the number of shares is increased.

C. Stock dividends and splits "cut a given amount of pie into smaller slices."

D. The rationale behind using stock splits and dividends to reduce share prices lies in the belief in an "optimal trading range" within which large numbers of investors will be able to purchase the stock, liquidity will be increased, and the price will be maximized.

E. Unless the total amount of dividends paid on shares is increased, any upward movement in the stock price following a stock split or dividend is likely to be temporary. The price will normally fall in proportion to the dilution in earnings and dividends unless earnings and dividends rise.

VIII. Stock repurchases are an alternative to dividends for transmitting cash to stockholders.

A. Stock repurchased by the issuing firm is called *treasury stock*.

B. Advantages of a repurchase to the stockholder include:
   1. Profits earned on repurchases are taxed at the capital gains rate, whereas dividends are not. This was a major advantage before 1987, when the capital gains tax rate was only 40 percent of the dividend tax rate.
   2. The stockholder is given a choice of whether to sell or to not sell his stock to the firm.
   3. The repurchase can remove a large block of stock overhanging the market.

C. Advantages of repurchase from management's point of view include:
   1. If an increase in cash flow is temporary, the cash can be distributed to stockholders as a repurchase rather than as a dividend, which could not be maintained in the future.
   2. It may be more efficient to use repurchased stock rather than newly issued stock for acquisitions on when stock options are exercised.
   3. If directors hold the firm's stock, they may favor repurchases for tax purposes (pre-1987).
   4. Repurchases can be used to raise the debt ratio quickly.
   5. Treasury stock can be resold when the firm needs more funds.

D. Disadvantages of repurchase from the stockholders' point of view include:
   1. Repurchases are not as dependable as cash dividends; therefore, the price of the stock may benefit more from cash dividends. A dependable repurchase program may not be practical due to the improper accumulation tax.
   2. Selling stockholders may not be aware of all the implications of the repurchase; therefore, repurchases are usually announced in advance.
   3. If a firm pays too high a price for the repurchased stock, it is to the disadvantage of the remaining stockholders.

E. Disadvantages of repurchase from management's point of view include:
   1. A repurchase program is often considered an indicator that management cannot locate good investments.
   2. If the repurchase is deemed to be primarily for the avoidance of taxes, the firm may be penalized under the improper accumulation of earnings provision of the tax code.

F. While repurchases on a regular basis do not appear feasible due to various uncertainties, occasional repurchases do offer some significant advantages over dividends, and repurchases can be valuable in making a major change in capital structure within a short period.

DEFINITIONAL QUESTIONS

1. MM argue that a firm's dividend policy has _____ _____ a stock's price.

2. Gordon and Lintner hypothesize that investors value a dollar of _____ more highly than a dollar of expected _____ _____.

3. A company may be forced to increase its _____ ratio in order to avoid a tax on retained earnings deemed to be unnecessary for the conduct of the business.

4. Some stockholders prefer dividends to _____ _____ because of a need for current _____.

5. If the _____ of a firm's stock increases with the announcement of an increase in dividends, it may be due to the _____ content in the dividend announcement rather than to a preference for dividends over capital gains.

6. The policy of using "extra" dividends is most appropriate for a firm with _____ earnings.

7. The stock transfer books of a corporation are closed on the _____-_____ date.

8. The _____ date occurs four days prior to the _____-____-_____ date and provides time for stock transfers to be recorded on the books of the firm.

9. Actual payment of a dividend is made on the _____ date as announced by the _____ _____ _____.

10. Many firms have instituted _____ _____ plans whereby stockholders can use their dividends to purchase additional shares of the company's stock.

11. A stock dividend requires that an accounting transfer be made from _____ _____ to the _____ _____ and _____-____-_____ accounts.

12. A stock split involves a reduction in the _____ _____ of the common stock, but no accounting transfers are made between accounts.

13. The assumption that some investors prefer a high dividend payout while others prefer a low payout is called the _____ effect.

14. The residual dividend policy is based on the fact that new common stock is _____ _____ than retained earnings.

15. Stock repurchased by the firm which issued it is called _____ _____.

CONCEPTUAL QUESTIONS

16. An increase in cash dividends will always result in an increase in the price of the common stock because D_1 will increase in the stock valuation model.

    a. True   b. False

17. A stock dividend will affect which of the following balance sheet accounts?

    a. Common stock
    b. Paid-in capital
    c. Retained earnings
    d. Cash
    e. The accounts in a, b, and c will all be affected.

18. A stock split will affect the amounts shown in which of the following balance sheet accounts?

    a. Common stock
    b. Paid-in surplus
    c. Retained earnings
    d. Cash
    e. None of the above accounts

19. If investors prefer dividends to capital gains, then:

    a. The required rate of return on equity, k_s, will not be affected by a change in dividend policy.
    b. The cost of capital will not be affected by a change in dividend policy.
    c. k_s will increase as the payout ratio is reduced.
    d. k_s will decrease as the retention rate increases.
    e. A policy conforming to the residual theory of dividends will maximize stock price.

20. If investors are indifferent between dividends and capital gains, the farther to the left the IOS and MCC schedule intersect, the *higher* the dividend payout ratio should be.

    a. True   b. False

PROBLEMS

21. Express Industries' expected net income for next year is $1.0 million. The company's target, and current, capital structure is 40 percent debt and 60 percent common equity. The optimal capital budget for next year is $1.2 million. If Express uses the residual theory of dividends to determine next year's dividend payout, what is the expected payout ratio?

    a. 0%
    b. 10%
    c. 28%
    d. 42%
    e. 56%

22. Amalgamated Shippers has a current, and target, capital structure of 30 percent debt and 70 percent equity. This past year Amalgamated, which uses a residual theory dividend policy, had a dividend payout ratio of 47.5 percent and net income of $800,000. What was Amalgamated's capital budget?

    a. $400,000
    b. $500,000
    c. $600,000
    d. $700,000
    e. $800,000

ANSWERS AND SOLUTIONS

1. no effect

2. dividends; capital gains

3. payout

4. retained earnings; income

5. price (or value); information

6. volatile

7. holder-of-record

8. ex-dividend; holder-of-record

9. payment; board of directors

10. dividend reinvestment

11. retained earnings; common stock; paid-in capital

12. par value

13. clientele

14. more costly

15. Treasury stock

16. b. A dividend increase could be perceived by investors as signifying poor investment opportunities and hence lower growth in future earnings, thus reducing g in the DCF model. The net effect on stock price is uncertain.

17. e. A stock dividend requires an accounting entry transfer from the retained earnings account to the common stock and paid-in capital accounts. There is no cash involved in a stock dividend.

18. e. A stock split will affect the par value and number of shares outstanding. However, no dollar values will be affected.

19. c. This is the Gordon-Lintner hypothesis. If investors view dividends as being less risky than potential capital gains, then the cost of equity is inversely related to the payout ratio.

20. a. If investors are indifferent, firms should follow the residual theory. Thus, the smaller the optimal capital budget, the higher the dividend payout ratio.

21. c. The $1,200,000 capital budget will be financed using 40 percent debt and 60 percent equity. Therefore, the equity requirement will be 0.6($1,200,000) = $720,000. Since the expected net income is $1,000,000, $280,000 will be available to pay as dividends. Thus, the payout ratio is expected to be $280,000/$1,000,000 = 0.28 = 28%.

22. c. Of the $800,000 in net income, 0.475($800,000) = $380,000 was paid out as dividends. Thus, $420,000 was retained in the firm for investment. This is the equity portion of the capital budget, or 70 percent of the capital budget. Therefore, the total capital budget was $420,000/0.7 = $600,000.

CHAPTER 20
COMMON STOCK FINANCING

OVERVIEW

This chapter is more descriptive than analytical, but financial managers do need a working knowledge of the issues covered. Common stock constitutes the ownership position in a firm. As owners, the common stockholders have certain rights and privileges, including (1) the right to control the firm through election of directors and (2) the right to the residual earnings of the firm.

Firms generally begin their corporate life as closely held companies, with all the common stock held by the founding managers. Then, as the company grows, it is often necessary to sell stock to the general public (that is, go public) to raise more funds. At this point, the firm's managers must be familiar with securities markets, including their regulation by the Securities and Exchange Commission (SEC). Eventually, the firm may choose to list its stock on one of the organized exchanges.

OUTLINE

I. **Common stock represents the ownership of an incorporated business. It corresponds to the proprietor's capital or the partners' capital for an unincorporated business.**

   A. Legal and accounting terminology is important in analyzing the owners' position in a business firm.
      1. Shares of common stock are authorized by the owners of a business and issued by management.
      2. *Par value* is essentially the minimum price at which new shares can be sold.
      3. Any difference between the par value and what stockholders paid for common stock is shown on the balance sheet as *additional paid-in capital*.
      4. *Retained earnings* represent the net income earned over the years that has been reinvested in the business rather than paid out as dividends.
      5. The *book value* of each common share is equal to the net worth, or common equity (stockholder's equity), consisting of the sum of common stock, retained earnings, and paid-in capital, divided by the number of shares of common stock outstanding.

   B. The corporation's common stockholders have certain rights and privileges.
      1. Common stockholders have control of the firm through their election of the firm's directors, who in turn select officers to manage the business.
         a. In a large, publicly owned firm, neither the managers nor any individual shareholders normally have the 51 percent necessary for absolute control of the company.
         b. Thus, stockholders must vote for directors, and the voting process is regulated by both state and federal laws.

    c. Stockholders who are unable to attend annual meetings may still vote by means of a *proxy*. Proxies can be solicited by any party seeking to control the firm.
2. The *preemptive right* gives the current shareholders the right to purchase any new shares issued, in proportion to their current holdings.
    a. The preemptive right may or may not be required by state law.
    b. When granted, the preemptive right enables current owners to maintain their proportionate share of ownership and control of the business.
    c. It also prevents the sale of shares at low prices to new stockholders, which would dilute the value of the previously issued shares.

C. Special classes of common stock are sometimes created by a firm to meet special needs and circumstances. If two classes of stock were desired, one would normally be called "Class A" and the other "Class B."
1. Class A might be entitled to receive dividends before dividends can be paid on Class B stock.
2. Class B might have the exclusive right to vote.
3. Note that Class A and Class B have no standard meanings.

II. **The United States has highly developed markets for buying and selling common stocks. Institutional investors have long dominated the bond market, and in recent years they have become a major factor in the stock market. Pension funds and other institutional investors now own about 35 percent of the stock of large, publicly held firms, and they represent about 75 percent of the trading volume in stocks.**

A. The stocks of smaller companies are generally owned by management groups and are referred to as *closely held*, or *privately owned*, corporations. The stocks of larger firms are generally held by a large number of investors. These companies are called *publicly held corporations*.

B. Stock market transactions may be separated into three distinct categories.
1. The *secondary market* deals with trading in previously issued, or outstanding, shares of established, publicly owned companies. The company receives no new money when sales are made in the secondary market.
2. The *primary market* handles additional shares sold by established, publicly owned companies. Companies can raise additional capital by selling in this market.
3. The primary market also handles new public offerings of shares in firms that were formerly closely held. Capital for the firm can be raised by *going public*, and this market is often termed the *new issue market*.

C. Financing with common stock has the following advantages:
1. Common stock does not obligate the firm to make fixed payments to stockholders.
2. Common stock carries no fixed maturity date.
3. Common stock increases the credit-worthiness of the firm, thus increasing the future availability of debt at a lower cost.
4. Common stock can often be sold more easily than debt if the firm's prospects look potentially good, but risky.
5. Capital gains returns from common stock are not subject to taxes until they have been received, that is, until the stock is sold.
6. Financing with common stock serves as a reserve of borrowing capacity.

D. Financing with common stock has the following disadvantages:

    1. Issuing common stock extends voting rights, and thus control, to new stockholders.

    2. Common stock gives new stockholders the right to a percentage of profits rather than to a fixed payment in the case of creditors.

    3. The cost of underwriting and distributing common stock is high.

    4. If common stock is sold to the point where the equity ratio exceeds that in the optimum capital structure, a firm's average cost of capital will increase, and its stock price will not be maximized.

    5. Dividends paid to stockholders are not tax deductible as is interest paid to creditors.

III. Most businesses begin life as proprietorships, partnerships, or closely held corporations. However, if the business prospers and grows, at some point the decision must be made as to whether to go public. There are advantages and disadvantages to public ownership.

    A. Going public has the following advantages:

        1. The original owners are able to diversify their holdings by selling some of their stock in a public offering.

        2. Public ownership increases the liquidity of the stock.

        3. New corporate cash is more easily raised by a publicly owned company.

        4. Going public establishes the firm's value in the marketplace.

    B. Going public has the following disadvantages:

        1. A publicly owned company must file quarterly and annual reports with various governmental agencies.

        2. Publicly owned firms must disclose operating and ownership data.

        3. The opportunities for owners/managers to engage in questionable, but legal, self-dealings are reduced.

        4. If a publicly held firm is very small, its shares will be traded very infrequently, and a liquid market will not really exist.

        5. Managers of publicly owned firms with less than 50 percent control must be concerned about tender offers and proxy fights. This sometimes leads to operating decisions that are not in the best long-run interests of the shareholders.

IV. Stocks traded on organized exchanges are called listed stocks. While the decision to go public is significant, the decision to list is not a major event. In order to have a listed stock, a company must apply to an exchange, pay a relatively small fee, and meet the exchange's minimum requirements.

    A. The company will have to file a few new reports with an exchange.

    B. It will have to abide by the rules of the exchange.

    C. Firms benefit from listing their stock by gaining liquidity, status, and free publicity. These factors may cause the value of the stock to be increased.

V. Most participants in the securities markets, including the organized exchanges, brokers, investment bankers, and dealers, are regulated by the federal government through the Securities and Exchange Commission (SEC) and also by state governments through regulations known as "blue sky" laws. (The blue sky laws were enacted to prevent brokers from selling "blue sky" rather than tangible assets of value.)

A. The SEC has jurisdiction over all interstate offerings to the public in amounts of $1.5 million or more.

B. The SEC also regulates all national security exchanges. Firms listed on these exchanges must file financial reports with both the SEC and the exchanges.

C. New issues must be registered at least 20 days before they are offered to the public. A *prospectus* describing the company and the securities to be offered must be sent to prospective purchasers of the new issue.

D. The Federal Reserve System controls the flow of credit *(margin credit)* that may be used in purchasing securities.

E. The security industry realizes the importance of stable markets, sound brokerage firms, and the absence of stock manipulation. Therefore, the various exchanges and trade organizations work closely with the regulatory agencies to police the markets and protect customers.

F. The purpose of regulation is to insure that adequate and accurate information is available concerning securities offered to the public, and to prevent fraud. Regulation cannot insure that investments will be successful or that investors will exercise good judgment.

VI. **The financial manager must have a knowledge of the investment banking process, the process by which new securities are issued. Investment banking decisions take place in two stages.**

A. At Stage I, the firm makes some initial, preliminary decisions on its own.
   1. The dollar amount of new capital required is established.
   2. The type of securities to be offered is specified. Further, if stock is to be issued, will a *rights offering* be used, that is, will the stock be offered first to existing stockholders?
   3. The basis on which to deal with the investment bankers, either by a *competitive bid* or a *negotiated deal* is determined.
   4. Finally, the investment banking firm must be selected.

B. The Stage II decisions are made jointly by the firm and the selected investment banker.
   1. First, the two parties will reevaluate the Stage I decisions.
   2. The firm and its investment banker must decide whether the banker will work on a "best efforts" basis or will "underwrite" the issue.
      a. On a *best efforts sale*, the banker does not guarantee that the securities will be sold or that the company will get the cash it needs.
      b. On an *underwritten issue*, the company does get a guarantee. Essentially, the banker purchases the issue, then resells the securities at a higher price. The banker bears significant risks in underwritten offerings.
   3. The investment banker's compensation must be negotiated.
   4. The offering price must be set.

C. The costs associated with a new security issue are termed *flotation costs*.
   1. These costs include compensation to the investment banker plus legal, accounting, printing, and other costs borne by the issuer.

2. Flotation costs depend on the type of security issued and the size of the issue.
3. These costs, expressed as a percentage of gross proceeds, typically range from 1.1 to 14.0 percent for bonds, 1.6 to 2.6 percent for preferred stock, and 3.5 to 22.0 percent for common stocks.

D. Several factors must be considered when setting the offering price.
1. If the firm is already publicly owned, the offering price will be based upon the existing market price.
2. The investment banker will have an easier job if the issue is priced relatively low, while the issuer naturally wants as high a price as possible.
3. Investors must be attracted to new issues. This can be done by reducing the price, or by "promoting" the issue.
4. If *pressure* from a new stock issue drives down the price of the stock, all shares outstanding are affected, not just the new shares. This loss in firm value is also a flotation cost. However, it is not normally a permanent loss, so it may not be a cost of any real concern.

E. Because of potential losses from price declines caused by a falling market, underwriters do not generally handle issues single-handedly. Groups of investment bankers form an *underwriting syndicate* to spread the risk and minimize individual losses. Syndicates are also useful because an individual banker's clients may not be able to absorb a large issue.

F. For new issues, the investment banker will normally maintain a market in the shares after the public offering. This is done in order to provide liquidity for the shares and to maintain a good relationship with both the issuer and the investors who purchased the shares.

DEFINITIONAL QUESTIONS

1. Ownership interest in a corporation is reflected on the balance sheet by the _____ _____ accounts.

2. Amounts paid by stockholders in excess of the par value are shown as "additional _____-_____."

3. One of the fundamental rights of common stockholders is to elect a firm's _____, who in turn elect the operating management.

4. If a stockholder cannot vote in person, participation in the annual meeting is still possible through a _____.

5. The preemptive right protects stockholders against loss of _____ of the corporation as well as _____ of market value from the sale of new shares below market value.

6. Firms may find it desirable to separate the common stock into different _____. Generally, this classification is designed to differentiate stock in terms of the right to receive _____ and the right to _____.

7. A _____ _____ or _____ _____ corporation is one whose stock is held by a small group, normally its management.

8. The trading of previously issued shares of a corporation takes place in the _____ market, while new issues are offered in the _____ market.

9. _____ _____ refers to the sale of shares of a closely held business to the general public.

10. Going public establishes the firm's _____ in the marketplace.

11. Securities traded on the organized exchanges are known as _____ securities.

12. Before an interstate issue of stock amounting to $1.5 million or more can be sold to the public, it must be _____ with and approved by the _____.

13. Setting the _____ price for an issue of stock may present a conflict of interest between the issuer and the _____ _____.

14. In order to spread the risk of underwriting a sizable common stock issue, investment bankers will form an _____ _____.

15. Credit used to buy stock is known as _____ credit, and its use is controlled by the _____ _____ _____.

CONCEPTUAL QUESTIONS

16. A change in the dividend payout ratio will have the most direct, or most immediate, effect on a firm's

    a. Common stock account.
    b. Earnings per share.
    c. Paid-in capital account.
    d. Net operating income.
    e. Retained earnings account.

17. When stockholders assign their right to vote to another party, this is called

    a. A privilege.
    b. A preemptive right.
    c. An ex right.
    d. A proxy.
    e. A prospectus.

18. A firm may go public, yet the firm itself may not receive any additional funds in the process.

    a. True   b. False

19. Flotation costs are generally higher for bond issues than for stock issues.

    a. True   b. False

20. When new shares are being sold, if it appears that the investment bankers will be unable to sell the entire issue at the initial offering price, the only way the entire issue can be sold is to lower the price.

    a. True   b. False

PROBLEMS

(The following data apply to the next three problems.)

Pepple-Smith Company
Stockholders' Equity Accounts

Common stock (100,000 shares authorized, 80,000 shares outstanding, $1 par)	$ 80,000
Additional paid-in capital	720,000
Retained earnings	1,200,000
Total common stockholders' equity	$2,000,000

21. If all 80,000 shares outstanding were sold at one offering, how much did Pepple-Smith receive for each share?

    a. $1
    b. $5
    c. $10
    d. $20
    e. $25

22. What is the current book value per share?

    a. $1
    b. $5
    c. $10
    d. $20
    e. $25

23. Suppose the firm sold the remaining authorized shares and netted $20.00 per share from the sale. What is the new book value per share?

    a. $23
    b. $24
    c. $25
    d. $26
    e. $27

ANSWERS AND SOLUTIONS

1. stockholders' equity (or common equity)

2. paid-in capital

3. directors

4. proxy

5. control; dilution

6. classes; dividends; vote

7. closely held; privately owned

8. secondary; primary

9. Going public

10. value

11. listed

12. registered; SEC

13. offering; investment banker

14. underwriting syndicate

15. margin; Federal Reserve Board

16. e. Although a change in the dividend payout would, in the long run, affect every item listed, retained earnings would be affected most directly.

17. d. Recently, there has been a spate of proxy fights, whereby a dissident group of stockholders solicits proxies in competition with the firm's management. If the dissident group gets a majority of the proxies, then it can gain control of the board of directors and oust existing management.

18. a. An example, that of the Ford Foundation selling stock to the general public, is given in the text. Also, a firm may go public if its managers sell off a portion of their stock holdings. Then, the funds obtained go to the managers rather than the firm.

19. b. The investment banker normally must expend greater effort in selling stocks, thus must charge a higher fee.

20. b. The investment bankers may be able to increase the demand for the stock by "promoting" the issue. If not, then a price reduction may be required.

21. c. The offering of 80,000 shares resulted in the firm collecting $80,000 in par value and $720,000 in additional paid-in capital for a total of $800,000. Thus, each share must have brought Pepple-Smith $800,000/80,000 = $10.

22. e. The total common equity of $2,000,000 represents the total investment of the 80,000 shares outstanding. Thus, the book value per share is $2,000,000/80,000 = $25.

23. b. The firm now sells the remaining 20,000 shares and nets $20 per share for a total of $400,000. Thus, the new total common equity is $2,400,000, and 100,000 shares are outstanding. The new book value per share is $2,400,000/100,000 = $24. Note that selling new shares below book value results in a lower book value on all shares. The opposite holds if new shares are sold above book value.

CHAPTER 21
LONG-TERM DEBT

OVERVIEW

Most firms find it desirable to use long-term debt financing. The two most important classes of fixed income securities are *term loans* and *bonds*. These securities come in many types: secured and unsecured, zero-coupon and normal coupon, floating rate and fixed rate, and so on. The variety of types stems from the fact that different groups of investors favor different types of securities, and their tastes change over time. The astute financial manager knows how to "package" securities at a given point in time to attract the greatest number of potential investors, thereby keeping the firm's cost of capital to a minimum.

OUTLINE

I. **Funded debt is simply another name for long-term debt.**

II. **A term loan is an agreement under which a borrower agrees to make interest payments and to repay principal, on specific dates, to a lender.**

   A. The financial institution which lends the funds is usually a bank, an insurance company, or a pension fund.

   B. The *maturity* of a term loan is generally from 3 to 15 years, but it may be as short as 2 or as long as 30 years.

   C. Term loans have several advantages over publicly issued securities.
   1. Loan provisions can be worked out more quickly between the lender and the borrower.
   2. Loan provisions can also be more flexible.
   3. It is not necessary for a term loan to go through the SEC registration process.
   4. If necessary or desirable, changes in the contract can be negotiated with the lender.
   5. Issue costs are generally lower for term loans.

III. **A bond is a long-term contract under which a borrower agrees to make a series of payments of interest and principal to the owner of the bond.**

   A. Bonds differ from term loans in that they are generally offered to the public rather than to a single lender or a small group of lenders.

   B. A bond's indenture sets forth the terms and conditions to which the bond is subject.

   C. The indenture is filed with a *trustee* who represents the bondholders and who sees that the terms of the indenture are carried out. Normally, a bank serves as the trustee.

D. When real estate or other property is pledged as collateral for a bond issue, the bond is referred to as a *mortgage bond*. In case of bankruptcy, the mortgage bondholders have first claim on the proceeds from the sale of the pledged assets.

E. A *debenture* is an unsecured bond, and holders are general creditors of the corporation. The use of debentures depends on the firm's general credit strength and the nature of its assets.

F. *Subordinate debt* has claims on assets, in the event of bankruptcy, only after senior debt as named in the subordinate debt's indenture has been paid off. Second mortgage bonds are subordinate to first mortgage bonds. Also, subordinated debentures may be subordinated to designated notes payable, or to all other debt.

G. There are several other important types of bonds.
　1. *Convertible bonds* are securities that can be converted into a fixed number of shares of common stock at the option of the bondholder.
　2. Bonds issued with *warrants* provide the investor with an option to buy the common stock of the firm *at a stated price*. The warrants are detachable from the bonds, and the bonds remain outstanding even after the warrants have been exercised.
　3. *Income bonds* pay interest only when covered by the earnings of the firm.
　4. *Indexed bonds* have their coupon rates tied to an inflation index, such as the consumer price index.

IV. **The cost of a debt security to the issuer is a function of the specific features of the debt contract. These features determine the riskiness of the debt.**

A. An *indenture* is the legal document which spells out the rights of both the bondholders and the issuing corporation. It contains the basic terms of the issue as well as any special provisions such as *restrictive covenants, call provisions*, and *sinking funds*. A *trustee*, the person who represents the bondholders, makes certain that terms of the indenture are carried out.

B. A *restrictive covenant* is a provision in a bond issue that requires the issuer to meet certain stated conditions.
　1. Standard provisions typically include minimum levels for the current ratio and the debt-to-assets ratio.
　2. These requirements are designed to help insure that the credit standing of the firm and the bond issue remains high.

C. A *call provision* gives the issuing corporation the right to call the entire bond issue for redemption before its regular maturity.
　1. When a bond is called, the company must normally pay an amount greater than the par value. This extra payment is referred to as a *call premium*.
　2. Bonds are frequently called when the issuing firm can *refund* the issue at a lower interest rate. The call premium is thus a penalty for depriving investors of the higher rate of interest.

D. A *sinking fund* provision requires that a firm retire a portion of a bond issue each year. Its purpose is like that of an amortization schedule for a term loan.

1. Failure to make a sinking fund payment constitutes technical default, so lenders can require immediate payment on the entire issue and possibly force the firm into bankruptcy.
2. Generally, sinking funds permit the firm to call a specific number of bonds for redemption or to buy the required number of bonds in the open market. The firm will select whichever method which is the least expensive.
3. Note that a sinking fund call involves a small percentage of the issue, say one-thirtieth of a 30-year issue, while a regular call involves the entire issue.

V. **In the 1980s, there have been several innovations in long-term financing.**

A. *Zero coupon bonds* are offered at substantial discounts below their par values.
  1. The advantages to the issuer are as follows:
    a. No cash outlays are required until maturity.
    b. These bonds often have a lower required rate of return than coupon bonds.
  2. Zero coupon bonds have the following advantages for investors:
    a. There is little danger of a call.
    b. Zero coupon bonds guarantee a "true" yield to maturity since there is no reinvestment rate risk.

B. When interest rates are volatile, lenders are reluctant to lend long term. Thus, they charge very high maturity risk premiums. On the other hand, borrowers, in general, would rather borrow long term so that they do not have to worry about having to continually refund their debt.
  1. The answer to the dilemma is *long-term floating rate debt.*
  2. The debt may have a 5- or 10-year maturity, but the interest rate changes periodically to reflect current market conditions.
  3. Floating rate debt is advantageous to lenders because it causes the market value of the debt to be stabilized, and it provides lenders with more income to meet their own obligations.
  4. Floating rate debt is also advantageous to corporations because they can obtain debt with a long maturity without committing themselves to paying an historically high rate of interest for the entire term of the loan. However, if interest rates rise, borrowers will face increasing interest expense.

C. Another type of debt which offers creditors protection against rising interest rates is a *bond* that is *redeemable at par.*
  1. The holder of a redeemable-at-par bond has the option of returning the bond to the issuer for the par value.
  2. If interest rates rise, the bondholder will turn in the bond and reinvest the proceeds at the higher rate.

VI. **Bond issues are normally assigned quality ratings by both Moody's Investors Service and Standard & Poor's Corporation. These ratings reflect the probability that a bond will go into default. Aaa (Moody's) and AAA (S&P) are the highest ratings.**

A. Bond ratings influence investors' perceptions of default risk and therefore have an impact on the interest rate paid, and hence on the firm's cost of capital.

B. Institutions are often limited to investing in investment grade securities, that is, those rated BBB or Baa, or higher. It is important, therefore, that a firm maintain a good quality rating on its bond issues.

C. Rating assignments are based on qualitative and quantitative factors, including the firm's debt/assets ratio, current ratio, and coverage ratios.

D. Rating agencies review outstanding bonds on a periodic basis, occasionally upgrading or downgrading a bond as the issuer's circumstances change. Also, is a company issues more bonds, this will trigger a review by the rating agencies.

VII. Most firms use several types of long-term securities.

A. The various types of securities offer different risk/return combinations to investors, and hence have different costs to the firm.

B. In theory, a firm should be indifferent between different types of securities because each would have a cost commensurate with its risk.
   1. However, changes in supply/demand conditions can cause some securities to be "cheaper" than others at times.
   2. Additionally, innovative, or new, securities often offer firms a particular bargain rate until "pent-up demand" for them is satisfied.

VIII. Long-term financing decisions are difficult because they are influenced by many factors, most of which are subjective. Additionally, these factors vary among firms at any point in time and for any given firm over time.

A. One of the foremost considerations is the firm's *target (optimal) capital structure.*
   1. Over the long haul, firms try to maintain their target structures.
   2. However, from year to year, firms may stray from the target to minimize flotation costs, to take advantage of market conditions, or because of its own internal situation. As examples, a firm would not want to issue long-term debt if it was convinced interest rates were about to fall, and it would not want to issue stock if it felt that its earnings were about to rise sharply, and more than the public anticipated.

B. Firms also must consider the *maturity of the assets being financed.*
   1. If a firm uses 30-year bonds to finance 10-year assets, the bond payments would continue long after the asset was retired.
   2. If a firm uses 10-year bonds to finance 30-year assets, it would have to "roll over" the debt after 10 years.
   3. Each of the above strategies involves significant risks. In general, the least risky strategy is to match the maturity of the debt to the maturity of the assets being financed.

C. *Current interest rate levels and forecasts of future interest rates* also play an important role in the financing decision.
   1. If current rates are high, and are expected to drop, it might be wise to use short-term financing until rates drop, and then lock in the lower rates with long-term financing.
   2. Conversely, if current rates are low and expected to rise, use long-term financing now to lock in the rates.
   3. However, interest rates are difficult, if not impossible, to forecast. Thus, pursuing one of the above strategies could prove to be disastrous if the forecasts were wrong.

D. Sometimes *covenants* in existing debt contracts restrict a firm's ability to use a particular type of financing at a given time.

E. The firm's *current condition and earnings outlook* also have an effect on the choice of securities.
   1. A firm may delay debt financing which would trigger a review by the rating agencies.
   2. Debt issued when in a poor financial condition would probably cost more and have more severe restrictive covenants.

F. The *amount of financing required* and the *availability of assets which could be pledged as collateral* also impact the financing decision.

IX. Appendix 12A of the text discusses bankruptcy and the process of reorganization.

X. Bond refunding decisions involve two separate questions: (1) Is it profitable to call an issue now, and (2) would it be even more profitable to wait and call at a later date? Appendix 12B discusses the analyses required to answer these questions.

DEFINITIONAL QUESTIONS

1. Long-term debt is sometimes referred to as _____ debt.

2. A _____ loan is a contract to pay _____ and _____ on specific dates to a lender.

3. Term loans are generally negotiated directly with a _____, _____ _____, or _____ _____. They are not sold to the _____ at large.

4. The process of paying off a term loan in equal _____ over the life of the loan is called _____.

5. A _____ is a long-term contract under which the _____ agrees to make payments of interest and principal to the holder.

6. The legal document setting forth the terms and conditions of a bond issue is known as the _____.

7. The _____ represents the bondholders and sees that the terms of the indenture are carried out.

8. A bond secured by real estate is known as a _____ bond.

9. Failure to make a sinking fund payment places the company in _____ _____, and could ultimately lead to _____.

10. In meeting its sinking fund requirements, a firm may _____ the bonds or purchase them on the _____ _____.

11. Except when the call is for sinking fund purposes, when a bond issue is called, the firm must pay a _____ _____, or an amount in excess of the _____ value of the bond.

12. A restrictive _____ is a provision in the bond's _____ which requires the issuer to meet certain stated conditions.

13. A bond issue is most likely to be called if interest rates have _____ substantially since the time of issue.

14. Firms issue various securities because investors have different _____/_____ trade-offs.

15. Over the long-run, a firm should finance in accordance with its _____ _____ _____.

16. The least risky financing strategy is to match the _____ of the debt with the _____ of the asset being financed.

17. It is very _____, if not _____, to forecast interest rates.

CONCEPTUAL QUESTIONS

18. There is a direct relationship between bond ratings and the required rate of return of bonds; that is, the higher the rating, the higher is the required rate of return.

    a. True   b. False

19. Which of the following would tend to *increase* the coupon interest rate on a bond that is to be issued?

    a. Adding a sinking fund
    b. Adding a restrictive covenant
    c. Adding a call provision
    d. A change in the bond's rating from Aa to Aaa
    e. Both a and c above

20. Zero coupon bonds have become quite popular over the last several years. These bonds are advantageous to the *issuer* because

    a. The bond is, in effect, not callable.
    b. These bonds generally have a higher yield to maturity than normal coupon bonds.
    c. The bond's cash outflows are spread over the life of the bond.
    d. The bonds are initially sold above par value.
    e. None of the above statements is correct.

21. The "penalty" for having a low bond rating is *less severe* when the Security Market Line is relatively steep than when it is not so steep.

    a. True   b. False

PROBLEMS

22. J. C. Nickel is planning a zero coupon bond issue. The bond has a par value of $1,000, matures in 10 years, and will be sold at an 80 percent discount, or for $200. The firm's marginal tax rate is 40 percent. What is the annual after-tax cost of debt to Nickel on this issue? (Assume that the discount can be amortized over the life of the bond and deducted from taxable income.)

   a. 9.59%
   b. 10.00%
   c. 11.62%
   d. 14.79%
   e. 17.46%

(The following data apply to the next two problems.)

The Privy Company has just issued a 10-year bond with a 10 percent annual coupon. The $100,000 issue sold at its par value of $1,000 per bond. The indenture has a sinking fund provision which stipulates that one-tenth of the issue will be redeemed at the end of each year.

23. Assume that interest rates fall after the issue date, causing the market value of the bonds to rise, and that Privy exercises the sinking fund provision by calling one-tenth of the issue (10 bonds) each year. What is the effective before-tax cost of the issue?

   a. 8.0%
   b. 9.2%
   c. 10.0%
   d. 11.2%
   e. 12.0%

24. Now assume that interest rates rise after the issue date, causing the market value of bonds to fall, and that the firm retires the issue over time by buying 10 of the bonds outstanding each year on the open market. Further, assume that Privy can repurchase each bond (with a face value of $1,000) for $950, so its total expenditure to purchase 10 bonds is $9,500. Now what is the effective before-tax cost of the issue?

   a. 8.0%
   b. 9.2%
   c. 10.0%
   d. 11.2%
   e. 12.0%

ANSWERS AND SOLUTIONS

1. funded

2. term; interest; principal

3. bank; insurance company; pension fund; public

4. installments; amortization

5. bond; borrower

6. indenture

7. trustee

8. mortgage

9. technical default; bankruptcy

10. call; open market

11. call premium; par

12. covenant; indenture

13. fallen

14. risk/return

15. target capital structure

16. maturity; maturity

17. difficult; impossible

18. b. The relationship is inverse. The *higher* the rating, the lower is the default risk, and hence the *lower* is the required rate of return. Aaa/AAA is referred to as high, and as we go down the alphabet, the ratings are lower.

19. c. Sinking funds, restrictive covenants, and an improvement in the bond rating all indicate lower risk for the bond, and hence would lower the coupon rate.

20. e. The primary advantages to the issuer are (1) that zero coupons have a lower required rate of return, and (2) that annual interest payments are avoided.

21. b. A steeper SML implies a higher risk premium on risky securities, and thus a greater "penalty" on lower-rated bonds.

22. a. Look at the cash flows to the firm. At Year 0, the firm receives $200. At Year 10, the firm must pay out $1,000. For each of the 10 years, Nickel is declaring a ($1,000 - $200)/10 = $80 interest expense, even though it is not actually paying interest in the interim period. The tax benefit of that expense is 0.40($80) = $32. Putting these cash flows on a time line, we get the following:

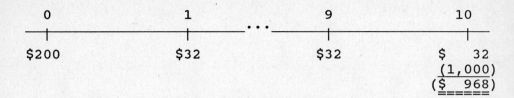

The cost of debt to the firm is that discount rate which equates the present values of the cash inflows and outflows, or the IRR. (The calculator solution is 9.59 percent.)

23. c. Each year, Privy will retire $10,000 face value in bonds. Thus, its interest expense would also decrease by one-tenth each year:

Year	Debt Outstanding at Beginning of Year	Interest Expense
1	$100,000	$10,000
2	90,000	9,000
-	------	------
9	20,000	2,000
10	10,000	1,000

Thus, Privy pays 10 percent on the outstanding balance throughout the life of the issue and it is being retired at par value. Its effective before-tax cost is also 10 percent.

24. b. To answer this, you must lay out the cash flows over the life of the issue:

Year	Debt Outstanding at Beginning of Year	Interest Expense	Sinking Fund Expense	Total Service Requirement
1	$100,000	$10,000	$9,500	$19,500
2	90,000	9,000	9,500	18,500
3	80,000	8,000	9,500	17,500
4	70,000	7,000	9,500	16,500
5	60,000	6,000	9,500	15,500
6	50,000	5,000	9,500	14,500
7	40,000	4,000	9,500	13,500
8	30,000	3,000	9,500	12,500
9	20,000	2,000	9,500	11,500
10	10,000	1,000	9,500	10,500

Now, the firm receives $100,000 at Time 0, and pays out the cash flows shown above in the righthand column. The IRR of this cash flow stream, 9.2 percent, is Privy's before-tax cost of debt in this case. The ability to repurchase the bonds at less than par reduces the cost of the issue. (Note that Privy would not actually be able to repurchase the final $10,000 worth of bonds for $9,500. The market value of the bonds would equal par value at maturity.)

CHAPTER 22
PREFERRED STOCK, LEASING, AND
OPTION-TYPE SECURITIES

OVERVIEW

Firms can use types of long-term financing other than common stock and debt. Other types of securities include 1) preferred stock, which is a hybrid security that represents a cross between debt and equity; 2) leasing, which is an alternative to borrowing; and 3) options-type securities, especially warrants and convertibles, which allow debtholders to share in the capital gains if a business is especially successful. All of these methods are widely used today, and an understanding of them is essential for the financial manager.

OUTLINE

I. **Preferred stock is a hybrid type of long-term financing. It is called a hybrid because it represents an equity investment in a business, yet it has many of the characteristics associated with debt.**

   A. If an analysis is being made by a common stockholder, preferred is treated like debt, because it entails fixed charges which must be paid ahead of common stock dividends.

   B. However, if the analysis is being made by a creditor studying a firm's vulnerability to failure, preferred stock is viewed as part of the equity base.

   C. Preferred stock has the following characteristics:
   1. Preferred stock has a par value.
   2. The preferred dividend can be stated as a percentage of the par value or in dollars.
   3. Dividends on preferred stock must be paid before dividends can be paid on common stock. For protection, dividends on most preferred stock are *cumulative* from year to year. That is, unpaid dividends accumulate and must be paid before common stockholders can receive dividends.
   4. Nonpayment of preferred stock dividends, however, does not force a company into bankruptcy.
   5. In the event of bankruptcy, preferred stockholders have priority over common stockholders but below creditors.
   6. Some preferred stock is *convertible* into common stock.

   D. There are advantages and disadvantages associated with preferred stock financing for both issuers and investors.

1. Preferred stock is a fixed cost form of financing, yet the firm avoids the danger of bankruptcy if earnings are too low to pay the preferred dividend. Preferred also allows a firm to avoid sharing control, as it must do when selling common stock.
2. Although advantageous to a firm, preferred stock does have a higher after-tax cost of capital than debt, mainly because preferred dividends are not tax deductible.
3. For the investor, preferred stock provides reasonably assured income. Also, for corporate investors, 80 percent of preferred dividends received are not taxable.
4. The disadvantages to the investors are (1) that returns are limited on preferred stock even though a substantial portion of ownership risk is borne by the preferred stockholders, and (2) that there are no legal rights to dividends even if a company earns a profit.

II. **The ownership of assets is not as important as the ability to use them in a profitable manner. Leasing provides the same ability to use capital assets as outright ownership.**

A. Historically, land and buildings were the types of assets most often leased, but today it is possible to lease almost any kind of fixed asset.
1. *The lessor* is the owner of the leased property and receives such tax benefits of ownership as the depreciation write-offs and, when they apply, investment tax credits.
2. The *lessee* buys the right to use the property by making lease payments to the lessor.

B. There are three common types of leasing arrangements.
1. *Sale and leaseback.* In this type of lease, a firm owning an asset sells the property to a leasing company and simultaneously leases it back for a specified period at specific terms.
   a. The sale and leaseback is an alternative to simply borrowing against the property on a mortgage loan basis.
   b. The seller receives the purchase price but retains the use of the property in exchange for rental payments.
   c. The lease payments are sufficient to return the purchase price to the lessor plus provide a return on the investment.
   d. The lessor owns the property when the lease expires; this is the *residual* value. The lessor may, as a part of the basic lease, be given the right to renew the lease (at a reduced rental) or to purchase the asset.
2. *Operating leases.* These leases include both financing and maintenance services.
   a. Operating leases ordinarily call for the lessor to maintain the equipment; the cost of maintenance is built into the lease payments.
   b. The lease contract is written for less than the useful life of the equipment; that is, the lease is not fully amortized.
   c. The lessor expects to recover the cost of the equipment through renewal payments or by selling the leased equipment.
   d. Operating leases often contain a cancellation clause to protect the lessee against obsolescence.
3. *Financial, or capital, leases.* These leases are fully amortized; however, they do not provide for maintenance and are not cancellable. They differ from a sale-leaseback only in that the equipment is purchased by the lessor from a manufacturer rather than from the lessee.

III. **Lease payments are deductible expenses for income tax purposes providing the IRS does not challenge the lease as simply being an installment sale in another form.**

   A. The IRS would consider the transaction to be a sale if the following conditions hold:
   1. The lease payments are made over a relatively short period and approximate the price of the asset.
   2. The lessee may then continue to use the asset after the original lease period for a nominal (small) payment.

   B. These restrictions prevent a company from using a lease arrangement to depreciate equipment over a much shorter period than its useful life.

IV. **Using lease financing rather than debt to purchase assets could have an impact on the firm's balance sheet.**

   A. Leasing is referred to as *off balance sheet financing* because often neither the leased assets nor the lease liabilities appear on the firm's balance sheet.

   B. A firm with extensive lease arrangements would have both its assets and its liabilities understated in comparison with a firm which borrowed to purchase the assets. The firm that leases would show a lower debt ratio.

   C. FASB #13 requires firms to *capitalize* certain financial leases and thus to restate their balance sheets.
   1. Leased assets must be reported under fixed assets.
   2. The present value of future lease payments must be shown as debt.

   D. Lease financing is comparable to debt financing in that a specified series of payments is to be made, and failure to meet these payments results in bankruptcy.

   E. Leased assets are equivalent to assets purchased using all debt financing. Suppose a firm's target capital structure is 50 percent debt and 50 percent equity. Further, assume that 50 percent of the firm's assets are leased. Then, to maintain its target capital structure, the firm must use all-equity financing for the non-leased assets.

   F. The lease decision is a financing decision, and not a capital budgeting decision. Thus, lease analysis is not generally conducted unless the decision has already been made to acquire the asset.

V. **Leases must be evaluated by both the lessee and the lessor. The lessee must determine whether leasing is less costly than borrowing and buying the asset, while the lessor must determine if the lease will provide some target rate of return.**

   A. For the lessee, leasing is a substitute for debt financing.
   1. In an NPV-type analysis, the lessee estimates the cost of leasing and the cost of owning. If the PV cost of leasing is less than the PV cost of owning, the asset should be leased.
      a. All cash flows must reflect tax effects.
      b. Since leasing is a substitute for debt financing, and since lease cash flows have approximately the same risk as debt cash flows, the *appropriate discount rate is the after-tax cost of debt.*

VI. Other issues often arise in leasing decisions.

    A. The value of the asset at lease termination is called its *residual value*.
        1. It might first appear that assets with large residual values would most likely be owned since the owner gets the residual value.
        2. However, competition among leasing companies forces lease contracts to reflect expected residual values. Thus, large residual value assets do not necessarily imply that firms should buy them rather than lease them.

    B. It is sometimes argued that firms which lease can get more favorable debt terms than firms which do not lease.
        1. This premise rests on the assumption that credit analyses do not recognize the full impact of leasing on a firm's financial strength.
        2. However, this contention is of questionable validity for firms with audited financial statements.

    C. Tax considerations are the dominant motives behind most nonoperating leases that are written today.
        1. A firm that is unprofitable, or that is expanding rapidly and generating large depreciation write-offs, cannot immediately use the full tax benefits of ownership.
        2. On the other hand, firms in high marginal tax brackets can use the tax benefits associated with owning.
        3. Therefore, companies that make extensive use of lease financing are typically doing poorly and are unable to effectively use tax benefits (such as U.S. Steel), while lessors include successful companies which can fully utilize the tax benefits (such as General Electric).

VII. An option is a contract which gives its holder the right to buy (or sell) an asset at some predetermined price within a specified period of time. Pure options are instruments that are created by outsiders rather than the firm itself.

    A. There are many types of options and option markets.
        1. *Call options* convey the right to buy a share of stock at a set price called the *exercise*, or *striking*, *price*.
        2. *Put options* give the holder the right to sell the stock at the striking price.
        3. An option, whether a call or a put, has both a buyer and a seller.
            a. The buyer has the right to exercise the option.
            b. The seller, who is called the writer, must execute the transaction if the option is exercised.
            c. A seller who writes call options on stock he or she holds is said to write *covered options*. A similar option written by someone who does not hold the stock is called a *naked option*.
        4. Corporations on whose stock options are written have nothing to do with the options market--they do not raise money in this market nor have any direct transactions in it.

    B. The *formula value* of an option is defined as follows: Formula value = Current stock price - Striking price. The formula value can be thought of as the value of the option if it expired today.

1. For example, if a stock sells for $25, and the option's exercise price is $20, the option's formula value is $25 - $20 = $5.
2. However, the actual price as set in the options market will be higher than the formula value.
3. An option's market price is higher than its formula value because options offer investors greater leverage and less loss potential than do the underlying stocks.

C. The *premium* of an option's market value over its formula value depends on:
1. *Time to maturity.* The longer the option period, the greater its market value over its formula value.
2. *Stock price variability.* The greater the volatility of the underlying stock's price, the greater the premium.

VIII. **A warrant is an option issued by a company which gives the holder the right to buy a stated number of shares of stock at a specified price. Thus, warrants are essentially company-issued call options.**

A. Often warrants are attached to debt instruments as an incentive for investors to buy the combined issue at a lower interest rate than would otherwise be the case. Additionally, warrants may eliminate the need for extremely restrictive indenture provisions.

B. Warrants were originally used as "sweeteners" by small, risky firms to make their bonds or preferred stocks more attractive. However, in 1970, AT&T became the first important and financially strong corporation to use warrants, and many others have since followed.

C. Most warrants are *detachable* and can be traded separately from the bond or preferred stock with which they were issued.

D. Warrants generate additional equity capital when they are exercised.
1. The option price is generally set 10 to 30 percent above the market price of the stock at the time the warrant is issued.
2. If the market price of the stock is above the exercise price, and the warrants are about to expire, holders will exercise their options and purchase stock.
3. Since warrants pay no dividends, holders will be inclined to exercise them and obtain common stock as the common dividend is increased.
4. A *stepped-up option* price will also induce holders to exercise their warrants.

E. Warrants generally produce additional funds if a company is successful and grows, for then the stock price will increase over the exercise price.

IX. **Convertible securities are bonds or preferred stocks that are exchangeable into common stock at the option of the holder and under specified terms and conditions.**

A. Conversion of a bond or preferred stock, unlike exercise of a warrant, does not produce additional funds for the firm. However, conversion does lower the debt ratio.

B. The conversion ratio specifies the number of common shares that will be received for each bond or share of preferred stock that is converted.

C. The *conversion price*, P_c, is the effective price paid for the common stock when conversion occurs. For example, if a bond is issued at its par value of $1,000 and can be converted into 40 shares of common stock, the conversion price would be

$$P_c = \$1,000/40 = \$25 \text{ per share.}$$

Someone buying the bond for $1,000 and then converting it would, in effect, be paying $25 per share for the stock.

D. The conversion price is typically set at about 10 to 30 percent above the market price of common stock when the bond is sold. Thus, if the common stock is selling for $20.83 at the time the convertible is issued, the conversion price might be set at 1.2($20.83) = $25. This would produce a *conversion ratio* of R = 40:

$$R = \$1,000/P_c = \$1,000/\$25 = 40.$$

E. Convertible issues have certain advantages and disadvantages to the issuing corporation:
   1. By giving investors an opportunity to realize capital gains, a firm can sell debt with a lower interest rate.
   2. Convertibles provide a way of selling common stock at prices higher than those currently prevailing.
   3. The sale of a convertible issue may be thought of as having the effect of selling common stock at a higher-than-market price at the time the convertible is issued.
      a. However, if the stock price does not increase, investors will not convert and the company will be stuck with debt rather than equity in its capital structure, but the interest rate on this debt will be comparatively low.
      b. If the stock price does rise, the company can force conversion by including a call feature in the bond's indenture.
   4. Note that if the firm's stock price rises sharply, it would have been better off to have waited and sold the common shares at the higher price.

F. The actual market price of a convertible bond will always be equal to or greater than the higher of its *straight debt value* or its *conversion value*. The higher of these two values is called the *floor value*.

G. The expected rate of return on a company's convertible debt should lie between its cost of straight debt and its cost of common equity.

X. **Firms with warrants or convertible securities outstanding must reflect these securities when they calculate and report earnings per share to stockholders.**

A. *Primary EPS.* Earnings available are divided by the average number of shares that would be outstanding if those warrants and convertibles likely to be exercised or converted had actually been exercised or converted.

B. *Fully diluted EPS.* This shows EPS as if *all* warrants and convertibles had been exercised or converted prior to the reporting date, regardless of the likelihood of this occurring.

C. For firms with large amounts of warrants and/or convertibles outstanding, there can be substantial differences between these two EPS calculations. Thus, the SEC requires that both primary and fully diluted earnings be shown.

DEFINITIONAL QUESTIONS

1. Preferred stock is referred to as a hybrid because it is similar to _____ in some respects and to _____ _____ in others.

2. The dividend on a share of _____ stock may be indicated as a _____ of par or in dollars.

3. Most preferred stock dividends are _____, and thus must be paid before dividends can be paid to common stockholders.

4. Preferred stocks are attractive to _____ investors because of the 80 percent dividend exclusion.

5. Issuing preferred stock decreases the danger of _____ if operating income is low.

6. Conceptually, leasing is similar to _____, and it provides the same type of financial _____.

7. Under a _____-_____-_____ arrangement, the seller receives the purchase price of the asset but retains the _____ of the property.

8. _____ leases include both financing and maintenance arrangements.

9. A financial, or capital, lease is similar to a _____-_____-_____ arrangement, but financial leases generally apply to the purchase of _____ equipment directly from a manufacturer.

10. The IRS would disallow a "lease" which effectively pays for the asset in a relatively _____ period, and then permits the lessee to retain the use of the asset for a _____ payment.

11. If the IRS allows the lease, then the _____ _____ is fully deductible.

12. Capitalizing a lease requires that the asset be listed under _____ _____, and that the _____ _____ of the future lease payments be shown as a _____.

13. _____ among leasing companies will tend to force leasing rates down to the point where _____ values are fully reflected in the lease rates.

14. Since some leases do not appear on the _____ _____, a firm may be able to use more _____ than if it did not lease.

15. A firm with low profits may be able to transfer the depreciation write-off to another firm and be compensated in the form of lower _____ _____.

16. The leasing decision is normally a _____ decision rather than a _____ _____ decision.

17. _____ are the dominant factors behind most financial leases.

18. Warrants and convertibles securities may make a company's securities more attractive to a broader range of _____ and lower its _____ _____ _____.

19. A _____ is an option sold with a bond or preferred stock permitting the owner to buy a stated number of shares of _____ _____ at a specified _____.

20. The formula value of an option equals the _____ price minus the _____, or _____, price.

21. When they are exercised, warrants add additional _____ _____ to a firm's capital structure.

22. Warrants will certainly be exercised if the stock price is above the _____ price and the warrant is about to _____.

23. Holders of warrants will have an extra incentive to exercise if the company sharply increases the _____ on its common shares.

24. Almost all warrants are _____ and can be traded separately from the debt or preferred stock with which they were issued.

25. Convertible bonds or preferred stocks may be exchanged for _____ _____ at the option of the _____.

26. The _____ _____ specifies the number of shares of common stock that will be received for each bond that is converted.

27. Selling a convertible issue may be thought of as selling _____ _____ at a price higher than the market price prevailing at the time the convertible is issued.

28. If a firm's stock price does increase, the company can force _____ of the convertible bonds by including a _____ _____ in the bond indenture.

29. In reporting its earnings, a firm with warrants and convertible securities must report both _____ EPS and _____ _____ EPS.

CONCEPTUAL QUESTIONS

30. When one is evaluating a lease proposal, cash flows should be discounted at a relatively *high* rate because lease flows are fairly certain.

    a. True   b. False

31. Generally, operating leases are fully amortized, and the lease is written for the expected life of the asset.

    a. True   b. False

32. A firm which uses extensive lease financing will have a substantially lower debt ratio than an otherwise similar firm which borrows to finance its assets and does not capitalize its leases.

    a. True   b. False

33. Firms may or may not capitalize a financial lease, at their own option.

    a. True   b. False

34. The coupon interest rate on convertible bonds is generally *higher* than the rate on nonconvertible bonds of the same riskiness and rating.

    a. True   b. False

35. Primary EPS shows what EPS would have been if *all* warrants and convertibles outstanding had been converted prior to the reporting date.

    a. True   b. False

36. Investors are willing to accept lower interest (or dividend) yields on convertible securities in the hopes of later realizing capital gains.

    a. True   b. False

37. The conversion of a convertible bond replaces debt with common equity on a firm's balance sheet, but it does not bring in any additional capital.

    a. True   b. False

PROBLEMS

(The following data apply to the next three questions.)

Treadmill Trucking Company is negotiating a lease for five new tractor/trailer rigs with International Leasing. Treadmill has received its best offer from Betterbilt Trucks for a total price of $1 million. The terms of the lease offered by International Leasing call for 5 payments of $240,000, with each payment occurring at the beginning of each year. As an alternative to leasing, the firm can borrow from a large insurance company and buy the trucks. The $1 million would be borrowed on an amortized term loan at a 12 percent interest rate for 5 years. The trucks fall into the ACRS 5-year class and have an expected residual value of $100,000. Maintenance costs would be included in the lease. If the trucks are owned, a maintenance contract would be purchased at the beginning of each year for $10,000 per year. Treadmill plans to buy a new fleet of trucks at the end of the fifth year. Treadmill Trucking has a total tax rate of 20 percent.

38. What is the present value of the cost of owning to Treadmill?

    a. $707,189
    b. $742,354
    c. $827,929
    d. $825,726
    e. $885,247

39. What is Treadmill's present value of the cost of leasing?

    a. $707,189
    b. $742,354
    c. $805,922
    d. $851,863
    e. $885,247

40. Treadmill should lease the trucks.

    a. True   b. False

41. The Clayton Corporation has warrants outstanding that permit the holder to purchase one share of common stock per warrant at $30. What is the formula value of Clayton's warrants if the common stock is currently selling at $20 per share?

    a. -$20
    b. -$10
    c. $5
    d. $10
    e. $20

42. Refer to Problem 41. Calculate the formula value if the common stock is now selling at $40 per share.

    a. -$20
    b. -$10
    c. $0
    d. $10
    e. $20

43. White Corporation has just sold a bond issue with 10 warrants attached to each bond. The bonds have a 20-year maturity, an annual coupon rate of 12 percent, and they sold at the $1,000 initial offering price. Interest is paid annually. The current yield to maturity on bonds of equal risk, but without warrants, is 15 percent. What is the value of each warrant?

    a. $22.56
    b. $21.20
    c. $20.21
    d. $19.24
    e. $18.78

Central Food Brokers is considering issuing a 20-year convertible bond that will be priced at its par value of $1,000 per bond. The bonds have a 12 percent annual coupon interest rate, and each bond could be converted into 40 shares of common stock. Interest is paid annually. The stock currently sells at $20 per share, has an expected annual dividend of $3.00, and is growing at a constant 5 percent rate per year. The bonds are callable after 10 years at a price of $1,050, with the price declining by $5 per year. If, after 10 years, the conversion exceeds the call price by at least 20 percent, management will probably call the bonds.

44. What is the conversion price?

    a. $20
    b. $25
    c. $33
    d. $40
    e. $50

45. If the yield to maturity on nonconvertible bonds of similar risk is 16 percent, what is the straight-debt value?

    a. $1,000.00
    b. $907.83
    c. $812.22
    d. $762.85
    e. $692.37

46. If an investor expects the bond issue to be called in Year 10, and he plans on converting it at that time, what is the investor's expected rate of return upon conversion?

    a. 12.0%
    b. 12.2%
    c. 13.6%
    d. 14.4%
    e. 15.3%

ANSWERS AND SOLUTIONS

1. bonds; common stock

2. preferred; percentage

3. cumulative

4. corporate

5. bankruptcy

6. borrowing; leverage

7. sale-and-leaseback; use

8. Operating

9. sale and leaseback; new

10. short; small (nominal)

11. lease payment

12. fixed assets; present value; liability

13. Competition; residual

14. balance sheet; leverage

15. lease payments

16. financing; capital budgeting

17. Taxes

18. investors; cost of capital

19. warrant; common stock; price

20. market; striking; exercise

21. common equity

22. exercise (striking); expire

23. dividend

24. detachable

25. common stock; holder

26. conversion ratio

27. common stock

28. conversion; call provision

29. primary; fully diluted

30. b. The cash flows are fairly certain, so they should be discounted at a relatively *low* rate, generally, the after-tax cost of debt.

31. b. Operating leases are frequently not fully amortized. The lessor expects to recover all costs either in subsequent leases or through the sale of the used equipment at its residual value.

32. a. However, analysts would recognize that leases are as risky as debt financing, and thus include the impact of lease financing on the firm's debt costs and capital structure. Also, if the company which leases capitalizes the leases, then the debt ratios will be similar.

33. b. FASB #13 spells out in detail the conditions under which leases must be capitalized for an unqualified audit statement.

34. b. The coupon interest rate is *lower* because investors expect some capital gains return upon conversion. Note, however, that the overall required rate of return is probably higher for the convertible issue than the straight debt issue because the capital gains portions of the convertible's total return is more risky.

35. b. Primary EPS includes only those shares from warrants and convertibles likely to be converted in the near future. Fully diluted EPS includes all shares.

36. a. However, the investor is including the expected capital gain as part of his required return, so the total required return on convertibles is higher than on a straight security.

37. a. The bond is turned in to the company and replaced with common stock. No cash is exchanged. When a warrant is exercised, the firm gets additional capital.

38. d. Place the cash flows associated with ownership on a time line:

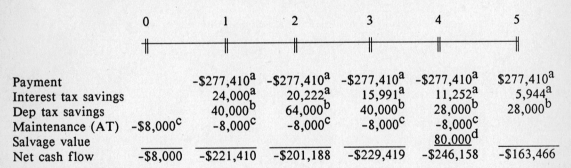

	0	1	2	3	4	5
Payment		$-\$277,410^a$	$-\$277,410^a$	$-\$277,410^a$	$-\$277,410^a$	$\$277,410^a$
Interest tax savings		$24,000^a$	$20,222^a$	$15,991^a$	$11,252^a$	$5,944^a$
Dep tax savings		$40,000^b$	$64,000^b$	$40,000^b$	$28,000^b$	$28,000^b$
Maintenance (AT)	$-\$8,000^c$	$-8,000^c$	$-8,000^c$	$-8,000^c$	$-8,000^c$	
Salvage value					$80,000^d$	
Net cash flow	$-\$8,000$	$-\$221,410$	$-\$201,188$	$-\$229,419$	$-\$246,158$	$-\$163,466$

PV cost of owning at 9.6 percent after-tax cost of debt is $825,726.

^{a}Net cost = $1,000,000.

Payment = $1,000,000/(\text{PVIFA}_{12\%,5})$ = $277,410.

Amortization Schedule

Year	Payment	Interest	Principal	EOY Balance	Interest Tax Savings
1	$277,410	$120,000	$157,410	$842,590	$24,000
2	$277,410	101,111	176,299	666,291	20,222
3	$277,410	79,955	197,455	468,836	15,991
4	$277,410	56,260	221,150	247,686	11,252
5	$277,410	29,722	247,688	-2	5,944

[b]Depreciable basis = $1,000,000.

Year	Factor	Depreciation Expense	Tax Savings
1	0.20	$200,000	$40,000
2	0.32	320,000	64,000
3	0.20	200,000	40,000
4	0.14	140,000	28,000
5	0.14	140,000	28,000
		$1,000,000	$200,000

[c]After-tax maintenance cash flow = $10,000(1 - T) = $10,000(0.8) = $8,000.

[d]After-tax residual value = $100,000(1 - T) = ($100,000)(0.8) = $80,000.

39. c. Place the cash flows associated with leasing on a time line:

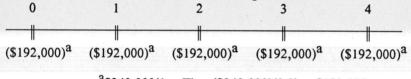

[a]$240,000(1 - T) = ($240,000)(0.8) = $192,000.

PV cost of leasing at 9.6 percent after-tax cost of debt is $805,922.

40. a. The PV cost of leasing is $825,726 - $805,922 = $19,804 less than the cost of owning.

41. b. Formula value = Market price - Exercise price. When P_0 = $20, Formula value = $20 - $30 = -$10. Note that negative prices cannot actually exist, so the formula value would be considered to be zero.

42. d. When P_0 = $40, Formula value = $40 - $30 = $10.

43. e. First, find the straight-debt value:

$$V = I(PVIFA_{k,n}) + M(PVIF_{k,n}) = \$120(PVIFA_{15\%,20}) + \$1,000(PVIF_{15\%,20}) = \$812.22.$$

Thus the value of the attached warrants is $1,000 - $812.22 = $187.78. Since each bond has 10 warrants, each warrant must have a value of $18.78.

44. b. P_c = Par value/Shares received = $1,000/40 = $25.00.

45. d.

$$V = I(PVIFA_{k,n}) + M(PVIF_{k,n}) = \$120(PVIFA_{16\%,20}) + \$1,000(PVIF_{16\%,20}) = \$762.85.$$

46. c. This is solved by finding the value of k_c in the equation:

Price paid = $I(PVIFA_{k_c,n})$ + Stock's expected market value $(PVIF,_{k_c,n})$.

Stock's expected market value = $(1.05)^{10}$ X $20 X 40 shares = $1,303.12.

Therefore, find the value of k_c for the following:

$$\$1,000 = \$120(PVIFA_{k_c,10}) + \$1,303.12(PVIF_{k_c,10})$$

$$k_c = 13.6\%.$$

CHAPTER 23
CORPORATE RESTRUCTURING:
MERGERS, DIVESTITURES, AND HOLDING COMPANIES

OVERVIEW

A *merger* involves the consolidation of two or more firms. Mergers can provide economic benefits through economies of scale, but they also have the potential for reducing competition, and for this reason mergers are carefully regulated by governmental agencies. Of the several rationales for mergers, perhaps the most common is the existence of synergy. When synergy is present, the value of the combined enterprise is greater than the sum of the values of the separate firms. Merger analysis may be regarded as a specialized form of capital budgeting analysis, with the most difficult part of the analysis being the estimation of the incremental cash flows that would result from the merger. Investment banking firms have specialists who can assist both the acquiring firm and the target firm in the valuation process. *Divestitures*, the opposite of mergers, also occur frequently. The reasons for divestiture are varied, and they range from the need for cash to governmental insistence (antitrust). *Holding companies* are firms whose sole purpose is to own operating interests in the stock of other firms. The holding company structure has both advantages and disadvantages over the conventional divisional structure.

OUTLINE

I. **Several reasons have been proposed to justify corporate mergers.**

   A. The primary goal of most mergers is to increase the value of the combining firms.
      1. If Companies A and B merge to form Company C, and if C's value exceeds that of A and B taken separately, then *synergy* is said to exist.
      2. Synergism can arise from four sources:
         a. Operating economies
         b. Financial economies
         c. Differential management efficiency
         d. Increased market power
      3. Operating and financial economies, as well as increases in managerial efficiency, are socially desirable. However, mergers to increase market power are both undesirable and illegal.

   B. *Tax considerations* can provide incentive for mergers.
      1. A highly profitable firm might merge with a firm which has accumulated tax losses so as to put these losses to immediate use.
      2. A firm with excess cash and a shortage of internal investment opportunities might seek a merger rather than pay the cash out as dividends, which would result in the shareholders paying immediate taxes on the distribution.

3. The 1986 Tax Reform Act increased the taxes that must be paid when a merger occurs. First, companies can no longer write up assets acquired for more than their book value and depreciate them on the higher cost basis. Second, the capital gains tax rate has been increased from 20 percent to 28 percent, so selling stockholders will get to keep less. These two effects will probably slow the rate of merger activity after 1986.

C. Occasionally, a firm will merge with another because it thinks it has found a "bargain."
   1. However, if the capital markets are efficient, stock prices represent the fair market value of the underlying assets.
   2. The fact that a firm's market value is far below its replacement value does not, in itself, make the firm an attractive acquisition candidate.

D. *Diversification* is often cited by managers as a rationale for mergers. Although diversification may bring some real benefits to the firm, stockholders can generally diversify more easily and efficiently than can firms by simply holding portfolios of stocks.

II. **There are four primary types of mergers:**

A. *Horizontal.* This type of merger occurs when one firm combines with another in its same line of business.

B. *Vertical.* A vertical merger exists when firms combine in a producer-supplier relationship.

C. *Congeneric.* This type of merger occurs when somewhat related enterprises, but not horizontally or vertically, merge.

D. *Conglomerate.* When completely unrelated enterprises combine, a conglomerate merger occurs.

III. **The high level of merger activity in the 1980s has been sparked due to:**

A. The relatively depressed condition of the stock market during that period.

B. The unprecedented level of inflation that existed during the 1970s and early 1980s, which increased the replacement value of firms' assets.

C. The Reagan administration's view that "bigness is not necessarily badness."

D. The general belief among the major natural resource companies that it is cheaper to "buy reserves on Wall Street" than to explore and find them in the field.

E. Note, though, that the 1986 tax law changes may slow down merger activity.

IV. **In most mergers, one company, the target company, is acquired by another, the acquiring company.**

A. In a *friendly merger*, the management of the target company approves the merger and recommends it to their stockholders.

    1. Under these circumstances a suitable price is determined, and the acquiring company will simply buy the target company's shares.

    2. Payment will be made either in cash or in shares of the acquiring company.

B. A *hostile merger* is one in which the target firm's management resists the takeover. The target firm's management either believes the price offered is too low, or it may simply want to remain independent.

    1. Under these circumstances, the acquiring company may make a *tender offer* for the target company's shares. This is a direct appeal to the target firm's stockholders, asking them to exchange their shares for cash, for bonds, or for stock in the acquiring firm.

    2. The number of tender offers has increased greatly during the past several years.

V. While merger analysis may appear simple, there are a number of complex issues involved.

A. The acquiring firm must perform a capital budgeting analysis. If it appears that the target firm can be purchased for less than its intrinsic value, then the offer should be made.

B. However, the target firm's shareholders must believe that a "fair" price is being offered. Otherwise, they will not tender their shares.

C. From a financial standpoint, there are two basic types of mergers.

    1. Operating mergers, where the operations of two companies are combined in hopes of synergistic gains.

    2. Financial mergers, where the two operations are not combined and where no operating economies are expected.

D. The primary expected benefit of an operating merger is higher cash flows. Financial mergers may result in a greater ability to employ leverage, greater liquidity for the stock, or a matching of capital needs and resources.

E. The terms of a merger include two important elements:

    1. Postmerger control of the firm. This is of great interest to managers due to their concern for their jobs

    2. Price to be paid. The second key element, price, determines whether the shareholders of the acquiring company or the shareholders of the target company reap the greater benefits from the merger.

VI. The valuation of the target firm involves two key items: (1) a set of pro forma financial statements and, (2) a discount rate to apply to the projected cash flows.

A. In a financial merger, the expected post-merger cash flows are the sum of the independent cash flows of the two companies.

B. In an operating merger, cash flow projections are more difficult, but essential to the merger analysis. Synergistic effects may result in greater cash flows than would have been achieved by summing the cash flows of the two independent companies. For example, economies of scale may result in lower operating costs per unit of production, hence higher cash flows.

C. Merger cash flows, unlike capital budgeting cash flows, must include interest expense.
1. The target firm usually has embedded debt that will be assumed by the acquiring company.
2. This debt does *not* generally have the same cost as marginal debt.
3. Thus, debt costs must be explicitly included in the cash flow analysis.

D. With debt costs included in the cash flow analysis, the resulting net cash flows accrue solely to the equity holders of the acquiring firm. Thus, the appropriate discount rate is a *cost of equity* rather than an overall cost of capital. The cost of equity used must reflect:
1. The underlying riskiness of the target company's assets.
2. The riskiness of the financing mix used for the acquisition.

E. The Security Market Line can be used to determine a firm's post-merger cost of equity once the firm's post-merger beta has been established.

F. The present value of the incremental merger cash flows is the maximum price that the acquiring firm should pay for the target company.

VII. **Investment bankers play an important role in merger activities.**

A. The major investment banking firms have merger and acquisition (M&A) departments which help to match merger partners.

B. These same investment bankers can also help a firm fend off an unwanted suitor.
1. Sometimes a "white knight" will be lined up to acquire a firm that is trying to avoid being taken over by an unfriendly suitor.
2. Investment bankers can also recommend "poison pills," which are actions that effectively destroy the value of the firm in the event of merger, and hence drive off unwanted suitors.

C. Finally, investment bankers are used to help establish the offering price. Generally, both acquiring and target firms will use investment bankers to help establish a price and also to participate in the negotiations.

VIII. **Joint ventures involve the joining together of parts of companies to accomplish specific, limited objectives.**

A. Joint ventures are controlled by a combined management team formed from the parent companies.

B. Joint ventures are operated independently from the parent companies.

IX. **Although corporations do more buying than selling of productive assets, selling, or divestiture, does take place.**

A. There are four primary types of divestitures.
1. A division may be sold intact to another firm. This is the most common form of divestiture.

2. A division may be sold to its managers. Managerial buyouts are often called *leveraged buyouts*, or LBOs, because the managers generally put up only a small percentage of the purchase price in personal funds, while borrowing the remainder and paying off the loan with cash flows from the business.
3. A division may be set up as a corporation, with the parent firm's stockholders then being given stock in the new corporation on a pro rata basis. This type of divestiture is called a *spin-off*.
4. Sometimes, when a firm cannot find a buyer for an entire division, the division's assets must be sold off piecemeal. This is a *liquidation*.

B. There are a variety of reasons cited for divestitures.
   1. It appears that, on occasion, investors do not properly value some assets when they are buried within a conglomerate. Thus, divestiture can occur to enhance firm value.
   2. Often, firms will need to raise large amounts of cash to finance expansion in their core business, or to reduce an onerous debt burden, and divestitures can raise the needed cash.
   3. Sometimes, assets are just no longer profitable and must be liquidated.
   4. Firms that are struggling against bankruptcy often have to divest profitable divisions just to stay alive.
   5. The government sometimes mandates divestiture on antitrust grounds.

X. A holding company is a firm that holds large blocks of stock in other companies and exercises control over those firms. The holding company is often called the parent company and the controlled companies are known as subsidiaries or operating companies. Holding companies may be used to obtain some of the same benefits that could be achieved through mergers and acquisitions. However, the holding company device has some unique disadvantages as well as unique advantages.

A. Advantages of holding companies include the following:
   1. *Control with fractional ownership*. Effective control of a company may be achieved with far less than 50 percent ownership of the common stock.
   2. *Isolation of risks*. Claims on one unit of the holding company may not be liabilities to the other units. Each element of the holding company organization is a separate legal entity.
   3. *Legal separation*. Certain regulated companies such as utilities and banks find it easier to operate as holding companies in order to separate those assets under the control of regulators from those not subject to regulation.

B. Disadvantages of holding companies include the following:
   1. *Partial multiple taxation*. Consolidated tax returns may be filed only if the holding company owns 80 percent or more of the voting stock of the subsidiary. Otherwise, intercorporate dividends will be taxed. Note, though, that 80 percent of the dividends received by the holding company may be deducted from taxable income.
   2. *Ease of enforced dissolution*. It is much easier for the Justice Department to require disposal of a stock position than to demand the separation of an integrated business operation.

C. The holding company device can be used to control large amounts of assets with a relatively small equity investment. The substantial *leverage* involved in such an operation may result in high returns, but it also involves a high degree of risk.

DEFINITIONAL QUESTIONS

1. If the value of two firms, in combination, is greater than the sum of their separate values, then _____ is said to exist.

2. Synergistic effects may result from either _____ economies or _____ economies.

3. The Justice Department may be concerned about the _____ implications of a proposed merger.

4. A _____ merger takes place when two firms in the same business combine, while the combination of a steel company with a coal company would be an example of a _____ merger.

5. The merger of two completely unrelated enterprises is referred to as a _____ merger.

6. A firm which seeks to take over another company is commonly called the _____ company, while the firm it seeks to acquire is referred to as the _____ company.

7. A merger may be described as "friendly" or "hostile," depending upon the attitude of the _____ of the target company.

8. A _____ _____ is a request by the acquiring company to the target company's _____ to submit their shares in exchange for a specified price or specified number of shares of stock.

9. An _____ merger combines the business activity of the two firms with the expectation of _____ benefits.

10. _____ mergers do not combine the business operations of two firms, and no operating economies are expected.

11. Merger analysis is very similar to _____ _____ analysis.

12. In valuing the target firm, the analysis focuses on the cash flows that accrue to the stockholders of the _____ firm.

13. A _____ _____ occurs when two firms combine parts of their companies to accomplish specific, limited objectives.

14. A pro rata distribution of stock in a new firm which was formerly a subsidiary is called a _____.

15. Unless a holding company owns at least _____ percent of the share of a subsidiary company, it may be subject to multiple _____ . on a portion of any intercorporate _____ .

CONCEPTUAL QUESTIONS

16. In a financial merger, the expected cash flows are generally the sum of the cash flows of the separate companies.

    a. True   b. False

17. Interest expense must be explicitly included in a merger incremental cash flow analysis.

    a. True   b. False

18. The holding company device can be used to take advantage of the principle of financial leverage. Thus, the holding company can control a great deal of assets with a limited amount of top-tier equity.

    a. True   b. False

PROBLEMS

(The following data apply to the next four problems.)

TransCorp, a large conglomerate, is evaluating the possible acquisition of the Chip Company, a transistor manufacturer. TransCorp's analyst projects the following postmerger incremental cash flows (in millions of dollars):

	1988	1989	1990	1991
Net sales	$200	$230	$250	$270
Cost of goods sold	130	140	145	150
Selling/administrative expense	20	25	30	32
EBIT	$ 50	$ 65	$ 75	$ 88
Interest	10	12	13	14
EBT	$ 40	$ 53	$ 62	$ 74
Taxes	16	21	25	30
NI	$ 24	$ 32	$ 37	$ 44
Retained earnings	12	13	14	15
Cash available to stockholders	$ 12	$ 19	$ 23	$ 29
Terminal value				400
Net CF	$ 12	$ 19	$ 23	$429

The acquisition, if made, would occur on January 1, 1988. All cash flows above are assumed to occur at end-of-year. Chip currently has a market value capital structure of 10 percent debt, but TransCorp would increase the debt to 50 percent if the acquisition were made. Chip, if independent, pays taxes at 30 percent, but its income would be taxed at 40 percent if consolidated. Chip's current market-determined beta is 1.80. Its estimated post-merger beta is 2.67.

The cash flows above include the additional interest payments due to increased leverage and asset expansion, and the full taxes paid by TransCorp on the Chip income stream. Depreciation-generated funds would be used to replace worn-out equipment, so they would not be available to TransCorp's shareholders. Retained earnings would be used, in addition to new debt, to finance required asset expansion. Thus, the net cash flows are the flows that would accrue to TransCorp's stockholders. The risk-free rate is 10 percent and the market risk premium is 5 percent.

19. What is the appropriate discount rate for valuing the acquisition?

   a. 10.00%
   b. 15.00%
   c. 19.00%
   d. 21.75%
   e. 23.35%

20. What is the value of the Chip Company to TransCorp?

   a. $197.73 million
   b. $206.42 million
   c. $219.78 million
   d. $322.85 million
   e. $429.00 million

21. Chip has 5 million shares outstanding. Chip's current market price is $32.50. What is the maximum price per share that TransCorp should offer?

   a. $32.50
   b. $37.50
   c. $41.37
   d. $43.96
   e. $46.93

22.
TransCorp should offer Chip's stockholders $32.625 per share.

   a. True   b. False

ANSWERS AND SOLUTIONS

1. synergy

2. operating; financial

3. antitrust

4. horizontal; vertical

5. conglomerate

6. acquiring; target

7. management

8. tender offer; stockholders

9. operating; synergistic

10. Financial

11. capital budgeting

12. acquiring

13. joint venture

14. spinoff

15. 80; taxation; dividends

16. a. In a financial merger, no synergistic effects are anticipated.

17. a. The target firm generally has embedded debt that is being assumed by the acquiring firm. Since these costs are not marginal, they must be specifically included in the analysis.

18. a. This statement is true.

19. e. $k_s = 10\% + 2.67(5\%) = 23.35\%$.

20. c.
$$V = \frac{\$12 \text{ million}}{(1.2335)^1} + \frac{\$19 \text{ million}}{(1.2335)^2} + \frac{\$23 \text{ million}}{(1.2335)^3} + \frac{\$429 \text{ million}}{(1.2335)^4}$$
$$= \$219.78 \text{ million}.$$

21. d.

$$\frac{\$219.78 \text{ million}}{5 \text{ million}} = \$43.96.$$

22. b. It does not make sense to offer Chip's shareholders just a little above the current market price. Enough shares would not be tendered to gain control, the expenses would be for nought, and other firms could be induced to make competing bids.